NEGOTIATING WITH TERRORISTS

International Negotiation Series

Negotiating with Terrorists

edited by

I. William Zartman

MARTINUS NIJHOFF PUBLISHERS
LEIDEN/BOSTON

This volume is reprinted from the journal *International Negotiation*,
Volume 8 (3), 2003

ISBN 90 04 14857 4

Koninklijke Brill NV incorporates the imprints Brill Academic Publishers,
Martinus Nijhoff Publishers and VSP.

http://www.brill.nl

PRINTED AND BOUND IN THE NETHERLANDS

CONTENTS

Contributors

Steven M. Beres:
Evidence Based Research, Inc., 1595 Spring Hill Road, Suite 250, Vienna, VA22182, USA.

Moty Cristal:
E-mail: M.Cristal@lse.ac.uk.

Adam Dolnik:
Institute of Defence and Strategic Studies, Nanyang Technological University, Block S4, Level B4, Nanyang Avenue, Singapore 639798.
E-mail: isadolnik@ntu.edu.sg

William A. Donohue:
Department of Communication, Michigan State University, East Lansing, MI 48824-1212 USA.
E-mail: donohue@msu.edu

Guy Olivier Faure:
Université de Paris V – Sorbonne, Paris, France.
E-mail: go.faure@free.fr

Richard E. Hayes:
Evidence Based Research, Inc., 1595 Spring Hill Road, Suite 250, Vienna, VA22182, USA. E-mail: rehayes@ebrinc.com

Stacey R. Kaminski:
Evidence Based Research, Inc., 1595 Spring Hill Road, Suite 250, Vienna, VA22182, USA.

Richard F. Pilch:
Center for Nonproliferation Studies, Monterey Institute of International Studies, 460 Pierce Street, Monterey CA, 93940, USA.
E-mail: richard.pilch@miis.edu

Bertram Spector:
Center for Negotiation Analysis, 11608 Le Havre Drive, Potomac, MD 20854
USA. E-mail: negotiation@verizon.net

Paul J. Taylor:
Department of Psychology, University of Liverpool, Liverpool L69 3BX, United
Kingdom

I. William Zartman:
School of Advanced International Studies (SAIS), The Johns Hopkins University,
1740 Massachusetts Avenue, NW, Washington DC 20036, USA.
E-mail: izartma1@jhu.edu

Negotiating with Terrorists: Introduction

I. WILLIAM ZARTMAN

Officially, the subject does not exist: we do not negotiate with terrorists. Practically, however, there are negotiations and negotiations, and terrorists and terrorists. The subject is currently topical, but also analytically challenging, occurring more frequently than it is studied. What, then, does the fact of dealing with terrorists have to do with the negotiation process? Can negotiations take place with terrorists? How does one negotiate with terrorists? These are questions that this volume seeks to address. It does so through, firstly, four articles dealing with conceptual questions, two of them by Richard Hayes and associates (Chapter 1) and by Guy Olivier Faure (Chapter 2), presenting a literature review, and two others by Adam Dolnik (Chapter 3) and by William Donohue and Paul Taylor (Chapter 4), focusing on more specific analytical distinctions; secondly, through two case studies of the successful Bethlehem and the failed Moscow negotiations by Moty Cristal (Chapter 5) and by Adam Dolnik and Richard Pilch (Chapter 6), respectively; and, thirdly, through a research note on the broad question by Bertram Spector (Chapter 7).[1]

Terrorism is defined by the UN Security Council (UNSCr 1373) as violent or criminal acts designed to create a state of terror in the general public and by the US Government (Department of State 2002) as premeditated, politically motivated violence perpetrated against noncombatant targets by subnational groups or clandestine agents, usually intended to influence an audience. One may argue a bit with the second definition around the edges (as with any other), on aspects that perhaps derive from the fact that the definition is made by a government agency; it specifically excludes state terrorism, which leaves a veil of legitimacy on state actions of the same type that are inappropriate (Pape 2003: 345). That qualification having been noted, both definitions are acceptable approximate characterizations of the subject.

All terrorists are hostage-takers and all are their own victims. The standard hostage-taking terrorist takes identifiable hostages. The suicidal terrorist holds the people around him hostage, adding to the terror itself by the fact that they never know when they will be his chosen victims; fear makes the whole population hostage to the terrorist, among which some are the victims at any specific time. But

International Negotiation Series 1:
I.W. Zartman (ed.) Negotiating with Terrorists, 1–7
© 2006 *Koninklijke Brill NV. Printed in the Netherlands.*

the terrorists are all their own victims. The suicider kills himself along with his victims, just as the hostage-taker has taken himself hostage: he cannot escape from the barricade, kidnap hideout or hijacked plane anymore than his captives can.

Yet the key to the analysis (meaning "taking apart") of the subject is to draw distinctions within the broad concept.[2] This volume begins with a basic distinction, introduced by Hayes et al., between absolute and "traditional" terrorists, although it would be good from the start to replace the latter term by "contingent" or "instrumental," denoting their use of terror as a use of others' lives as exchange currency for other goals, as Faure indicates. Absolute terrorists are those whose action is non-instrumentalist, a self-contained act that is completed when it has occurred and is not a means to obtain some other goal (not to be confused of course with some broader cause). Suiciders – bombers and hijackers – are absolute terrorists, and so are beyond negotiation. They are generally even beyond dissuasion, and in this, they differ from non-terrorist suiciders, whose end is without a broader purpose and is not intended to influence behavior beyond their own.

But useful distinctions may be possible in order to better understand and deal with the phenomenon, between total (or revolutionary) and conditional absolutes. It is not only the suicidal tactics, but the unlimited cause that makes for truly absolute terrorism. When the cause is world social and political revolution, it becomes an unattainable millennial dream used to justify total indiscriminate tactics – "unlimited ends lead to unlimited means" (Crenshaw 2000). Other suiciders use the same tactics that are finite, dividable, exchangeable – aspects that will be relevant to later parts of this discussion – even though their act itself is as self-contained and absolute as any other suiciders'.[3]

The other side of the distinction holds greater ambiguity, replicating the ambiguity in its name. Instrumental or contingent or demonstrative terrorism covers much of the literature of the past century on negotiating with terrorists and involves mainly hostage-taking, as discussed by Faure, Dolnik, Hayes, and Donohue, and in the case studies by Cristal and by Dolnik and Pilch. The violence is therefore not definitive or absolute: it is accomplished only in part, as in the act of hostage-taking, but threatened or contingent in the rest, as in the fate promised for the hostages if the demands are not met. But some hostage-taking is no longer contingent terrorism. On one hand, airline suiciders are absolute terrorists: their goal is their own sacrifice as well as the sacrifice of their hostages, and there is no way of negotiating a compromise. On the other hand, once the hostage-taker has killed his hostage(s), he verges on the absolutist, for he has nothing more to negotiate about or with.

Contingent or even instrumental terrorism is preferable as a term to demonstrative terrorism (used by Pape 2003: 345), both because of the usual distinction between demonstrative/expressive violence (to get it off your chest) and instrumental violence (to accomplish something). "Non-absolute" terrorism seeks much more than demonstration: it seeks to exchange its victims for something – publicity, ransom, release of friends. Indeed, it is absolute terrorism, if anything, that is demonstrative, in the sense that it expresses the frustration of the suicider over the situation and his inability to change it by any other means.

Other kinds of distinctions are made within the category of terrorism that are relevant to understanding the phenomenon and its susceptibility to negotiation. Among contingent terrorists, the distinction made by Dolnik between barricade and kidnapping terrorists highlights an important difference – the sustainability and vulnerability of the situation, and beyond that the typical difference between the perpetrators-barricaders being more frequently mentally imbalanced and kidnappers either extortionists (criminals) or militants. In that typology, a third type should be added, as noted by Donohue: the non-suicidal aerial hijacker, whose situation is that of a barricader on the ground but more sustainable within limits in the air precisely because of the vulnerability of the hostages.

The distinctions among terrorists, as noted by Hayes and Faure, are also relevant but raise further questions that are particularly important in the present context. Criminals, militants (nationalists or revolutionaries), fundamentalists, and mentally unstable cases are categories that can often overlap but make a difference in regards to negotiability. The most important elision to make in these categories is between social revolutionaries and religious militants. Although the point of reference and inspiration of the latter is god-given revelation and of the former is political ideology, it would be wrong to ignore their more important similarities. Both revolutionaries and fundamentalists want to overthrow the given social system and build a new world in the image of their dreams, and as terrorists both are willing to kill others and die themselves to achieve their goal. Thus, the current emphasis on the fundamentalist basis of terrorism should not obscure their social revolutionary nature. Camus' *Les Justes* gives as important insights into religious as into ideological motivations.

The result is of importance in addressing the topic of this issue of the journal: negotiating with terrorists. Any attempt to negotiate with total absolute terrorists only encourages them; it achieves no other purpose (Pape 2003). They have nothing to negotiate about, they have nothing to negotiate with.[4] Indeed, it is notoriously difficult even to contact them and to talk them out of their act, while they are up in the air or even on the street heading toward their target. Since contact and communication are basic conditions of negotiation, inaccessibility is another component of absolute terrorism. Of course, even here a distinction needs to be made between the terrorists themselves (the suiciders) and their bosses or organizers. The organizers do not blow themselves up. They are not madmen and the point is gradually being understood that they are highly rational and strategic calculators

(Crenshaw 1981; Horgan and Taylor 2003). But their purpose is so broad that it is unlikely to lend itself to negotiation, and indeed negotiation and the compromises involved are likely to be seen as damaging to the galvanizing purpose of the terrorist organizer in a desperate, asymmetrical situation.[5]

On the other hand, contingent terrorists are seeking to negotiate. They want to get full price for their hostages, and for the most part live hostages are better bargaining material than dead ones. Hostages are hostage capital, as Faure puts it, or bargaining chips, that is, items of no intrinsic value to the bargainer but created for the purpose of bargaining away. Contingent terrorists try to overcome their essentially weak position by appropriating a part of the other side and trying to get the best deal out of the other side's efforts to get that part back, to make itself whole again. Absolute terrorists do not want society to be whole again, they want it wounded and bleeding. To be able to do so, terrorists must believe in their own right, whether that sense of justice that counterbalances their asymmetrical power position comes from god (as in the case of fundamentalists), from ideology (as in the case of social revolutionaries), or from their belief that the world owes them this right as a result of its own basic discrimination or corruption (nationalists and criminals, respectively).

In between the two groups are the conditional absolute terrorists, who do have something to negotiate about – territory, independence, conditions – even if their suicidal tactics are absolute. Conditional absolutes are not contingent: they do not seek negotiation as part of their act and their tactics are not divisible into two parts, grasping hostage capital and spending it. But their demands are potentially negotiable, leaving that potentiality to be developed by the negotiating partner. Here, the distinction between agent and organizer adds to the specialty of the conditional absolute case. The agent is still likely to be totally absolute, and partial absoluteness refers only to the organizer. But the distinction suggests appropriate negotiating – or pre-negotiating – tactics. It is important to divide the terrorists, pulling the contingents and conditional absolutes away from the absolutes, which means giving the prospect of something real and attainable, as was done in the case of the IRA in Ulster, as Hayes notes.

The problem in the case of contingent terrorists is not that they are not interested in negotiating but that the world does not accept their deal. But that is merely an extreme case of a typical negotiating situation. To that situation there are two appropriate negotiating strategies: to lower their terms or to change their terms. Cristal, Dolnik, Donohue, and Faure explore the first. They draw attention to a frequently neglected link between status and outcomes, showing that low status leads to offensive tactics, position politics, and hostile bargaining that is unproductive of integrative outcomes. They bring out the "need to achieve a gradual process of creating conditions which will enable the terrorists to securely conclude the crisis [. . .] undermining the terrorists' psychological safe-zone, constructing legitimacy for the negotiated agreement and building the terrorists' independent decision making capabilities", in Cristal's words. Treatment as equals, development of the legitimacy of a solution, and expansion of options are all ways of moving the hostage-takers off position bargaining and opening the possibility of a fruitful search for mutually satisfactory solutions, only available when they can think in terms of lowered expectations and so of lowered demands.

Changing terms are dealt with in Faure's and Dolnik's accounts and in Cristal's analysis of the Bethlehem negotiations. The key to successful negotiations is to change the terrorists' terms of trade from their demands to their fate. When they see that there is no chance of their demands being met but that their future personal situation is open to discussion, innumerable details become available for negotiation. The two must be carried out in tandem, indicating that while one avenue or problem is closed for discussion, the other is open and personally more compelling.

Terrorists tend to focus on their original terms of trade – release of hostages in exchange for fulfillment of demands – and are little open to looking for reductions and alternatives, options that need to be developed if negotiations are to succeed. As in any negotiations, when the two parties become convinced that a search for a solution is legitimate and acceptable to both sides, they become joint searchers for a solution to a problem rather than adversaries. To entice them into this common pursuit, they need to be convinced that the other side is willing to consider their interests. "If state leaders have the political will to promote negotiation as a response to terrorism, they will need to attend to terrorists' interests, not only their actions, strategies and tactics [. . .] To overcome the no-negotiation impediment, state leaders will need to respond in a special way, seek to understand terrorist interests, translate those interests into politically acceptable terms, and respond to them appropriately", notes Spector.

These two strategies may or may not be in contradiction with each other. On one hand, one strategy helps the terrorists look for lesser forms of an outcome on terms that interest them, whereas the other helps them look for other terms. The second option also reinforces the position of the authorities as holders of the upper hand – one-up negotiators, in Donohue's terms – rather than full equals. On the other hand, both strategies depend on removing obstacles to creative negotiating, indicating the legitimacy and interest of both parties in finding a solution, and developing a range of options. At this point, the problem returns to the other side, the official negotiator who needs to lead the terrorist against his will into the give-and-take of negotiation.

There is room for a wide range of tactics; at some point, take-it-or-leave-it offers are useful whereas at other times, invitations to further refinement and creative thinking are appropriate. At some points, firmness in the subject of negotiations is in order, whereas at other times, alternatives and options can be explored. Time, as Dolnik, Hayes, and Spector emphasize, is on the side of the negotiator, a point that the terrorist may seek to reverse by either killing or releasing some of his hostages. Once relations with terrorists get into the bargaining mode, however, they are open to the same shifts and requirements of tactics as any other negotiation.

All this is not to suggest either that terrorists' demands are to be considered legitimate in principle and only require some tailoring around the edges, or that concessions do not encourage contingent as well as absolute terrorists. The answer to the question of whether negotiations can be conducted with terrorists is that contingent terrorists in fact are looking for negotiations and that even conditional absolute have something negotiable in mind; but the answer to the next question of how much of their demands can be considered acceptable depends on their content and on the importance of freeing the hostages. This latter consideration again relates in turn to the danger of encouragement. Here, it is not the matter of negotiation per se that encourages contingent terrorism but rather the degree of their demands that they are able to achieve by negotiation. If negotiating leads the terrorist to a purely symbolic result – a radio broadcast or a newspaper ad presenting his position – he is more likely to decide that the result is not worth the effort, rather than to feel encouraged to do it again. Or if negotiating leads the terrorist to a bargain for his escape and totally neglect his original demands, he is not likely to feel encouraged to make another try. Thus, in the case of contingent terror, any encouragement would come from the results but not from the act of negotiating itself.

Similarly, the negotiator needs to offer the conditional absolute terrorist concessions to his demands as the payment for his abandonment of his violent terrorism and not as concessions to the pressure of the terrorism itself. If the negotiator should make concessions to the terrorist as part of the negotiation process, so must the terrorist, and the absolute terrorist organizer does have something to offer as payment: his choice of terrorist tactics. Thus, the answer of the negotiator to his public's fears of appeasing and legitimizing terrorism lies in the deal he is able to extract from the terrorist and in his need to focus on the fate of the victims, as Cristal, Faure, Hayes, and Spector show.

Negotiating with terrorists is possible, within limits, as the follow chapters show and explore. Limits come initially in the distinction between absolute and contingent terrorists, and then within these categories in the restrictions on strategies open to the terrorists' negotiating adversaries. Basically, the official negotiator is faced with the task of giving a little in order to get the terrorist to give a lot, a particularly difficult imbalance to obtain given the highly committed and desperate nature of terrorists as they follow rational but highly unconventional tactics. Such are the challenges of negotiating with terrorist that this volume explores and elucidates.

Notes

1. Undated references refer to the chapters in this volume.
2. Cf. Stedman's (2000) analysis of "spoilers" by breaking the concept down into several types.
3. Pape (2003) lumps together negotiable and nonnegotiable goals, which is a mistake; see Spector below on the role of goals. Representativity seems to be used by the European Commission for the Prevention of Torture as another distinction, but it is unoperationable; see Palma (2003).
4. Dolnik's suggestion that absolutes might be persuaded to give up their hostages since they had already made their splash, and then to seek an "honorable" death in fighting the police, seems a bit too calculating to be a real strategy.
5. The botched bombings in Casablanca in May 2003 bring out a new weakness in current terrorism, in highlighting the gap between the rational, skilled, dedicated organizers and the less sophisticated and less committed agents, who in some cases not only carried out their tasks badly but in others got cold feet and ran away. See also Atran 2003.

References

Atran, Scott (2003) "Genesis of Suicide Terrorism", *Science* CCIC 1534–39 (7 March).

Crenshaw, Martha (2000) "The Psychology of Terrorism: An Agenda for the 21st Century", *Political Psychology* XXI 2: 405–420.

Horgan, John and M. Taylor (2003) *The Psychology of Terrorism* (London: Frank Cass).

Palma, Mauro (2003) "European Strategy against Terrorist Insurgency and Local Armed Conflict", Rome University Conference on Terrorism, 15 November.

Pape, Robert A. (2003) "The Strategic Logic of Suicide Terrorism", *American Political Science Review* IIIC 3: 343–361 (August).

Reich, W. (1990) *Origins of Terrorism: Psychologies, Ideologies, Theologies, States of Mind* (Washington, DC: Woodrow Wilson Center Press).

Stedman, Stephen John (2000) "Spoiler Problems in Peace Processes", in Paul Stern and Daniel Druckman, eds., *International Conflict Management after the Cold War* (Washington, DC: National Academy Press).

US Department of State (2002) *Patterns of Global Terrorism 2001* (Washington, DC: Office of the Coordinator for Counterterrorism, US Department of State).

Zartman, I. William (1990) "Negotiating Effectively With Terrorists", in Barry Rubin, ed., *The Politics of Counterterrorism* (Washington, DC: The Johns Hopkins Foreign Policy Institute).

Negotiating the Non-Negotiable: Dealing with Absolutist Terrorists

RICHARD E. HAYES, STACEY R. KAMINSKI, and
STEVEN M. BERES

Background

The 20th century witnessed global expansion of markets ranging from energy and consumer goods to media and culture. By the end of the century, the United States had become the world's sole superpower, visibly present on every continent. Globalization created a multidimensional, dynamic, and highly complex environment in which many people felt dissatisfied and some believed turning to terrorism could alter the global political, social, and economic order. As Van Creveld (1991) notes, the enemies of Western civilization no longer have well-defined borders, clear identities, ties to nation-states that can be held accountable for their actions, or a clear and predictable way of operating. Terrorists have shown the capacity to adapt their organizations, processes, and communications to take advantage of the increasingly networked world in which we live.

Most terrorist organizations have goals, means, and behavior familiar to those who studied the subject during the 20th century. In an earlier article entitled "Negotiations with Terrorists" (Hayes 1988), the senior author of this piece reviewed the research and evidence in existence at that time on strategies and tactics effective in dealing with terrorists. The material reviewed dealt primarily with purely hostile or mixed-motive relations between governments and terrorists. It did not deal with terrorists bargaining with one another or with the governments that supported them. The authors of the current article make the assumption that for most terrorist groups these findings remain valid, relevant, and reliable. Hence, the material in that article is reviewed briefly here.

However, we also argue that an absolutist form of terrorism has emerged and become both more visible and more dangerous than the classic types that have often been associated with ethnic or political goals. These groups – and individuals since some of them are willing to act outside formal structures – are characterized as absolutist because they are not willing to enter into political discourse. Rather, their demands are immediate, unconditional, and universal. The tactics of absolutist terrorists are also much more likely to include suicide attacks. While desperation and

International Negotiation Series 1:
I.W. Zartman (ed.) Negotiating with Terrorists, 9–24
© 2006 *Koninklijke Brill NV. Printed in the Netherlands.*

suicidal tactics are not new to terrorism, the frequency with which absolutist terrorists employ them and their willingness to cause mass, indiscriminate casualties are unusual. Hence, we argue, a different approach must be taken for "negotiating" with them.

In this article, the term "negotiation" is not used in the traditional manner. The term is used as a way of characterizing the methods in which a group or organization ceases to inflict damage or cause harm as a means to influence policy, culture, or social structures. This can be achieved in a variety of ways without direct negotiations, ways that are outlined later in this piece. These methods can be used individually or in conjunction with standard methods for a combined and concerted effort that may create synergistic effects.

In "Negotiations with Terrorists", we utilized a definition of terrorism: "the use or threat of dramatic, public violence by non-state actors that is intended to influence the behavior of people or institutions beyond those immediately targeted or harmed by the violence". Sun Tzu (1962) would have been comfortable with this definition. His dictate "kill one, frighten ten thousand", demonstrates this, though he was largely writing in the context of state terrorism.

After the attack on the United States on 11 September 2001, American national security policy changed from one of deterrence and response to one that endorses preemptive strike against "terrorists of global reach and the states that harbor them" (Bush 2001). The concepts involved in this new approach were outlined in the National Security Policy of the United States (NSP 2002). This doctrine implies a recognition that the enemy has changed and also a commitment to a very different approach to ensure US national security. This new policy has been applied in the use of military force in Afghanistan starting from November 2001, and in Iraq starting from March 2003. However, use of the military instrument is only part of a larger strategy designed to influence countries, terrorist organizations, and individuals. This larger strategy is explored in the section on negotiating with absolutist terrorists.

Negotiating with "Traditional" Terrorists

Before looking at successful approaches, strategies, and tactics in the 20th century, we should make it clear that the phrase "traditional terrorists" is an unhappy one. It serves our purpose in distinguishing the absolutist terrorists from other groups. However, there is really nothing traditional about any terrorist or terrorist organization. The phrase, as used here, encompasses some very different groups, including those who see their cause as ethnic and those who see their cause as ideological.

The earlier article looked at a half dozen contexts in which governments negotiated with terrorists as individuals and organizations. They included:

- Amnesties
- Treatment of arrested terrorists
- Negotiations during terrorist events and campaigns
- Negotiations in larger political contexts
- Bargaining about types and targets of action
- The effects of other policies on terrorism

Amnesties

Governments frequently offer terrorists still in the field some combination of safe surrender, amnesty, reduced sentences for past crimes, rewards for cooperation, or guarantees of safety for the individual and his/her family members. The direct goals of such programs are a cost effective reduction of the number of terrorists in the field and improved intelligence about their members and organizations. These programs can be effective, particularly if the government demonstrates good faith in dealing with those who accept their offers. Mistrust and suspicion among the terrorists can also be a by-product. For example, the amnesty campaign of Philippines President Aquino that lasted from 1986 to 1997 resulted in bloody purges among some insurgent groups.

Treatment of Arrested Terrorists

When individual terrorists are arrested, the governments by which they are held may negotiate with them over their fate. These negotiations typically represent efforts to trade more lenient sentences and prison conditions (or protection for family members) for information. The most famous application of this technique was the Italian government's Repentant Terrorist Law, aimed at Red Brigade members. There is evidence (Hayes and Shiller 1983) that the principles of a classic Prisoner's Dilemma game were employed when this law was applied. First, the authorities were able to offer a huge difference between the rewards to those who cooperated and the punishments in store for those who did not. Second, communication among the prisoners was restricted. Finally, as a result of indiscriminant recruiting, trust among the prisoners was low. As a consequence, the authorities gained valuable intelligence that enabled them to destroy the once very powerful terrorist organization.

Negotiations During Terrorist Events and Campaigns

The most visible negotiations occur during dramatic terrorist events. Where the location of the victim(s) is known (hostage/barricade) the authorities generally have significant advantages. The senior leaders of the terrorist organizations are usually not present. More inexperienced personnel must make all the decisions. Skilled negotiators can often wear them down, making relatively minor concessions (food, water, other comfort items) in return for hostage release; persuading them to release what both sides agree are "innocent" hostages (women, children, the elderly, or those from groups the terrorists do not want to harm), which often enables the authorities to gain valuable information about the numbers, locations, arms, and security procedures of the terrorists. It is also possible to prolong the situation until fatigue and psychological pressures result in positive outcomes. The evidence from hostage/barricade situations indicates that making relatively minor concessions, up to and including safe passage for the terrorists if no one has been harmed, has not been correlated with an increase in terrorist attacks of the same type. However, where major political concessions have been made or where safe passage has been granted after hostages have been harmed, the likelihood of more attacks of the same type rises significantly.

In situations like kidnapping, when the location of the victims is not known, the authorities have much less leverage and the situation is more dangerous for the victims. When the terrorist group uses kidnapping as a means of raising funds, they will usually attempt to bargain with the victims' families or employers, rather than with governments. Governments typically attempt to find the victims and carry out rescues, an approach which historically has had mixed results. However, the broad result of making concessions also applies to these cases. Namely, substantial concessions increase the likelihood of similar attacks against the same targets and the same types of targets, both from the same group and other groups. This is particularly true if the concessions receive wide publicity.

Individual terrorist acts that continue over time (as opposed to time specific attacks such as bombings) have been termed "negotiated acts" by Oots (1986) or "counterterrorism opportunities" by Hayes (1982) because they create an opportunity for tacit or explicit bargaining. Moreover, campaigns of terrorism (series of linked attacks) are also very real opportunities for negotiation. These terrorist campaigns are generally based on decisions by leaders and involve planned and controlled activities. Hence opportunities exist to influence or terminate them through communication with the terrorist organization. Turk (1982) argues that most campaigns of terrorism are attempts at deterrence. That is, the terrorist organization seeks to alter some government policy or forestall some government actions by threatening to or engaging in illegal activities. Governments seek to decouple their policies from the terrorist campaign and to stress the illegal nature of the behavior. This can be effective as a way of isolating the terrorists from the general population.

Negotiations in Larger Political Contexts

Terrorist events are not isolated. They always occur in a larger political context. There is evidence that terrorism spreads, grows, and declines by contagion and diffusion processes (Midlarsky, Crenshaw, and Yoshida 1980; Heyman and Mickolus 1981). Terrorist groups often seek political change, autonomy, different treatment by the government, or other obviously political goals. While bargaining in these cases is typically tacit or indirect (involving negotiations with "responsible leaders" not closely linked with the terrorist activity), ignoring it and its effect on the types and levels of terrorism is naïve and reduces the likelihood of conflict resolution. Governments that can create an effective dialogue with leaders not associated with violence and demonstrate that legal political activity can be effective in resolving grievances, increase the likelihood that they can isolate the terrorists. Creating political dialogue can demonstrate that the authorities are responsive to genuine concerns and that violence is counterproductive. Bringing the "Greens" into the mainstream political life in Europe is an example of governments removing the perceived need for violence.

While Laquer (1987) argues that concessions made to moderate leaders can be used to isolate terrorists and strengthen the moderates' role, powerful forces are often at work to make such strategies difficult. Terrorist leaders are usually reluctant to enter legitimate politics themselves. Their self-concept, base of support, and experience lie in the violent arena. Moreover, when substantive concessions are made by the authorities, terrorist leaders are likely to believe they are the result of the pressure from terrorism. Dedicated terrorists can also be expected to attack those involved in efforts at negotiated settlements. They will seek both to intimidate the "responsible moderates" and to outrage the public that is supporting the government. Both Colombia and Israel have experienced this phenomenon repeatedly.

Bargaining About Types and Targets of Action

Terrorist groups adapt the types of attack they make, who they target, and where they attack based on their experience and the defensive capabilities demonstrated by governments. Landes (1978) and Gurr (1979) report that skyjackings declined after the installation of metal detectors in US airports. Steiner and Hayes (1984) have shown that once West Germany demonstrated the capability and will to defeat skyjackings, terrorists ceased to target the country utilizing that technique. Moreover, successful acts of terrorism are likely to be repeated against the same governments (Hayes 1982) and imitated (Oots 1986) by other groups. Rubenstein (1987) has suggested that the repeatability of acts may be a decision criterion for some groups because they believe there exists a large population ready to rebel, but which lacks a model of how to do so successfully.

The Effects of Other Policies on Terrorism

The existing evidence suggests that a variety of other policies also has measurable effects on the likelihood and frequency of terrorist attacks. For example, inconsistent behavior by a government toward terrorists or terrorism is likely to produce more violent behavior (Lichbach 1987). Incomplete destruction of terrorist organizations leaves behind a core of experienced, determined terrorists who will prove troublesome over time (Laquer 1987) and may rebuild the group (Hayes 1982). Harsh penalties tend to loose impact over time (Hewitt 1982) as they come to be expected and even discounted by the terrorists and their supporters. To be effective, governments need to act firmly against individuals convicted of specific criminal acts, without engaging in arbitrary actions that impact others, particularly innocent members of society. Very tough policies are needed, but the rule of law must visibly prevail. Stated another way, the appearance of arbitrary behavior must be avoided if the terrorists are to be isolated from popular sympathy and support.

Negotiating with Absolutist Terrorists

The way in which absolutist terrorists are discussed in this piece mirrors much of what others refer to as "new" terrorists. Hoffman (1999) distinguishes "new" terrorism from "old" terrorism in three fundamental ways:

• The goals of the new terrorists are less tangible;
• The new terrorist organizations use technology and build global networks;
• The new terrorists tend to be united by common religious fanaticism.

These "new" terrorists are also more willing to commit mass murder and devastation than "traditional" terrorists. Traditional terrorists seek to publicize what they perceive to be a just cause and win supporters. Hence, they have an incentive to target narrowly rather than broadly and to avoid mass killings that might deprive them of support. The absolutists see no such constraints. They plan suicide attacks routinely, partly because they believe this approach constitutes the path to a religious afterlife and partly because they view everyone who is not part of their movement as an enemy. Suicide bombers in crowded areas, car and truck bombs intended to devastate major facilities, and even chemical attacks have been carried out by these "new" terrorists.

Though "new" terrorism encapsulates the characteristics of the absolutist terrorist as described in this article, there is little evidence to support the claim that this "new" terrorism is really new (Crenshaw 2000). Non-tangible goals and terrorist acts based on religious fanaticism have been occurring throughout the 20th century, though the context and purpose of these actions may have changed.

We have chosen to call these people "absolutist" terrorists primarily because they have such radical, impossible demands. They are not merely fully committed to their causes, but also fully committed to forcing the rest of the world to accept their demands and adopt their values and way of life. In a discussion with students from a major university on the subject of the 11 September bombings, the senior author found himself explaining how Western civilization itself – from blue jeans and rock music to educated women – was an affront to those who carried out the attacks. Rappaport's (1984) discussion of historical religious terror and Mickolus's (1987) early observations about modern Shiite terrorist groups demonstrate that this is not an isolated or new phenomenon.

The absolutist terrorists' strategy is exemplified by the phrase: "unlimited ends lead to unlimited means" (Crenshaw 2000). Hoffman (2001) notes that the demands and goals of transnational terrorist organizations have become less attainable, even as they have organized themselves into networks that rely on global transportation, finance, and communications systems. Whine (2002) also notes that these groups do not necessarily give warning or claim specific responsibility. He argues, "[t]he new terrorist tends to strike, and to go on striking without publicity for himself or his cause, until he is caught. He does not need to claim responsibility perhaps because he acknowledges only God as his master, and God has seen his action. No one else matters". Of course, this lack of visible presence complicates the problem of opening dialogue or negotiations.

With direct negotiations infeasible, those who oppose terrorism have instead opted for a negotiation strategy that focuses on three targets:

- Negotiations with state supporters of terrorism
- Isolating the violent actors
- Penetrating the veils

Negotiations with State Supporters of Terrorism

State support has long been one of the most important enablers of terrorism. States can provide safe havens where terrorists can organize and train, funds, travel and identity documents, diplomatic pouches by which weapons and documents can be moved without inspection, and the support of intelligence services. These services enable terrorists to overcome many of the key barriers to success and to maneuver around many of the defenses that their targets employ. While a few governments have employed agents of their national governments to carry out terrorist attacks (North Korea, Iraq under Saddam Hussein, and Libya are obvious examples), the more common practice is to create deniability by allowing terrorist organizations with goals that are aligned with those of the state to operate from national territory. This was the approach of the Taliban and similar charges have been made against Syria, Libya, Iraq under Hussein, and others.

Still other states have been charged with "making deals with the devil" in that they allow extremist terrorist organizations to organize and operate (often discretely) within their territory (recruiting, raising funds, and teaching hatred) as long as their activities do not target the regime in power. Allegations of this type have been leveled at Pakistan, Saudi Arabia, Yemen, and Indonesia, among others. In most cases these regimes have either dismissed the charges as erroneous or pled that the areas involved were remote and difficult for them to control. In other words, they have argued that they have taken those security measures that they could reasonably be expected to take, that hostility from within their populations arose from legitimate disagreements about the policies followed by those who oppose terrorism, and that the intelligence reports of terrorist activities and linkages within their countries were wrong or exaggerated.

After the 11 September attacks, the United States declared its intentions not only to pursue the individual terrorists and terrorist organizations that had carried out the attack, but also others that posed a similar threat and those governments that supported them or allowed them to use their territory. The obvious government supporting the Al Qaeda network was the Taliban regime in Afghanistan. The United States first attempted to deal with the Taliban as a legitimate, responsible member of the international community.

Early in 1998, Osama Bin Laden issued a *fatwa* (religious edict) from within the borders of Afghanistan, where he was building the Al Qaeda movement, authorizing attacks on US interests and citizens around the globe. Bill Richardson, then the US Ambassador to the United Nations, asked about this *fatwa* and its meaning in Afghanistan. He was formally told by representatives of the Taliban that the *fatwa* lacked religious authority and should be disregarded. During this same period, requests from the US that Bin Laden be expelled from Afghanistan went unanswered.

Following the bombings of the US embassies in Kenya and Tanzania during August of 1998, the US continued dialogue with the Taliban seeking Bin Laden's ouster and that he be brought to justice. The linkage of Al Qaeda to the embassy bombings gave new urgency to these efforts. In early 2001, two French journalists reported (Brisard and Dasquie 2001) that the US had offered to provide aid to the rebuilding of war-torn Afghanistan, possibly including a badly needed oil pipeline if the Taliban would cooperate on several issues. These issues included expulsion of or delivery of Bin Laden, a review of human rights issues, and the creation of a transitional government that would include the Northern Alliance (the Taliban's most important remaining foe within Afghanistan) within an agreed timetable of 2–3 years. Reportedly, the US even offered to delay its investigations seeking to link Al Qaeda and Bin Laden to the 12 October 2000 attack on the USS Cole. This effort represents a classic tactic in dealing with state supporters for terrorism – offering major rewards for cooperation while implying major penalties for continuing support for terrorism. However, these negotiations reportedly broke down because the Taliban refused to enter into formal negotiations with other possible rival political leaderships in Afghanistan. On its part, the US renewed the USS Cole investigation, which was taken as a sign by the Taliban that the offer was off the table.

With the bombing of the World Trade Center and the Pentagon in September 2001, US policy changed dramatically from one in which state support for terrorism was actively discouraged through diplomatic and economic means to consideration of military action where necessary to preempt the threat. President Bush's aforementioned statement that the US would strike at "terrorists of global reach and the states that harbor them" had special meaning in the context of US-Taliban relations. The American position turned rapidly from one of diplomatic contacts and dialogue to demands that Bin Laden and his lieutenants be arrested and turned over to responsible authorities. When these demands fell on deaf ears, the US turned to military action. By the end of November, military force had replaced negotiations as the tool for ending state sponsorship of terrorism within Afghanistan.

However, the use of force against the Taliban regime in Afghanistan must be understood as a major tacit bargaining move in the US relationship with other governments that were believed to be supporting Al Qaeda and other absolutist terrorists within global network(s). This use of force delivered messages both to regimes that were willingly allowing the use of their territories and resources and to those that had been claiming an inability to control their own territories and populations.

Pakistan is an important case and instructive about the general approach (and its limits). Some elements of the Pakistani regime had not only cooperated with the Taliban, but had been active supporters of that group's efforts to win control over Afghanistan. The civil war and lack of law and order that permeated Afghanistan following the end of the Soviet occupation cried out for some unifying force. The Taliban, which advocated strict adherence to *Sharia* law, or Islamic code, represented a "law and order" approach that was attractive to the more conservative elements in the Pakistani elite. However, events such as destroying more than 80 percent of Afghanistan's Buddha statutes shocked the world, including Pakistan (Associated Press 2001). The Taliban also placed bans on music and other forms of entertainment (Assistance Afghanistan 2001). Despite these actions and the massive human rights abuses, particularly against women, on the part of the regime, the Taliban continued to be seen as a reasonable neighbor by many in the Pakistani regime during 1991 until after the US diplomatic offensive.

Pakistan was not directly threatened with military action, though the aggressive US posture toward the Taliban certainly implied a willingness to take tough measures against those who were unwilling to cooperate. We cannot know in detail what promises were made in advance, but once Pakistan indicated a willingness to work with the US and cease support for the Taliban, major initiatives were undertaken. For example, the Bush administration promptly removed all sanctions imposed on Pakistan since 1990 with regard to its nuclear program. Washington also promised to reduce tariff barriers against Pakistani textile exports as well as write off $1 billion in bilateral debt. US economic assistance in 2002 totaled $600 million, with promises of more to come. In return, the US asked that Pakistan furnish intelligence information and cooperate actively in the war on terrorism, particularly against Al Qaeda.

Isolating the Violent Actors

Beyond the direct quid pro quo in which massive differences exist between the rewards made available by the US for cooperation and the threats (explicit or implicit) against those who support or condone absolutist terrorists, the US policy of looking for public and aggressive support also serves to drive a wedge between the governments it is negotiating with and the terrorists who want to operate on their territories. Pakistan is, again, an instructive case. There is no doubt that President Musharif has been forced to take positions that put him at risk politically at home. Those who helped put the Taliban into power in Afghanistan and the fundamentalist Islamists who support Al Qaeda are clearly unhappy with his actions and looking for ways to force him from power. Moreover, cooperation with the US has forced him to deploy troops into the Northwest Territories that are controlled by tribal leaders who have long been considered so difficult to control and dangerous that that have been essentially ignored by the Pakistani government. In addition, cooperation with the US allows his political opponents to charge that he has given in on security issues that compromise the sovereignty of the country. Most important, and often overlooked by political commentators, is the fact that the absolutist terrorists and their supporters are forced, by their very belief system, to attack the Pakistani regime that is cooperating with the US against them. Hence, by their own actions, these absolutists make political dialogue all but impossible, burning bridges that compel the government to take them on. In other words, one of the successful outcomes of the US approach of major carrots and sticks will tend to be an unambiguous and deepening chasm between the absolutists and the governments they need for support.

Yemen is another fairly obvious example of this strategy. This is a country that has a long history of being unable to control the remote reaches of its territory. It has become famous as the birthplace of Osama Bin Laden. It most recently was in the terrorism headlines because of the attack on the USS Cole in a Yemeni port. Hence, there seems little doubt that this country was a place Al Qaeda operatives were able to operate.

Penetrating the Veils

Shortly after the September 2001 attacks, President Saleh of Yemen gathered his military entourage and announced that his country would side with the United States in the war on terrorism. The US is providing $400 million in military and economic assistance to Yemen in return for intelligence and cooperation on this important security issue. This is a small country that clearly feared the US would be willing and able to use military force if its regime did not cooperate. The difference between the rewards for cooperation and the potential punishments for non-cooperation was large enough to sway the Yemeni regime even though it knew some elements in the country would resist its decisions.

A number of other governments has also found itself in a position where the undoubted presence of absolutist terrorists within their territories has made the decision to cooperate with the United States a wise one. Indonesia, for example, despite a long-term and strong desire to maintain a non-aligned posture, has found itself embroiled in the global war on terrorism because of the attack in Bali and charges that its territory has been used for training camps related to Al Qaeda.

At this writing, the Saudi Arabian government finds itself under pressure despite the fact that it has sought to walk a fine line between its global alliance with the US (in the form of moderation in the oil market and reliance on the US as guarantor of its security from the Saddam Hussein regime in Iraq) and the demands on it as host to the most sacred cities of Islam. US critics have long charged that the Saudi tolerance and export of Wahhabism has fostered virulent anti-US and anti-Western teaching that has resulted in major financial and popular support for Al Qaeda. The fact that many of the hijackers on September 11 and in other major attacks have been Saudi nationals has been cited as a reflection of this policy. The attacks of May 2003 within the Kingdom, despite the fact that they targeted primarily expatriate facilities and personnel, appear to indicate that the terrorists are unwilling to allow the Saudi royal family to continue their policy of creative ambiguity.

Indeed, as the attacks in Saudi Arabia and Morocco indicate, the absolutist terrorists, when cut off from state support, must focus their operations where they have a sympathetic population that will at least allow them to operate unimpeded, if not give them help. Those governments that have chosen to turn the other way except when there is direct and obvious evidence that absolutist terrorists are operating on their territory and have allowed popular sympathy to develop for those terrorists' causes, may be in the process of discovering that they will reap the whirlwind. They may be forced to choose between long term enmity with the sole remaining superpower and engaging in serious efforts to root out absolutist terrorism.

Isolating the Violent

Successful bargaining with states to end their support for and tolerance of absolutist terrorists is the most visible, and in many ways the strongest element in the battle against absolutist terrorists. It is also an important element in the second major tool – isolating those who counsel violence as the means of prevailing. Governments, because they control schools and (in much of the world) media and information flows, are powerful instruments for influencing people's attitudes toward terrorism as a political tool. Hence, part of what is expected of them is leadership in delegitimizing violence and ensuring the availability of alternative ways for responsible dialogue.

However, the Western world is not impotent when dealing with this issue. To take a simple example, one of the few instances when suicide bombing campaigns have been questioned in the Middle East occurred when arguments against this tactic were described as a means of saving the youth. Violence, particularly terrorism and suicide bombings, is a tactic of the desperate. Where hope exists, these extreme measures are not necessary. The absolutist terrorists understand this – they prey on the desperate and seek to ensure broad support for their acts by stressing not only the righteousness of their cause but also the absence of alternative means. Due to their righteousness and desperation, they also stress that there are no innocents – women, children, the aged, and others are legitimate targets.

To isolate these terrorists, those who oppose terrorism have attempted to publicize the viciousness of the attacks and the indiscriminant nature of the carnage they create. Stressing, as was done after the 11 September attacks, the number of countries whose citizens were killed, helped create international outrage.

Absolutist terrorists also depend on funding from around the globe. By changing their laws and enforcing some that have long been on the books, some nations have been able to impede the flow of money to Al Qaeda and other absolutist terrorist organizations. When confronted with how these funds are used, legitimate charities and donors have backed away from supporting these activities. Many governments have increased their cooperation in the financial arena. However, cooperation remains far from complete. Moreover, some populations remain willing to provide funds for what they see as legitimate causes so desperate that the only resort is terrorism.

The largest challenge to isolating the violent, absolutist terrorists is demonstrating that non-violent alternatives exist and can be productive in resolving genuine grievances. This approach will not work with the dedicated terrorists themselves, for they see political discourse and compromise as wrong. However, their uncompromising postures will help ensure they are isolated (indeed, that they isolate themselves) when meaningful political dialogue takes place.

Penetrating the Veils

Absolutist terrorists are difficult to defeat, in part, because we know so little about them and the way they are organized and operate. Moreover, their organizations are difficult to penetrate using traditional intelligence and police techniques because they are often based on family, clan, tribe, or other personal associations. Many of the leaders have known one another for decades. The lack of specific knowledge can be compared with the "seven veils" famous in Middle Eastern dancing. Penetration of the veils depends on a variety of tools and techniques. These include:

- international police work;
- cooperation among intelligence services;
- high technology investigations;
- incentives for individual cooperation;
- effective interrogation of captured terrorists; and
- thorough investigation of terrorist events.

To a remarkable extent, every one of these approaches involves some form of negotiation. Many of them involve negotiations among governments and government agencies in order to bring together the experience, expertise, skills and information necessary to develop the intelligence necessary to disrupt the terrorists' networks and convict those who are brought to justice.

Incentives for individual cooperation are also an important tool. Major rewards, often millions of dollars, are offered for information leading to the arrest of leaders and those who carry out major attacks. In the impoverished parts of the world where many of the absolutist terrorists live and operate, financial incentives for information can be important. Moreover, offering such incentives also creates a climate of distrust among the terrorists – forcing them to rely on those they have come to depend upon over the years and limiting their ability to expand their organizations for fear of exposure.

Working with captured absolutist terrorists remains a major challenge because their cooperation can be valuable, but their belief structure may make it difficult to gain their confidence, establish meaningful communication with them, or believe what they say is true. However, the press reports that many of them have been willing to tell what they know with respect to past operations and organizational arrangements. Incentives for such cooperation will obviously vary greatly from case to case, but seem unlikely to include full pardon for past terrorist actions. Of course, cross-checking what these individuals say against the results of investigations and the statements of others who are in custody provides a meaningful filter against which to test the information they provide.

Conclusion

In light of the events of the past decade, negotiating with terrorists and terrorist organizations has become increasingly difficult due to the radical nature of the groups involved. Since the organizations have cut themselves off from the ability to engage in traditional forms of negotiating, alternate means need to be explored and exploited. The methods used in dealing with terrorists and the groups and organizations that support them needs to be broadened. This can be implemented in the policy decisions of those nations that oppose these groups in order to erode the cohesive foundations that enable terrorists to operate.

References

Aldinger, C. and Steen, M. (2001) "Taliban say they'll surrender Kandahar". Reuters December 7.
Assistance Afghanistan (2001) "Taliban Music Ban Said Destroying Afghan Heritage". 1 May. <http://www.pcpafg.org/news/Afghan_News/year2001/2001_04_30/Taliban_Music_Ban_Said_Destroying_Afghan_Heritage.shtml>.
Associated Press (2001) "Taliban Destroys Buddha Statues". 11 March. <http://www.tibet.ca/ wtnarchive/2001/3/11_6.html>.
Brisard, Jean-Charles and Dasquie, Guillaume (2001) *Bin Laden: The Forbidden Truth*. Paris: Denoël.
CBS News (2001) "Bush Targets Hamas Money". 4 December. <http://www.cbsnews.com/stories/2001/12/04/attack/main320009.shtml>.
Chelalal, Cesar (1999) "Taliban Conducts a War Against Women". *Japan Times*, 17 July.
CNN.com/US (2000) "Transcript of President Bush's address". 20 September. <http://www.cnn.com/2001/US/09/20/gen.bush.transcript/>.
Crenshaw, Martha (2000) "The Psychology of Terrorism: An Agenda for the 21st Century". *Political Psychology* 21, 2: 405–420.
Crenshaw, Martha (2001) "Counterterrorism Policy and the Political Process". *Studies in Conflict and Terrorism* 24, 5: 329–337.

Gurr, T.R. (1979)"Some Characteristics of Terrorism in the 1960s". In M. Stohl (ed.), *The Politics of Terrorism*. New York: Dekker.

Hayes, R.E. (1982) *The Impact of Government Behavior on the Frequency, Type, and Targets of Terrorist Group Activity*. McLean, VA: Defense Systems.

Hayes, R.E. (1988) *Models of Structure and Process of Terrorist Groups: Decision-Making Processes*. Vienna, VA: Evidence Based Research.

Hayes, R.E., and Schiller, T. (1983) *The Impact of Government Behavior on the Frequency, Type, and Targets of Terrorist Group Activity: The Italian Experience, 1968–1982*. McLean, VA: Defense Systems.

Hewitt, C. (1982) *The Effectiveness of Counter-Terrorist Policies*. Washington, DC: US Department of State.

Heyman, E.T., and Mickolus, E.F. (1981) "Imitation by Terrorists: Quantitative Approaches to the Study of Diffusion Processes in patterns of International Terrorism". In Y. Alexander and J. Gleason (eds.), *Behavioral and Quantitative Perspectives on Terrorism*. New York: Pergamon Press.

Hoffman, Bruce (2001) "Change and Continuity in Terrorism". *Studies in Conflict and Terrorism* 24, 5: 417–428.

Hoffman, Bruce (2002) "Rethinking Terrorism and Counterterrorism Since 9/11". *Studies in Conflict and Terrorism* 25, 5: 303–316.

Huang, Reyko (2002) "South Asia and the United States: Assessing New Policies and Old Problems". Center for Defense Information. <http://www.cdi.org/terrorism/southasia.cfm>.

Human Rights Watch (2001) "Afghanistan Human Rights Denied Systematic Violations of Women's Rights in Afghanistan". 15, 5. <http://www.hrw.org/reports/2001/afghan3/afgwrd1001-04.htm>.

Khalaf, R. (2002) "Yemen develops its own type of campaign: President Saleh wants US help, not troops". *Financial Times*, 18 February.

Krebs, Valdis E. (2002) "Mapping Networks of Terrorist Cells". *Connections*. <http://www.orgnet.com/MappingTerroristNetworks.pdf>.

Kurth, James (2000) "Confronting the Unipolar Moment: The American Empire and Islamic Terrorism". *Current History* 101, 659: 403–408.

Landes, W.M. (1978) "An Economic Study of US Aircraft Hijackings, 1961–1976". *Journal of Law and Economics* 21:1–31.

Laquer, W. (1987) *The Age of Terrorism*. New York: Little, Brown.

Lichbach, M.I. (1987) "Deterrence or Escalation: The Puzzle of Aggregate Studies of repression and Dissent". *Journal of Conflict Resolution* 31: 261–297.

Mickolus, E.F. (1987) "Comment: Terrorists, Governments, and Numbers". *Journal of Conflict Resolution* 31: 54–62.

Middle East Media and Research Institute (2001) "Radical Islamist Profiles (2): Sheikh Omar Bakri Muhammad – London". Inquiry and Analysis Series 73, 24 October.

Middle East Media and Research Institute (2002) "'Why We Fight America': Al-Qa'ida Spokesman Explains September 11 and Declares Intentions to Kill 4 Million Americans with Weapons of Mass Destruction". Special Dispatch 388, 12 June.

Midlarsky, M., Crenshaw, M. and Yoshida, F. (1980) "Why Violence Spreads: The Contagion of International Terrorism". *International Studies Quarterly* 24: 262–306.

The National Security Strategy of the United States of America (2002). <http://www.whitehouse.gov/nsc/nss.pdf>.

Oots, K.L. (1986) *A Political Organization Approach to Transnational Terrorism*. Westport, CT: Greenwood Press.

Pillar, P.R. (2001) *Terrorism and US Foreign Policy*. Washington, DC: Brookings Institute Press.

Quillen, Chris (2002) "A Historical Case Study of Mass Casualty Bombers". *Studies in Conflict and Terrorism* 279–292. Taylor and Francis.

Rappoport, D.C. (1984) "Fear and Trembling: Terrorism in Three Religious Traditions". *American Political Science Review* 78: 658–677.

Rubenstein, R.E. (1987) *Alchemists of Revolution: Terrorism in the Modern World*. New York: Basic Books.

Sanger, David E. (2002) "Threats and Responses: Security; Bush to Outline Doctrine of Striking Foes First". *New York Times* Section A, Page 1, Column 3, 20 September.

Simon, Steven and Benjamin, Daniel (2000) "America and the New Terrorism". *Survival* 42, 1: 59–75.

Steiner, M. and Hayes, R.E. (1984) *The Impact of Government Behavior on the Frequency, Type and Targets of Terrorist Group Activity: The West German Experience, 1968–1982*. McLean, VA: Defense Systems, Inc.

"Suicide Terrorism: A Global Threat". (2000) *Janes Intelligence Review*, 20 October. <http://www.janes.com/security/international_security/news/usscole/jir001020_1_n.shtml>.

Turk, A.T. (1982) "Social Dynamics of Terrorism". *International Terror, Annals of the American Academy of Political and Social Science* 119–128.

Tzu, Sun (1962) and Griffith, Samuel B. (trans.), *The Art of War*. Oxford: Oxford University Press.

Van Creveld, Martin (1991) *The Transformation of War*. New York: The Free Press.

Whine, Michael (2002) "The New Terrorism". 20 January. <http://www.ict.org.il/articles/articles/articledet.cfm?articleid=427>.

Negotiating with Terrorists: The Hostage Case

GUY OLIVIER FAURE

Originally, the word "hostage" comes from the Latin *hospes* that means "hospitality". Obviously, the concept has evolved a great deal in meaning and substance. Historically, the practice dates back to high antiquity, as exemplified in its practice in ancient Egypt, Persia, the Middle East, Greece and the Roman Empire. It was even then present as a clause in treaties. The first "hostages" were most often prominent people handed over to adversaries in order to guarantee fulfillment of commitments such as the exchange of prisoners or evacuation of territories. It was also a way to ensure that allies would remain as such. "Diplomatic hostages" were often members of royal families and were treated as persons of distinction. The practice of hostage-taking became illegal in the 18th century. At the same time, a much more sordid practice continued to occur and is still in use: abduction for the purpose of obtaining political advantage. Since 1949, the Geneva Conventions strictly forbid hostage-taking as contrary to human rights. Usually, the practice is considered a criminal offense and severely punished. Some countries, such as Colombia, have even outlawed any contact with hostage-takers.

Today, it remains a common practice on a great variety of occasions. Hostage-taking can be defined as the detention of individuals whose release is conditional on the realization of certain conditions determined by their captors. Thus, the hostage is the guarantor of a trade-off; he is a currency of exchange. This illegal control is a *fait accompli* on the freedom of the hostages and threatens their lives. This situation created by the hostage-takers is meant to strengthen their bargaining position.

Hostage-taking is part of a broader action, that of random terror which is meant to create or to perpetuate a power situation (Arendt 1962). This is typically a weapon of the weak. It is also a way of substituting violence for the rule of law. By doing so, the hostage-taker challenges the prevailing legal authority, weakens it, and discredits it. Acting in this fashion, hostage-takers knowingly and dramatically are ready to transgress the first taboo of our societies by committing murder.

Several hostage-taking situations can be distinguished: skyjacking, hostage-barricade incidents such as attacks on embassies, and kidnapping (Hayes 2002). According to the definition adopted by the European Union in 2001, hostage-taking falls into the category of terrorist offenses and includes activities such as extor-

International Negotiation Series 1:
I.W. Zartman (ed.) Negotiating with Terrorists, 25–49
© 2006 *Koninklijke Brill NV. Printed in the Netherlands.*

tion, seizure of aircraft, kidnapping for the purpose of seriously intimidating a population, and attempts to alter or destroy the political, economic, or social structure
of a country. Even if negotiating to free hostages deals more with the symptoms of
the problem than with its cause, in the short term, legal authorities are bound to act
to save human lives. Negotiation is one among the various tools that can be used
even if terrorists are among the least likely negotiators. Research has already shed
light on some aspects of this highly uncertain and complex activity (Baldwin
1976; Faure 1988, 2002; Hayes 2002; Miller 1980; Waugh 1982).

For several decades, hostage-taking has been a widespread activity. Drawing
from experience, a number of technical manuals has been published for the purpose
of providing advice on specific negotiation skills and methods that should be used
in particular circumstances (McMains and Mullins 2001; Lanceley 1999; Davidson
2002; Thomson 2001; MacWillson 1992; Bolz and Hershey 1980; Clutterbuck
1987; Cooper 1981; Poland and McCrystle 1999; Adang and Giebels 1999). These
guides are often written by police negotiators. They cover topics such as barricaded
subjects incidents, high-risk suicide attempts, jail riots, violence in the workplace,
stress management, verbal tactics in crisis communication, dealing with emotionally disturbed people, selecting the negotiation team, intelligence gathering, sniper
operations, assaults, media relations, and post-traumatic debriefing.

Falling short of providing a real structure for action, these guidelines refer to
basic principles drawn from experience that should be followed by any negotiator
dealing with hostage-takers. Among the main elements emphasized are the need to
avoid engaging in verbal conflict, to actively listen, to avoid deadlines, to give nothing away while appearing to make trade-offs, to understand that lies and deception
are acceptable in such critical matters, to gain time, to distract the captors from the
hostages, to reassure hostage-takers that the site will not be assaulted, to minimize
the seriousness of the crime, not to use the word "hostage", not to suggest exchang-
ing oneself for hostages, and not to expose oneself physically.

Objectives

The purpose of this article is to offer an overview of negotiation concerning
hostage-taking from an analytical perspective drawn from negotiation theory. The
point is to present insights on this type of negotiation and in doing so test the relevance of concepts and models.

The work is structured according to the rationale of the negotiator. Various
background components of the hostage negotiation are surveyed and studied.
Among these elements are the parties involved, the hostage-takers' motivations and
profiles, the negotiators' objectives and what is considered to be "negotiable", the
legitimacy issue, and the context. The second section deals with the negotiation

process, addressing the different phases of negotiation, the attitudes of the hostages, information gathering, and the role of the media and public opinion. A third section focuses on two other essential dimensions of the negotiation, namely, the intercultural aspects and the psychological dimension. A final section deals with the end-game scenarios and assessment of the outcome of this complex and uncertain form of negotiation.

Each of these themes is dealt with and illustrated with examples. In addition to the existing scientific literature in this domain, the content of this article is based on interviews with practitioners and on the personal observations of the author.

Background Components

The Parties Involved

A hostage-taking situation is a complex setting that includes many stakeholders. The major and most visible parties to the negotiation are – besides the hostages who sometimes play an active as well as a passive role in the drama – the hostage-takers and the entity that is the target of the whole operation. Hostages may be prominent personalities, children of famous people, political figures, or a group of unknown people such as airplane passengers including crew and pilot, clients and staff of a bank, train passengers, children at school or in a school bus, or diplomats and guests in an embassy.

Hostage-takers can be political militants, but also may be people suffering from psychological problems or simply bank robbers who are trying to escape from the site of their crime. The target of the whole operation of hostage-taking may be a government, a company, or a wealthy individual – basically, whoever is in possession of a resource coveted by the hostage-takers.

There may be other actors involved in the situation, such as public opinion, the government of the country where the incident is taking place, or the hostages' families. Hostage-takers may have constituencies such as political groups. Figure 1 depicts a general model of the overall hostage situation.

If we consider the negotiation process itself, we have to include the negotiators, whose task it is to directly interact with the hostage-takers. They may be police officers, government representatives, and special units that may include psychologists or prominent people who are asked to intervene as mediators.

The overall logic of the system relies on the threat principle. The hostage-takers are people who appropriate the lives of other people by violent means and intend to make use of these lives as a currency of exchange. They create this situation to be able to issue a credible threat. The point is to be able to seriously harm the hostages if the target does not comply. Harming the captives may consist in protracting their

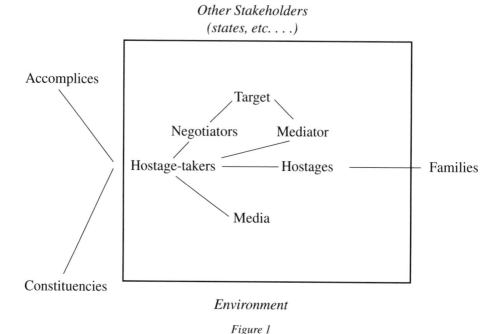

Figure 1

captivity – sometimes for years – in crippling them, in letting them die of illness and care deprivation, or simply in killing them.

As underlined by Faure (2002), a hostage-taking situation has very specific attributes:

- Dramatic stakes to manage: namely, human lives;
- Positions on both sides of an abyssal gap reflecting the extremely conflicting values of the parties;
- The impossibility of officially recognizing the hostage-taker as a legitimate counterpart;
- Trust as a mechanism that normally has no place in such a setting and cannot be established and implemented during the negotiation process;
- The safety of the negotiators themselves when they work within a hostile context; and,
- Third-party intervention from, for example, the media or the families of the hostages.

These various elements make it extremely difficult to conceive of negotiation as a win-win game. The formal structure of the problem is much more adequately described with a concave curve representing the zone of possible agreements rather than the usual convex curve setting the stage for a Pareto optimal result. Thus, it becomes very unlikely that a situation in which everyone's needs are met will be constructed.

Hostage-Takers' Motivation and Profile

Three types of hostage-takers can be distinguished, each one corresponding to a different set of motivations. The three prototypes are the criminal, the political militant, and the mentally ill person (Pearce 1977; Stratton 1978; Goldaber 1979). *The criminal*, who is often called a gangster, a felon, or an extortionist, is mainly motivated by money. A bank robber who finds the police waiting for him at the entrance of the building and who takes hostages to negotiate safe conduct belongs to this category. In fact, most often the gangster neither wants to be caught nor face a murder charge. His margin for maneuver is thus rather narrow. The hostages are meant to provide an alternate means of escape. This situation involves the risk of escalation from a simple armed robbery to murder, but if the hostage-taker behaves rationally, he will not resort to that extreme option.

Kidnapping with the intention of seeking ransom belongs to the same category. This type of criminal tends to view his action as a kind of business transaction. Someone will have to pay for the hostage's right to continue living.

There are also mixed types of hostage-takers whose public discourse is based on religious or separatist arguments, yet who in fact do no more than extort financial resources from governments. In this domain of kidnapping for ransom, the Abu Sayyaf Group, a Muslim radical organization operating in the southern islands of the Philippines, is a typical example of a group resorting to terror for financial profit. Since April 2000, this group has carried out a series of hostage-taking activities, mostly aimed at foreigners, with fruitful results. Aboard speedboats, the Abu Sayyaf Group attacked a tourist resort in Malaysia and kidnapped 21 foreigners. In July of the same year, this group seized three French journalists. Later in the year, all prisoners were released after a ransom payment of US $10–25 million, allegedly from European governments funneled through the Libyan government. In May 2001, the terrorist group kidnapped three Americans and 17 Filipinos from a tourist resort in the Philippines. Several of them were murdered while the others were freed after a year of detention at the price of a ransom of US $1 million per person. The same group went on in the following years to kidnap a number of Filipinos, releasing some after more ransom was paid and executing others.

The political militant is most often motivated by power, influence, fame, political recognition, political trade-offs such as the freeing of prisoners of his own group, or the acquisition of resources for his cause. What is typical of actions taken by political militants is their collective and planned nature. The collective aspect does not only include the coordinated action of several highly committed people, but also the existence of a sponsoring group and a situation that dramatically modifies the power relations between parties. Evidence of long and careful preparation, detailed planning, calculated expectations, and the use of standard operating procedures which have stood the test of time leave very little room for spontaneous moves and unforeseen events. Such a reality and observed behavior differ considerably from the scenarios offered in movies and television programs in which the terrorists are often portrayed as neurotics or psychopaths whose behavior is hardly predictable.

As observed by Miller (1980), such terrorists can be clients of a United Nations member state and use terrorism as an extension of diplomacy. In quite a few cases, political militants are willing to die if their demands are not met, even if they are not basically suicidal. In this category, one must include "free-lance revolutionaries" who seek political outcomes but are not backed by any established organization (Baldwin 1976).

Defined as "ideologues", political militants are akin to "religious terrorists", the most unlikely negotiators since extremist ideologies tend to obscure the ability to compromise (Hayes 2002). The hostage-taker who is a political militant may be portrayed as a popular hero or a sort of Robin Hood figure (Oettgen and Spinazzola 1987). He considers himself as a representative of victims seeking justice. He thus believes he is justified to use any means that helps him achieve what he considers to be righteous ends. He has the option of turning a defeat into a victory and thus projecting a new identity for the group he represents. If he succeeds in taking hostages, he will be seen by his followers as having ultimately triumphed. If he fails, he will be remembered for his sacrifice. In both cases he will end up as a hero, a symbol, or a role model for the group.

The mentally ill individual includes those who may be classified as psychopaths, paranoid-schizophrenics, maniacs, or suicidal persons, and is motivated by releasing anxiety or satisfying some perverse need. Often defined as "insane", his most erratic behavior makes him an extremely difficult case to deal with (Baldwin 1976).

Considering the three profiles, uncertainty about the real objectives of the hostage-takers is a major variable in the management of this type of negotiation. These objectives can be extremely diverse. They may be political, psychological, symbolic, social-emotional, or simply monetary in nature. The search for a specific tangible compensation is among the most common goals of a hostage-taker. The sought compensation may be money, but also may be evasion from legal punishment, freedom for accomplices, release of political prisoners, weapons, or medicine. Sometimes, the objective may be more difficult to decipher as in cases demanding public exposure and publicity, ending one's life with external assistance (that of the police, for instance), constructing a new identity, taking revenge in a lose-lose rationale, or playing out an apocalyptic scenario.

The Negotiators' Objectives and What is "Negotiable"

The negotiators' purpose is to free hostages. Negotiators thus manage two conflicting constraints: securing the freedom of the hostages and deterring other terrorists from taking more hostages. There is no way to free hostages without giving something to the hostage-takers. If there is a gain and no negative consequences, hostage-takers will learn that their action is worthwhile and may make more attempts of the same kind. On the one hand, if concessions and exchanges are conceded, deterrence is not effective. Thus, the counter-threat of a possible police or army intervention may introduce a new balance into the overall system. On the other hand, if the target remains inflexible, the hostages may be killed and the responsibility of the massacre consequently may be borne by the authorities as much as by the hostage-takers.

Defining the real objectives of the hostage-takers is a crucial step because this information will govern the actions to be taken. In complex cases, the French for instance have specialized teams of intervention (the RAID for the police or the GIGN for the army) that have developed computer programs to analyze the psychological profile of the hostage-taker. Based on a limited amount of verbal exchanges, it becomes possible to detect, for example, if the individual is a paranoid psychopath or a melancholic, and thus select an appropriate mode of argumentation and intervention.

A considerable range of issues can be explored during the negotiation process. The hostages are not only a currency of exchange but also a shield against any physical intervention from the police, army, or specialized units. The hostage-takers manage a kind of "hostage capital". Although official authorities normally deny it, there are many things that are traded off in the course of this type of negotiation including not only safe conduct for the hostage-takers, release of jailed terrorists, money, and weapons (Faure 1988), but also recognition, reputation, and the furnishing of political symbols (Miller 1980). There are some limits to the trade-offs. Normally, face-saving is part of the final deal as no open capitulation could be accepted on either side. In order for this to be possible, no hostage should be killed, no negotiator murdered, and no hostage-taker executed.

The Legitimacy Issue

Prior to entering the negotiation process, the issue of bestowing legitimacy on the negotiating counterpart as a consequence of the negotiation itself may be raised.

This is an especially delicate, embarrassing, and thorny point for governments. Formally, no government recognizes a terrorist group, an extortionist, or a hostage-taker as a legitimate counterpart. One should not deal with the devil without the risk of losing one's soul. In addition, there is a widely acknowledged principle that consists of stipulating that one does not negotiate under threat. In doing so, one can jeopardize reputation or future effectiveness.

Though these principles are clear, reality intervenes with an insurmountable priority: the onus to save lives. This moral duty of intervening has been formalized by a UN resolution (March 1987), which not only categorically condemns all hostage-taking irregardless of the motivation but which also asks governments to take all necessary measures to put an immediate end to confinement of victims. In practice, governments often intervene directly or through a third party. There is a moral legitimacy in "interacting" with the hostage-takers, if not in negotiating with them. This double language can be applied to a great variety of issues. Usually no concessions are made officially and the final deal is not made publicly because often the country involved has to make concessions that, if known, would create problems for it with other countries or with its own public opinion (Faure 1988). Here, more than in any other situation, the iceberg principle, which consists of disclosing only a small portion of the information known, applies. If one considers again, for instance, the actions of the Abu Sayyaf Group in the Philippines, no government has acknowledged having paid a ransom to obtain the freedom for its own nationals. For its own part, the Filipino government strictly opposes payment of ransom for hostages.

The legitimacy issue refers to a broader domain, that of values. There is very little in common between hostage-takers who appropriate the lives of innocent people and representatives of legitimate organizations whose action is carried out according to the law. This characteristic will have obvious consequences for the negotiation process. The empathy process by which one side stands in the shoes of the other and tries to understand (if not to share) their views can hardly operate. The moral gap created by the hostage-taking act is an element that structures the negotiation in terms of relational incompatibility and raises a major obstacle to the implementation of a mechanism for exchange and concessions. Thus, the negotiation concession-convergence model is a necessary tool, but extremely difficult to set up.

The moral disqualification of the counterpart on both sides may authorize behaviors that would otherwise not be present in a negotiation, such as lying, playing tricks, manipulating, or using deceptive devices. A number of people highly familiar with this type of negotiation, such as heads of police, considers that hostage-takers should be promised everything and delivered nothing (Miller 1980). Thus, not only the ends, but the "quality" of the counterpart, may morally justify lying and cheating. However, if the negotiation unfolds in several stages, or if the police will have to deal with identical cases later, the question of this tactic's credibility is raised. If there is not a minimum of credibility among parties, no serious and effective negotiation can be carried out in the future.

The Context

One of the most significant factors in understanding negotiations with terrorists is context. Hostage-takers may act in a friendly context or in a hostile context. Negotiators who have to deal with them usually adopt totally different strategies and sometimes even very different goals. In the case of a context friendly to the terrorists, the pressure is on the intervening negotiators to free the hostages because they have very narrow room for maneuver and do not control the negotiation environment. They can be subjected to harassment, attrition, threats, or other coercive tactics. They can even be made to fear for their own lives. There are cases that end tragically for negotiators when they are not protected or when the other side does not care about possible punishment. As soon as one side has absolutely nothing to lose, it becomes extremely difficult to maintain a reasonable power balance in the negotiation process.

In the case of hostage-takers operating in a hostile environment such as a hostage-barricade situation, the "fishbowl theory" applies (Baldwin 1976). The means available to the hostage-takers are much more limited. They face a much higher risk and usually put much more pressure on the hostages. Hijackers, for instance, and those who seize hostages in bank vaults or embassies, are bargaining in a fishbowl with an adversary who is outside and "can change the water in the bowl" anytime he likes. The hostage-takers' answer to this unfavorable situation is, when possible, to move to a more welcoming environment. This is typical of hostage-taking in airplanes and leads the terrorists to bring the airplane to an accomplice country where the context can be reversed (Faure 1988). This was the case when a TWA flight was hijacked en route to Rome from Athens by two Lebanese Hezbollah terrorists and forced to fly to Beirut where 15 more terrorists got on board. Of the 145 passengers, 32 male Americans were kept as hostages for 17 days. Passengers with Jewish names were taken to secret sites in the Shiite part of Lebanon and ultimately rescued by a US delta force unit.

Another fishbowl case was the takeover of the Grand Mosque of Mecca in 1979 by a religious group of more than a thousand men denouncing the misdeeds of the Saudi royal family. Fifty thousand people were held hostage at first, soon reduced to 170, a significant but far more manageable number. A siege was organized and the Saudi King obtained a *fatwa* to launch an assault on the premises of the holy shrine. The storming of the site proved so costly in lives that, after several unsuc-

cessful attempts, the governor of Mecca requested the intervention of a French specialized unit, the GIGN. Members of this unit were quickly "converted" to Islam
so as not to infringe upon Muslim law. They used various techniques such as flooding the basement of the mosque and then trying to electrocute those who were still
alive. At the end, gas was used to neutralize the survivors. Altogether, an estimated
4000 people lost their lives during the two-week battle. 63 rebels were captured
alive. Examples were made of them, with their public beheading at different locations around the Kingdom.

Commitment and capabilities are basic conditions that govern the entire negotiation process. On the hostage-taker's side, there are a wide range of commitments:
determination to obtain some objective, to have all demands met, to kill, or to die.
Determination is only credible and effective if the corresponding threat can be
implemented, which raises the question of the capabilities of the hostage-takers
and the resources they have at their disposal. Do they have enough means, weapons, men, external support, know-how, and information to conduct their action
effectively?

The 1979 hostage case at the US Embassy in Teheran demonstrates the essential role played by a highly favorable context to the captors. Iranian militants
attacked the US Embassy and took 90 hostages. 54 of these prisoners remained in
captivity for 444 days. The 500 militants, often described as "students", and the
Iranian government were total accomplices. All negotiation attempts were fruitless.
A rescue mission was launched and aborted after heavy casualties. The hostages
were only released after a protracted negotiation made easier by Algerian mediation, the death of the former Shah, and the invasion of Iran by the Iraqi army. It was
a case in which no fishbowl rationale could be applied, hostage-taker determination was extremely high, resources were fully available to them, and the risk level
was nil.

The Negotiation Process

The Three Phases

Attempts to obtain the release of hostages through bargaining is a process which
occurs under conditions of high conflict and which may have dramatic consequences. Life and death are the stakes behind the interaction and risk-taking is a
major dimension in the actors' behavior. In addition, a psychological component –
the level of stress to which parties to the situation are exposed – also comes into
play because the lives of captives, captors, and negotiators are at risk. Thus, this
type of negotiation exhibits a set of characteristics that opens up an extremely wide
range of possible consequences.

Zartman's three-phase model of 1) pre-negotiation, 2) formula, and 3) details can be applied with much relevance to this type of negotiation. The *pre-negotiation* phase consists of accepting the idea of negotiation. It is the basic assumption on which the hostage-taker strategy is devised. On the side of the authorities, officially there cannot be any negotiation with illegitimate counterparts, but in fact "contacts" are established. To this end, it can be quite necessary to set up a direct communication system such as a phone line and organize a way to supply the captives and their captors with food and daily necessities through an intermediary third party. If such contacts were not established, the authorities in charge would be regarded by public opinion and by the hostages' families as indifferent to the fate of the victims or incapable of action. This is why authorities most often act with discretion about the content of the exchanges, but at the same time, are interested in appearing active.

Establishing the *formula for agreement* is particularly difficult to manage because negotiators are confronted with outrageous demands from the hostage-takers. This is due not only to the economic or political cost of meeting those demands but because such demands often infringe on national laws and international conventions. The demand may be, for instance, to ask for the release of hundreds of political prisoners jailed in a third country, to obtain highly sophisticated weapons, to receive amounts of money equivalent to the annual budget of a small country, to get access to world television networks to issue proclamations, to ask for political figures to replace the hostages, to require the resignation of a government, to compel a country's government to criticize itself publicly, or to insist on official recognition from the UN or even for a seat in that body.

This kind of situation represents a very conflictual interaction. Often, tough tactics such as threats and *faits accomplis* are used to make one's determination more credible and put more pressure on the other party. The hostage-takers live under the permanent threat of being stormed in an assault by an intervention team, whereas the authorities fear the execution of captives. The goal for the authorities is to lower the level of the captors' expectations by mobilizing harassment and fatigue tactics, and information manipulation.

One of the most effective tools in speeding the search for a formula of agreement is applying the most feared threat that underlies the hostage situation – killing one or several hostages. Several incidents in the Middle East offer illustrations of this tactic.

Timing is an extremely important factor in the negotiation because it structures the process and drastically influences behaviors. Thus, Miller (1980) points out that "time is an expandable commodity; life is not". Unless captors keep their hostages in a friendly environment, time usually works to the advantage of the authorities. This is why issuing imperative deadlines is part of the panoply of constraints raised by the hostage-takers who thus aim to impose their own tempo onto the discussions.

Baldwin (1976) observed that as the situation evolves, fatigue becomes an increasingly important variable. Rationality and motivation are likely to change on the hostage-takers' side. With fatigue, the overarching formula offered by the authorities may begin to appear more acceptable to the captors. There also may be a shift in priorities as the situation decomposes. This can happen, for instance, because of an unexpected intervention, for example, on the part of a religious leader respected by the captors or the parents of the hostage-taker if he is acting alone. This is why captors tend to seek to maintain their anonymity, whereas the authorities strive to discover their true identity in order to multiply the means of pressure.

However, time does not always play against the captors, especially if they are operating in a friendly context. In fact, with the passage of time, public opinion expects positive results, commiserates with the hostages, and may accuse the authorities of being incapable of resolving the situation. If one considers the overall situation, its evolution over time may lead the hostage-takers to experience the Damocles complex. The captors realize that they have somehow been turned into prisoners. The experience of confinement in a bank or an airplane, for instance, may increasingly modify their perception of the problem. This reframing may lead them to abandon their hopes for an outcome within minutes or hours. In a protracted situation, the context may come to bear heavily upon the hostage-takers, playing an essential role in ongoing negotiations.

Lengthening the duration of the negotiation may also introduce a reversal effect between the position of culprit and victim. The authorities become reprehensible for not having dealt with the problem with the necessary effectiveness and rapidity. This phenomenon is accentuated if the hostages are ordinary citizens with whom common people can identify.

In a negotiation, the security point denotes the minimum gains that a party has determined acceptable. The existing gap between the goals of a negotiator and his security point plays an essential role in the management of the negotiation process. If a hostage-taker is truly ready to die for his cause, it means that his goals and security points are identical. There is no more room for maneuver for the other side. An effective technique for the terrorist can be to make the authorities believe that his goal and his security point are the same. Conversely, the negotiator will try to make the hostage-taker believe that exile is a better option than death because he will thus still have leverage to serve his cause.

The *details phase* is still highly competitive and often the process moves to the edge of the abyss. Parties to the conflict, especially political militants, are caught in a lose-lose game in which the only satisfaction becomes that of inflicting more suffering or casualties on the other side. Within such a situation, hidden or overt violence prevails at the negotiation table. Such means are not the most suitable for reaching an agreement or even limited forms of cooperation.

Tricks of all sorts are used; cheating is the most common currency, and deep distrust remains throughout the process. Negotiators apply the reciprocity principle with the "salami" tactic to reach their goals. Anything given to the hostage-takers must receive compensation, even water, food and other commodities such as light and electricity. The trade-off may be a hostage if there are many of them, or the sending of a messenger or a doctor.

This phase of fine-tuning concessions is an ambivalent moment in negotiations because everyone believes he has done the most difficult part of the task and true hope for a solution has appeared. At the same time, the obstacles have not been really overcome because each side will try to compensate quantitatively for what it has conceded in the previous phase. Like the authorities, terrorist groups have closely studied the negotiation techniques used by these authorities and have a precise plan to control the ultimate phase. This stage unfolds under the threat of dirty tricks, even if none are really implemented, which makes this phase extremely antagonistic. The prevailing suspicion of ill intent, especially on the side of the captors is the unspoken rule, for the word of the other is deemed questionable. In such a case, negotiation cannot be defined as a process of gradual reduction of uncertainty, because uncertainty will remain until the very last moment.

The Attitude of the Hostages

Most of the captives fall into the category of "passive hostages", which means people who do not have the possibility of exerting any important personal initiative with regard to their own situation. The hostages come to realize that their position was created against their own will and that they have become a financial or political stake. They experience the hostage condition as an overwhelming unfairness being done to them. They do not control their movements or their own lives. Their destiny will be played out for them. Beyond being simple prisoners, they are suspended dead people at the captors' mercy. As such, they have two basic reactions: either they prostrate themselves or they try to act. Thus, some hostages manage, at great risk, to escape from their place of detention. There are cases of hostages with strong enough personalities or sufficient charisma to directly influence some of their captors (Miller 1980). When the head of the hostage-takers realizes this, he has to remove them. Basic precautions are often taken by captors so that they do not show themselves to the hostages unless wearing a hood and they forbid all verbal exchange and visual contact. Sometimes hostages are kept tied up, isolated or in quasi-darkness.

Some hostages establish relations with their captors and may even come to espouse their cause. The psychological process is known as the "Stockholm syndrome" (Wilson and Smith 1999; Wilson 2002). Dependent, humiliated, cut off from the outside world, and overcome by feelings of abandonment and psychological weakness, the hostage may begin to identify with the captor. This is the outcome of a mental process in which hostage and jailer develop a sense of mutual attachment. With the passing of time and the suspension of contact with the outside world, both find themselves locked in a common fate. Each one needs the other to achieve freedom and satisfaction of demands. Deprived of power, the hostage identifies with the captor and feels that both have similar interests. The authorities outside are thus perceived as the enemy who imposes obstacles to the release of captives. If something dramatic happens, these authorities are considered responsible.

This psychological process was first observed in Stockholm in the case of a failed bank robbery that resulted in hostage-taking. Several of the hostages ended up identifying with the criminals and a woman even initiated sexual relations with her jailer. These attitudes were not a submissive response to normal feelings of fear but were produced by a kind of intimacy that developed during the captivity phase during which both parties shared the same difficult situation in the same physical space under conditions of high stress. Thus, an emotional bond was created. Patricia Hearst, the daughter of a press tycoon, provided a spectacular illustration of the Stockholm syndrome. First, she was kidnapped and held for ransom. Later, she joined the cause of the captors, lived with one of the men, and helped the gang to attack banks at gunpoint.

Another expression of this hostage identification syndrome was observed in the hostage-taking at the residence of the Japanese ambassador in Lima, Peru in 1996 by a Marxist-Leninist commando. Labeled the "Lima Syndrome", it describes a gradual identification of some of the captors with the hostages throughout the days, weeks or months of detention. As a consequence, their original hostility softened. The unity of the terrorist group was thus challenged.

The Stockholm syndrome may lead the hostages to adopt an antagonistic attitude toward the authorities, such as refusal to cooperate in a rescue attempt (Ochberg 1980), providing inaccurate information about the hostage-takers and the siege site if they are released during the negotiation process, or afterwards, refusing to testify against their captors. However, the Stockholm syndrome can also offer possibilities for positive reciprocal feelings that may prevent hostage-takers from killing their hostages. An illustration can be found in the South Moluccan hijacking of a train in the Netherlands in 1975. A passenger was chosen for execution if the authorities did not meet a deadline. Before being killed, this hostage asked his captor to deliver an oral farewell message to his family. The content of the message was so moving that the terrorists changed their mind and did not kill him (Ochberg 1978).

The Stockholm syndrome has been most often explained as a phenomenon of identification with the captor. Another explanation considers the syndrome as a regression process. The hostage regresses to a state of extreme dependence on the captor and develops a strong sense of gratitude toward those controlling his life (Strentz 1979; Ochberg 1980). Indebtedness may thus play an important role, especially when the gap between what is expected or dreaded by the captive and what really happens to him is significant. In 1513, Machiavelli provided an explanation of the phenomenon by pointing out that when men receive good instead of the expected evil, they feel more indebted to their benefactor (Lanceley 1999).

Information Gathering

Whatever the degree of antagonism, a hostage negotiation requires a communication system, some kind of interaction, a minimum attempt to "understand", and information collection. If the positions of the parties on fundamental aspects are in extreme conflict, it may be advisable to appear more cooperative than one's actual position. The point is to avoid throwing oil on the fire. Importantly, by bridging the divide in communication, the negotiator can encourage the hostage-takers to reveal themselves. This may yield useful data on the hostage-takers themselves, their objectives, means, strategy, and sources of external support.

Information gathering is the role of the police and specialized services at both the national and international levels. It includes on-site observation made with the help of optical probes, high-sensitivity microphones, bugs, and micro-lasers able to register conversations held a street away. Telephone exchanges and other conversations are normally tapped and analyzed to identify significant elements such as intonations, hesitations, slips, etc.

Knowing the adversary enables negotiators to drill a hole in the shell behind which the hostage-taker protects himself psychologically, as well as practically. To see the captors or to take pictures of them may lead to their identification and thus greater leverage, especially in the case of kidnapping or hostage-barricade situations, such as a bank robbery gone wrong. If the hostage-taker realizes that he has been spotted and identified, his spirits and demands may lower considerably.

The 1975 Spaghetti House case is one in which the collection of personal information played a crucial role. Three armed robbers bungled a raid and held seven hostages in a London restaurant for six days. Sensitive microphones were put in appropriate places, a great deal of information was collected, and the identity of the captors was discovered. At the end, the gangsters simply surrendered.

The Media and the Public Opinion

The purpose of the media is to inform the public about events happening in the world. The media often displays a special interest for hostage-taking because its dramatic and spectacular dimension generates much public attention. The hostage-takers are aware of this and strive to take advantage of this fact. They often resort to the media as an amplifier of their claims and a megaphone for their propaganda. Thus, the leader of the Palestinian Peoples' Liberation Front stated that in dramatic circumstances such as hostage-taking, it is more useful to keep one Jewish prisoner alive than to kill one hundred in a classic battle.

The media, especially the television, may gradually transform the hostage-taker from a mediocre unknown, an anonymous person among the crowd, into a hot-headed star in the limelight whose words and actions are heard all over the world. A quasi-symbiotic relation may thus be established between hostage-takers and the media, each one providing something essential to the other.

When a journalist identifies himself with the hostages, the public may feel involved in the drama. Public opinion may play a non-negligible role in the strategy adopted by negotiators. In the 1976 case of the hijacking and landing of the Air France airplane in Entebbe, Israeli public opinion was opposed to a military solution until the terrorists raised their demands, thereby casting doubt on the possibility of reaching a negotiated agreement. It was only from this new situation that the Israeli authorities were able to implement their policy of firmness. The militants from the People's Front for the Liberation of Palestine, embarking in Athens, hijacked the plane to Benghazi where all non-Israeli passengers were released. The hijackers then went to Entebbe. The Israeli government sent two airplanes of para-troopers who managed within 90 minutes to kill all the captors, destroy 11 Ugandan military planes, and release all the hostages.

Sometimes the media plays a direct role in the hostage-taking situation by inter-vening among the protagonists. Thus, in New York, in a case in which negotiation had led to an agreement including the release of the hostages and the surrender of the terrorist, a reporter almost derailed the entire operation. He managed to reach the captor by telephone and interviewed him on the reasons behind his conduct. The immediate effect was to reactivate the grievances of the captor who then questioned the agreement.

The intervention of the media may also lead to death. A Lufthansa flight was hijacked to Mogadishu, Somalia in October 1977. During the detention of the air-plane, the pilot managed to surreptitiously send critical information about the ter-rorists to the control tower. A journalist came to know about it and reported what the pilot was describing to a radio channel. One of the hostage-takers on board was listening to that channel and had no difficulty guessing where the leak was coming from. The terrorist killed the pilot. As a basic principle, authorities in charge of the hostage situation try their utmost to keep the media away from the negotiation scene. This strategy is not easy to maintain as hostage families and captors tend to seek more leverage on the negotiation process by resorting to the media.

Dimensions of the Negotiation

The Cultural Issue

When the negotiation brings together protagonists from different countries, the cultural dimension may play an important part (Faure 2002). The gap between North and South, as well as the role of major political actors may, on one hand, function as a trigger for hostage-taking activities and, on the other hand, serve as an obstacle to dialogue in the negotiation. Existing stereotypes often tend to widen the gap and entrench the antagonism. Furthermore, the terrorist group as a social unit may have developed a culture of its own which in many ways is incompatible with any national or global culture. It may have been established as a defense mechanism to shield the group and justify its actions, and it may negate dialogue and communication. Thus, a siege mentality may develop (Faure and Rubin 1993).

At stake are conflicting sets of values on which attitudes are based and behaviors justified. Very often, identity problems arise on the terrorist side. Any counteroffer from the authorities can be perceived as an attempt to checkmate the global project of the terrorist group, challenging its values, its *raison d'être*, and its identity. Opportunities for communicating are reduced and channels that have been established for the purpose of helping the negotiation process are simply used as means of conducting verbal warfare.

Negotiation to free hostages juxtaposes two groups who also belong to different organizational cultures. The culture of the legal authorities dealing with the situation is based on official legitimacy, the group's institutional position, and the laws in force. The hostage-takers' culture is rooted in shared values that have been adopted by the members of their group and produce specific representations of the world. Huge discrepancies may exist and bear on the negotiation. Not least of these is the definition given by each party to the overall situation. The authorities face a criminal case, abduction, which is a totally unacceptable action that must be punished accordingly. For the hostage-takers, the situation represents a courageous and just initiative.

The actors in the situation are also perceived in highly contrasting ways. The negotiators define themselves as representatives of the only legitimate authority embodying the values of society, whereas for the terrorists, the official negotiators are just agents of a repressive power. For the negotiators, the hostage-takers are viewed as criminals and terrorists, whereas the hostage-takers define themselves as freedom fighters. Thus, culprits and victims are two sides of the same coin. The hostages themselves are also conceived differently by each side – innocent hostages by some and guests by the other.

The nature of the demands reveals the same conflicting perceptions. For one group, the act is mere extortion. For the other group, it is a compensation mechanism, an action undertaken in order to be recognized. The ethical dimension also exhibits considerable discrepancies. In the view of the legal authorities, terrorists' methods discredit their aims. For the terrorists, the impossibility of reaching a substantial outcome through normal channels justifies their means.

A disjunction in values can also be observed when considering the main variables in hostage-taking. Legitimacy, law, justice, violence, and death are interpreted in radically incompatible ways. The legitimacy of the authorities is denied and at best viewed as serving the interests of a small number of influential people. The law of one group is defined by the other as a repressive apparatus. What is justice for some is viewed as the very expression of unfairness by others. The condemnation of violence by some is considered ideological manipulation by others. Death is viewed as a failure for some but a crowning achievement for others. This set of disjunctive perceptions makes communication in the negotiation setting extremely difficult.

The Psychological Variable

In a wide range of hostage negotiation cases, including those involving political militants and mentally ill people, the psychological dimension plays a major role and clearly distinguishes hostage situations from other types of negotiations. This dimension considerably increases the level of complexity of the negotiator's task because, like the ideological dimension, it tends to break the basic rationale that governs most negotiations.

The psychological profile of hostage-takers may include tendencies towards megalomaniac attitudes, paranoid behavior, or suicidal actions. Terrorist groups may sense an overwhelming sense of power and self-image by making outrageous demands directly of a government. Paranoid attitudes result from a Manichean vision of the world, with good and evil caught in a fight to the death. This can leave no room for compromise, because it would betray the terrorist's mission. Suicidal conduct is implemented with either the idea of accomplishing an altruistic sacrifice or playing out the great "end scenario". The altruistic sacrifice demonstrates an extremely strong identification of the member with his group or a pathological weakening of the personality. Orchestrating the "end scenario" is a way to implement, on a small scale, the end of the world prophecy.

Devaluation of the victims may be used to reduce the seriousness of the act of murder if the hostages are to be killed. Bewildering as these beliefs may be, they are spread and maintained by individuals and groups to feed contempt and create a differentiated image of other, providing easy excuses for the worst acts.

The Final Stage

The End Scenarios

After a few hours, days, weeks, or even months, the negotiation comes to a final stage. Two scenarios can result: a settlement is found or no agreement is reached. When a settlement has been found, it includes the release of the hostages as well as various concessions to the captors. The most common concessions in the case of a hostage-barricade situation or kidnapping are the provision of a sum of money, safe conduct, and/or the promise of a fair trial. If the hostage-taking has political overtones, trade-offs may include money, weapons, medicine, safe passage, asylum for the hostage-takers, the freedom of political prisoners, and access to media networks by the hostage-takers to make public proclamations.

An interesting mechanism of the negotiation process – the sowing of differences to produce an internal division within the hostage-taker group – can facilitate agreement. The unity of the group is weakened and sometimes destroyed by the fact that some offers made by the authorities appear acceptable to some group members but not to others. Another similar trigger for agreement is to convince the captors that the authorities have reached their extreme upper limits of conceivable concessions.

As underlined by Baldwin (1976), it is essential to offer an exit to the hostage-takers, and to time this offer at the right moment. This tactical maneuver combined with efforts to reduce the range of options and lower the level of expectations of each hostage-taker may be quite effective.

When a settlement has been found, there are still two types of endings. The terms of the agreement can be implemented faithfully or they may be abandoned. The non-implementation of the agreement by the captors may for instance lead to the murder of the hostages, as was the case with Aldo Moro, a former Italian prime minister, by the Red Brigades. Kidnapping cases also offer examples of a number of murders at the end of negotiations or during the period of detention. One reason for defection may be that the hostage-takers seek to suppress information that may be used to track them down later.

The authorities may also defect from the agreement, resorting to armed intervention. In this case, negotiation was only a means to soften the hostage-takers. The aim was to collect information on the hostage-takers, their weapons, their degree of preparation, their attitudes, the particulars of the place of confinement, and their possible external allies. Negotiators maintained continuous communication with the terrorists, depriving them of sleep and exhausting them in order to reduce their ability to analyze new events and lower their level of vigilance.

When hostage-taking is perceived as an act of war, the response of authorities is likely to be in a similar vein. This position is reflected in Israeli policy, which clearly prioritizes deterrence and long-term views. An example of this is the 1974 case when children at a school in Maalot, Israel were taken hostage by a Palestinian group. Three Arabs from the Democratic Front for the Liberation of Palestine attacked the school, killing the guard and several children. The assault, led by an elite brigade, resulted in a tragic outcome not only for those hostage-takers who were killed but also for the 21 children.

The 1975 Savoy Hotel incident in Tel Aviv was the scene of another dramatic ending. Eight PLO gunmen landed by sea in Tel Aviv. They took dozens of hostages at the Savoy Hotel. The same day, security forces stormed the site but were unable to avoid bloodshed. Eight hostages were killed and 11 wounded. Three Israeli soldiers were also killed. At the end, the terrorists retreated to a room and blew themselves up.

The case of the Lufthansa flight hijacked to Mogadishu in 1977 ended with a more positive outcome. None of the 82 passengers were hurt during the storming of the airplane. By contrast, the case of a Moscow theater where over 700 people were held hostage by Chechen commandos in October 2002 resulted in a massacre (see Dolnik and Pilch, this issue). A group of 40 heavily armed Chechen militants, some with explosives strapped to their bodies, took control of the theater, threatening to kill the hostages if the Russian government did not meet their demand to end the war in Chechnya. After three days, the Russian Special Forces pumped sleeping gas into the main hall and stormed the building. At least 90 hostages were killed during the assault, some of them due to the gas used to neutralize the captors.

Among hostage-barricade situations resolved by military intervention is the highly successful case of the revolutionary group that occupied the residence of the Japanese ambassador to Lima, Peru in December 1996 for over four months. Fourteen rebels from the Tupac Amaru Revolutionary Movement took 700 hostages during a traditional celebration. They kept 74 of these prisoners during the whole duration of the detention. The government rejected their demand for the release of 300 prisoners, a change in the government economic policy, and a ransom ("war tax"). The storming of the residence, which was well planned and well executed, resulted in the deaths of all the rebels and only one hostage.

When the act of hostage-taking is committed by a small number of abductors, assault is a frequent solution. Due to the surprise effect and fatigue, the intervening group is often able to kill the hostage-takers. This not only puts an end to the hostage situation but also deters other potential hostage-takers from engaging in the same activity. This type of action is reminiscent of a popular movie, "Dog Day Afternoon". The film was based on a real case in a New York bank where the gangsters asked for an airplane, but were subsequently "neutralized" (one was killed and the other arrested) on the tarmac of the airstrip.

A last category is the absence of any agreement. Two scenarios may be observed:

either the hostage-takers, exhausted and demotivated, give themselves up and release the hostages; or these hostage-takers, infuriated by the absence of a result, kill the hostages and try to escape. Cases of no agreement are mostly found in situations of hostage-barricade and kidnapping, when demands from the captors are exorbitant or when the authorities consider that they can solve the problem through exhaustion instead of concessions. A final reason for hostage-takers to concede is when the publicity their cause has received is in itself considered a sufficient outcome. This was the case in 1981 when an Armenian commando occupied the Turkish Embassy.

Assessing the Outcome

It is extremely difficult to evaluate the "success" of a negotiation concerning hostages. Given the drama which accompanies a hostage crisis, a well-managed negotiation is positive not only for the hostages but for the negotiators themselves. As underlined by consultants in this domain, it develops confidence, self-esteem, and makes one less apprehensive with regard to the prospect of facing similar cases in the future.

Hayes (2002), referring to Sandler and Scott, as well as Atkinson, Sandler, and Tschirhart, defines "negotiated success" for the hostage-takers as the "achievement of *some, but not all*, of the terrorist groups' demands". The problem is that the measurement of "success" should not be in terms of the demands made. Any set of demands will always include a tactical dimension (that is, ask more to obtain less or insist on one issue to extract more on another). Thus, "success" should be measured in terms of the real, not the stated objectives of the hostage-takers. Unfortunately, we usually cannot have precise knowledge of these real demands and must work from assumptions, which make any conclusion questionable.

From the perspective of the authorities, a negotiation may be considered "successful" if it has led to the release of the hostages, the catching of the hostage-takers, and no other trade-off. This result is not the most common. Looking at quantitative criteria, should the size of a ransom paid to hostage-takers be considered in assessing success? On a qualitative level, can we consider as a "success" the Vienna negotiation with an Arab commando that resulted in the closure of a refugee center for Russian Jews from the USSR in return for the release of hostages?

Storming the place of detention also raises problems because it is difficult to find criteria for assessing the outcome. Statistical studies made at the Rand Corporation (Miller 1980) show that more hostages have been killed during assaults than killed by terrorists during their captivity. This, however, does not mean that it was not opportune to resort to that type of action when taking into account the context and the possible course of events.

The 1972 Munich Olympic Massacre is probably the most significant example in terrorist history of a complete failure. Eight Palestinians from the Black September group broke into the Olympic Village, killed two Israeli and took nine more athletes hostage. Later, the German police intervened with sharpshooters on an airbase. They had believed that there were only five hostage-takers. The assault turned into a total disaster with the death of all the Israeli hostages and one police officer. Only five terrorists were killed. The others were taken prisoners and later released as currency of exchange in another hostage-taking operation.

On the hostage-takers' side, there is a failure if no compensation of any kind has been given, if the hostages have been released, and if the captors have been caught or killed. A typical example is the Manila Coup, which occurred in the Philippines in 2003. Three hundred soldiers from the armed forces seized a shopping mall in the middle of the capital, taking 60 foreign nationals as hostages and setting up booby-traps and explosives all around the building. All hostages were released before nightfall and the rogue soldiers eventually surrendered. No shot was fired in this hostage-barricade situation. The rebels demanded that President Arroyo step down, accusing her of corruption and of sponsoring terrorism by selling weapons to Muslim separatists and communist guerrillas. The threat of an all-out attack by the loyal Armed Forces surrounding the mutineers was enough to convince them to give up their project. None of their demands were taken into account and they were destined to be court-martialed. The firm, but restrained attitude of the President, authorizing use of reasonable force to dislodge the group, proved to be a credible threat. However, the hostage-takers may have achieved one of their goals, if they sought to draw international media attention to the current situation in their country.

Still, on the hostage-takers' side, a typical case illustrating success over time is evident in a series of kidnappings carried out by the Revolutionary Armed Forces of Colombia (FARC) group. FARC has organized 27 kidnapping operations within the past decade. Missionaries and US businesspeople were among the main targets. Some were exchanged for ransom and some have been executed. A former Colombian senator and presidential candidate, Ingrid Betancourt, was also kidnapped after she entered territory under FARC control. As a French-Colombian dual citizen, Paris made a failed attempt to exchange her for "humanitarian support" to the captors.

Kidnappings which occur in carefully chosen places can yield quite a high return for hostage-takers. Thirty-one European tourists visiting the Algerian part of the Sahara "vanished" at the beginning of 2003. The Algerian government identified the *Groupe Salafiste pour la Prédication et le Combat* (GSPC), an Islamist group, as the organization behind the kidnappings. After five months of discussions, new developments, and unexpected events including the death of one hostage by sunstroke, the 14 remaining captives (mostly German) were freed in the north of Mali 1200 km from the place where they had been kidnapped. Reportedly, a ransom of Euro 4.5 million was paid to the captors by the Malian government. This amount is supposed to be reimbursed with development aid. The German government denies having paid anything.

All the hostages had been carefully "selected" to be German-speaking people, under the assumption that they would be citizens of countries that would be easier to negotiate with than the United States. A former payment of a considerable amount to the Islamist Group Abu Sayyaf in another kidnapping case may have played an important role in the choice of the victims. Two major concerns may have guided the action of the hostage-takers: obtaining a large amount of money and ensuring a safe way out. This second factor explains why the situation ended in a third country, Mali. With regard to these two criteria, the hostage-takers of the GSPC have arguably had a complete success. However, in the mid-term, they may have contracted some debts with those who facilitated their operation.

Conclusion

Unfortunately for mankind, negotiation with terrorists is an expanding activity. Considering the number and variety of hostage-taking situations, the wide range of rationales used to support them, and their occurrence in all geographic regions, research into hostage-taking negotiation is a fascinating area.

There is a wide diversity of rationales at work motivating this activity. For groups that want to achieve a great deal with few means, transgressing basic universal values is an ongoing temptation. Generating distress, terror or panic is a powerful way to increase one's leverage and create a new situation. Terrorism is the word most commonly used to describe this action, but in reality it is just a situation in which an unethical tool is used for what the perpetrators believe to be ethical ends.

Negotiating with hostage-takers, given its ideological and psychological aspects, is one of the most unusual and most difficult engagements. The dramatic issues at stake make it a uniquely uncomfortable job. One of the major difficulties arises from what are often absolutely incompatible goals and values espoused by the parties. The negotiation must manage this paradox. The situation makes it impossible to forget about values, but at the same time, it seems to be necessary to set values aside if one wants to progress.

Considering the structure of hostage-taking negotiations, the dominant paradigm is of a shifting nature – either a prisoner's dilemma or a chicken game. When the negotiation starts, the hostage-takers base their actions on the prisoner's dilemma paradigm because they expect a transaction and assume that there can be room for cooperation. The first impulse of the authorities is to turn down the idea of any common ground or cooperation with the captors and thus operate from a chicken par-adigm, where there is no room for cooperation. Then, as time passes, psychologi-cal attrition, frustration, and the exacerbation of tensions cause the situation to change. The hostage-takers, out of spite or desperation, come to operate along the rationale of the chicken paradigm. The authorities, as circumstances require, may gradually reframe their approach to the problem. Thus, a paradigm shift may take place and create conditions for a catastrophic outcome; if win-win formulas are very thin in terms of content, the lose-lose formulas lie in wait for the negotiator at each turn of the negotiation process. The complexity of the task comes from the multi-dimensional aspect of this type of negotiation. One has to orchestrate several instruments at the same time because of the number of factors in play.

Terrorism is no more than a tool, even if it is a traumatic one, and hostage-tak-ing is a tactical device. The root problem has to be resolved and fundamental issues have to be addressed. Ultimately, hostage-taking is a symptomatic expression of the agenda of leaders who rank above the actual hostage-takers. Thus, negotiators may need to engage these higher level decision makers as well.

References

Adang, O.M.J. and Giebels, E. (eds.) (1999) *To Save Lives*. Amsterdam: Elsevier.

Arendt, H. (1962). *The Origin of Totalitarianism*. New York: Meridian.

Baldwin, D.A. (1976) "Bargaining with airline hijackers". In I.W. Zartman (ed.), *The 50% Solution*. New York: Doubleday.

Bolz, F. and Hershey, E. (1980) *Hostage Cop: The Story of the New York City Police Hostage Negotiating Team and the Man who Leads It*. New York: Rawson, Wade Publishers.

Clutterbuck, R.L. (1987) *Kidnap, Hijack, and Extortion: The Response*. New York: St Martin's Press.

Cooper, H.H. (1981) *The Hostage-takers*. Boulder, CO: Paladin Press.

Davidson, T.N. (2002) *To Preserve Life: Hostage-Crisis Management*. Auburn, CA: Cimacom 2002.

Faure, G.O. (2002) "Negotiating with terrorists". *PINPoints* IIASA Laxenburg 18, 2002.

Faure, G.O. (2002) "Negotiation: the cultural dimension". In V. Kremenyuk (ed.), *International Negotiations: Analysis, Approaches, Issues*. San Francisco: Jossey-Bass.

Faure, G.O. and Shakun, M. (1988) "Negotiating to Free Hostages: A Challenge for Negotiation Support Systems". In M. Shakun (ed.), *Evolutionary Systems Design, Policy Making under Complexity*. Oakland: Holden-Day.

Faure, G.O. and Rubin, J.Z. (eds.) (1994) *Culture and Negotiation*. California: Newbury Park.

Goldaber, I. (1979) "A typology of hostage-takers". *Police Chief* 46: 21–23.

Hayes, R.E. (2002). "Negotiations with terrorists". In V. Kremenyuk (ed.), *International Negotiation*. San Francisco: Jossey-Bass.

Lanceley, F.J. (1999) *On-Scene Guide for Crisis Negotiators*. New York: CRC Press.

Machiavelli, N. (1947) *The Prince*. T. Bergin (editor and translator). New York: Appleton-Century-Crofts.

MacWillson, A.C. (1992) *Hostage-taking Terrorism: Incident-response Strategy*. New York: St Martin's Press.

McMains, M.J. and Mullins, W.C. (2001) *Crisis Negotiations: Managing Critical Incidents and Hostage Situation in Law Enforcement and Corrections*. Cincinnati, OH: Anderson Press.

Miller, A.H. (1980) *Terrorism and Hostage Negotiations*. Boulder, CO: Westview Press.

Ochberg, F. (1978) "The victim of terrorism". *Practice of Medicine* 220: 293–302.

Ochberg, F. (1980) "Victims of terrorism". *Journal of Clinical Psychiatry* 41: 73–74.

Oettgen, W. and Spinazzola, B. (1987). *La négociation lors de la prise d'otages terroriste*. Paris: Sorbonne. René Descartes, mémoire de maîtrise de sociologie.

Pearce, K.I. (1977) "Police negotiations: A new role for the community psychiatrist". *Journal of the Canadian Psychiatric Association* 22: 171–175.

Poland J.M. and McCrystle, M.J. (1999) *Practical, Tactical, and Legal Perspectives of Terrorism and Hostage-taking*. Lewiston, NY: E. Mellon Press.

Stratton, J. (1978) "The terrorist act of hostage-taking: A view of violence and the perpetrators". *Police Science and Administration* 6: 1–9.

Strentz, T. (1979) "Law enforcement policies and ego defenses of the hostage". *FBI Law Enforcement Bulletin* 48: 1–12.

Thomson, L. (2001) *Hostage Rescue Manual*. London: Greenhills Books.

Waugh, W.L. (1982) *International Terrorism*. Salisbury, NC: Documentary Publications.

Wilson, M. (2002) "The psychology of hostage-taking". In A. Silke (ed.), *Terrorists, Victims and Society: Psychological Perspectives on Terrorism and its Consequences*. Chichester, UK: John Wiley.

Wilson, M. and Smith, A. (1999) "Rules and roles in terrorist hostage-taking". In D. Canter and L. Alison (eds.), *The Social Psychology of Crime: Groups, Teams and Networks*. Ashgate, Dartmouth: Aldershot.

Contrasting Dynamics of Crisis Negotiations: Barricade versus Kidnapping Incidents

ADAM DOLNIK

Introduction

In the past thirty years, negotiation has become the primary method of dealing with hostage incidents in many countries of the world. A wealth of literature has been published about the strategies, techniques, and dynamics involved in the process of crisis negotiations. However, most of the available accounts concentrate mainly on barricade situations, devoting minimal attention to kidnappings.[1] The primary difference between the two scenarios is that the location of the victim(s) as well as that of the perpetrator(s) is unknown in kidnappings, giving the terrorist more flexibility. As a result, many of the components of crisis negotiation that have been so successful in resolving barricade hostage incidents are inapplicable to kidnapping scenarios. In order to determine whether negotiation is the right approach to resolve a hostage crisis, FBI specialists have developed a list of conditions that must be present in order for an incident to be negotiable (McMains and Mullins 2001: 50). These criteria are summarized in Figure 1. It is interesting to note that at least 50 percent of the listed conditions are not satisfied in most kidnapping situations, implying that the negotiability of such incidents via traditional means is low. Yet, most kidnappings have been successfully resolved by crisis negotiations.[2]

This article seeks to provide a comparative analysis of the negotiation dynamics involved in barricade versus kidnapping incidents. This analysis should help the reader understand the differences between the two scenarios, and the implications of these differences for developing appropriate negotiation strategies. The question of a suitable response is increasingly important as the Bush administration continues to develop a new strategy for dealing with international hostage incidents (Miller 2002).

This article will utilize the analytical framework of interest-based negotiation developed by specialists at Harvard University. Both negotiation scenarios will be analyzed in terms of the people, interests, options, best alternatives to a negotiated agreement (BATNA), and objective criteria involved in the negotiations. Historical examples will be used to demonstrate the differing dynamics involved in both nego-

International Negotiation Series 1:
I.W. Zartman (ed.) Negotiating with Terrorists, 51–81
© 2006 *Koninklijke Brill NV. Printed in the Netherlands.*

tiation settings. Emphasis will be placed on premeditated incidents perpetrated by organized groups with a political, criminal, or religious motivation.

This article draws primarily on open source literature devoted to the topic of hostage-taking, kidnapping, terrorism, crisis negotiations, and negotiation theory in general. The greatest limitation of this analysis is its abstract nature. Since every negotiation is a unique and complex process, it is practically impossible to provide a universally applicable negotiation strategy. Consequently, this paper attempts to outline only the most significant differences in the two crisis scenarios and provide an assessment of how these differences are likely to influence the negotiations.

The first part of this study will provide an overview of trends, characteristics, and the evolution of kidnapping and barricade hostage-taking. The second part will focus on the five elements of negotiation. Typologies of kidnappers and hostage-takers will be provided with a special focus on their apparent and hidden interests, options, BATNAs and objective criteria, which can be exploited during the negotiation process. The third part will focus on other factors that influence the different dynamics of barricade and kidnap negotiations. In this part, the analysis will stress the contrasts between the two types of incidents with regard to time, duration, deadlines, demands, media, means of communication, tactics and psychological processes. The conclusion will provide a summary of findings and recommendations.

Overview

Unlike in barricade incidents, in kidnappings the location of the hostages and their captors is unknown. However, it is possible for either scenario to transform into the other, as a kidnapping incident may turn into a barricade situation if the location of kidnappers is discovered, and vice versa, if a hostage-taker manages to escape from the scene along with a hostage to an unknown location. Alternatively, a combination of the two scenarios can occur in the case of an airliner hijacking, in which the terrorists have a mobile platform.

Development of specialized hostage response teams dates back to an incident known as the 1972 Olympics "Munich Massacre", in which members of the Palestine Liberation Organization's (PLO) Black September Organization killed eleven Israeli athletes (Hoffman 1998: 72). A failed rescue operation underscored the need to investigate options for peaceful resolution of hostage incidents. However, even though barricade events are spectacular in terms of attracting media attention, for terrorists they remain a rarely used tool. Consequently, the emphasis among negotiation teams has gradually shifted from terrorists to emotionally disturbed individuals, trapped criminals, and domestic violence cases (McMains and Mullins 2001: 36). Very few of these incidents are actually pre-meditated, which seems to be the primary reason behind the staggering success rates of the negotiation approach. According to FBI's Hostage Barricade Database System (HOBAS), about 80 percent of incidents are resolved peacefully with no injuries to hostages or perpetrators (McMains and Mullins 2001: 5).

Unlike barricade incidents, kidnappings are used much more frequently by organizations with a political or criminal intent. There seems to be, in fact, a convergence of ideological and criminal motivations, resulting from the decline of state sponsorship of terrorism following the end of the Cold War. Many organizations with a political agenda have been forced to find new sources of financing, and kidnappings for ransom have become a major source of income for many ideologically motivated groups. This explains why worldwide reported kidnappings have risen by 70 percent over the last 10 years (Royal and Sun Alliance Insurance Group 2002). It is estimated that annually between 10,000–15,000 kidnapping incidents occur worldwide, 80 percent of them in Latin America (Hardgrove 1998). Only about 35 annual cases occur in the US, possibly due to the FBI's high success rate at uncovering and arresting the perpetrators – 95 percent of kidnappers in the US are caught, compared to only 1 percent in Colombia (Bolz, Dudonis and Schultz 2002: 118).

A disturbing trend in international kidnapping is its increasing sophistication. Kidnappers often research the financial capabilities of the victims by studying their bank information and tax returns. The ransom demand is than designed to be high enough to be profitable, but reasonable enough to be affordable.

Figure 1. Characteristics of a negotiable hostage incident (FBI)

1. The desire to live on the part of the hostage-taker.
2. The threat of force by the police.*
3. The hostage-taker must present demands for release of hostages.
4. The negotiator must be viewed by the hostage-taker as someone who can hurt but desires to help.*
5. The negotiator needs time to develop trust with hostage-takers.*
6. The location must be contained and stabilized to support negotiations.*
7. The hostage-taker and negotiator must have a reliable means of communication, either by phone or face to face.
8. The negotiator must be able to "deal" with the hostage-taker who controls the hostages and makes the decisions.*

* *Condition not satisfied in most contemporary kidnapping incidents*

(Added by author)

Source: McMains and Mullins. (2001) *Crisis Negotiations: Managing Critical Incidents and Hostage Situations in Law Enforcement and Corrections.* Anderson Publishing, 2nd edition

Elements of Negotiation: Kidnappings vs. Barricade Situations

Crisis negotiations differ from other negotiations in that the stakes are extremely high. With the life of at least one person in immediate danger, tension and stress is high for all parties. Such an environment impairs the rational decision-making ability of the actors and introduces perhaps more extreme positions than any other type of negotiation. As a result, the negotiation approach on the part of the hostage-taker is positional bargaining at its worst. It is the negotiator's task to break through these extreme positions and to facilitate a peaceful resolution of the incident. A particularly useful method of dealing with positional bargaining is the concept of interest-based negotiation. In this approach, the negotiator attempts to identify interests that lie behind the counterpart's positions and seeks to satisfy those interests by introducing new options (Fisher and Ury 1991). There are five basic elements of interest-based negotiation: people, interests, options, BATNA, and objective criteria.

People

a) *Perpetrators in Barricade Situations.* It has been estimated that between 52 to 85 percent of barricade hostage-takers are mentally disturbed individuals. Between 20 to 25 percent of barricade situations involve domestic violence (McMains and Mullins 1991: 231). Such a situation usually arises from an argument to which the police are called; the hostage-taker then tries to keep the police away by threatening to hurt his or her spouse. Criminals trapped by the police during a robbery make up the other major portion of barricade incidents. The crucial element that these incidents have in common is the low level of preparation on the part of the hostage-taker. This works in favor of the negotiator, as an unprepared counterpart is more likely to question his or her decision to have taken hostages as time passes.

Although marginal in number, premeditated incidents perpetrated by organized groups with a political or religious motivation are far more interesting from a negotiations perspective. Since the terrorists' have planned in advance, and since they typically do not have the authority to make autonomous decisions, it is a much more difficult task to convince the hostage-takers to release the hostages and surrender. The people involved in organized hostage incidents tend to be fairly low in the organization's ranks, since death or arrest of the perpetrators is a likely outcome and organized groups are reluctant to risk senior operatives for such high-risk operations. For the same reason, the hostage-takers are usually heavily indoctrinated and very determined, while at the same time rather inexperienced and inadequately trained for negotiating during a high pressure standoff.[3] This condition plays an important role is the hostage-takers' ideology. It not only influences target selection, but also lays the grounds for victim dehumanization – a necessary component of killing someone in cold blood (Bandura 1998: 163). The process of dehumanization causes a psychological transformation wherein the civilian hostage is perceived by the hostage-taker as a party in the conflict. Different ideological motivations enable different degrees of dehumanization. If forced to kill hostages, ethnic and nationalist groups are likely to pick a hostage of the ethnicity or nationality that matches that of their enemy. This phenomenon was demonstrated during the 1976 hijacking of Air France Flight 139 by members of the Popular Front for the Liberation of Palestine (PFLP) in conjunction with the Baader-Meinhof gang. Soon after the plane landed in Kampala, Uganda, Israeli citizens were separated from other passengers and demands were issued. Similarly, leftist revolutionary groups will most likely pick persons that they can identify as wealthy or as employees of large corporations. Religiously motivated terrorists, on the other hand, are likely to have the ability to successfully dehumanize the victims indiscriminately, based on the perceived divine sanction of their actions. Understanding the role of ideology in dehumanization of victims is crucial, as it makes it possible to identify the hostages who face the greatest risk of being selected for execution. Negotiators should concentrate on developing justifications for demanding the release of these hostages early, without attracting attention to their common identity.

b) *Perpetrators of Kidnapping Incidents.* Perpetrators of kidnapping incidents differ significantly from barricade hostage-takers due to the fact that kidnappings almost always constitute a pre-meditated act. Kidnapping cases include child abductions by parents for the purpose of gaining custody, by pedophiles for sexual reasons, and by emotionally disturbed persons for adoption purposes. Such cases, however, will not be discussed in this study, as few are resolved through crisis negotiations.[4]

Most kidnappings involve well-organized groups. While guards and snatch operation participants are fairly low in the organization's ranks, negotiators are usually experienced and employ a business-like approach (Auerbach 1998). Victims are typically selected on basis of their family's or employer's willingness and ability to pay a large ransom, as well as on the basis of ease of abduction. For politically motivated groups, ideology and the victim's symbolic importance in terms of generating wide media coverage are other important factors influencing target selection.

c) *Negotiators in Barricade Situations.* The initial negotiators in hostage situations are usually the first-responders who try to control the situation until the arrival of a special crisis unit. Upon arrival, a trained police negotiator takes over the situation. The principal negotiator is usually supported by a backup who acts as an advisor and note-taker, and who also monitors the psychological state of the primary negotiator. An important factor is the existence of a triad between the negotiator, the tactical assault team and the command post. The negotiator should never be the same person as the commander of the operation, as the possibility of deferring demands onto a higher authority is one of the most important tools in the negotiator's toolbox (Fisher and Ury 1991). In incidents that are under the jurisdiction of state or federal authorities, local police negotiators are sometimes exchanged for a state or a federal level representative. In incidents with international implications, government officials are also involved in the negotiations.

d) *Negotiators in Kidnap Situations.* Since most Western governments refuse to "negotiate with terrorists", the majority of kidnapping situations are handled by experienced negotiators from the private sector. An important moment in kidnapping negotiations is the response to the initial contact with the kidnappers. If conducted through a telephone, the initial reaction to the notification can set the tone for future negotiations (Clutterbuck 1978: 76).

Once the initial contact has been made the situation is usually handed over to a professional negotiator. In contrast to barricade situations, where the negotiator handles the communication personally, kidnap negotiators usually act as advisers to the "voice", typically a person who is familiar with the local language and culture, and who is also sufficiently emotionally detached from the victim and his or her family (Hardgrove 2002).

Interests

When discussing interests in negotiations, it is important to keep in mind that interests are the underlying factors behind positions, and that every party has multiple interests.

a) *Perpetrators in Barricade Situations.* Interests of hostage-takers vary greatly and are contingent on the perpetrators' motivations. Suicidal individuals may be motivated by the desire to provoke a confrontation with the armed forces in order to commit "suicide by cop". At the same time, the decision to publicly commit suicide is influenced by hidden interests, such as the unsatisfied need for self-actualization or the desire to feel needed. Trapped criminals may be motivated by the prospect of financial gain and by the desire to avoid a prison sentence.

Interests of organized hostage-takers with a political or religious motivation also vary. These can be separated into two categories: interests of the organization and interests of the actual perpetrators.

The organization's decision to publicly take hostages is usually motivated by the desire to attract media coverage in order to bring worldwide attention to their struggle. Traditionally, organizations also attempt to use hostages as leverage in gaining the release of imprisoned comrades. Other interests include the desire to demonstrate capability and to spark fear and a sense of vulnerability in a broader audience. At the same time, the organization is usually concerned with gaining a favorable public image for its "freedom fighters", as opposed to the pejorative label of "terrorists". An organization's campaign of public hostage-taking is usually also directed inwards, often designed to reinforce group cohesion. This helps to explain why many terrorist organizations sometimes conduct operations of minimal strategic value. Such operations are designed to raise morale within the organization and to preserve or improve self-perception.

The actual perpetrators of organized barricade incidents also have different motives. Some may try to avenge the deaths of their friends and relatives; others may be influenced by propaganda or by psychological idiosyncrasies. A common denominator seems to be the desire to risk one's own life in the name of a "greater good". An evident hidden interest is to be admired by others, especially within the organization and its support group, and to demonstrate commitment to the cause. This has important implications for crisis negotiators – the terrorists are likely to view a negotiated solution mainly in light of how their performance will be judged by their peers, and not necessarily on the objective level of how much benefit the settlement actually brings to their cause. For this reason it is desirable to gain access to the terrorist hostage-taker as an individual, even though as Zartman notes, in terrorist cases such access is usually denied (Zartman 1990: 173).

In relation to the outcome of the standoff, perpetrators will also be concerned with avoiding capture. Escape is usually the preferable option, as one has to stay alive in order to further participate in the struggle for the cause, even though some individuals may prefer to die and become martyrs. In such cases, however, it is essential to make the distinction between the *willingness* to die and the *desire* to die. Most terrorists are willing to die for their cause; but only a few see their death as the preferred outcome. According to Corsi's statistical analysis of hostage incidents recorded in the ITERATE database, terrorists engaged in barricade hostage incidents were suicidal in only 1 percent of the cases, while in 94 percent of incidents they were willing to give up their lives, but preferred not to (Corsi 1981). This implies that even when terrorists repeatedly express their determination to die during the incident, this claim alone should not be understood as an insurmountable barrier to the negotiability of the incident. In most instances, this is a rather rational course of action aimed at denying the counterpart threat level: the proclamation of the desire to die weakens the deterrent value of threats by the government to resolve the situation forcefully (Zartman 1990: 170).

b) *Perpetrators in Kidnapping Incidents*. The primary goal for most organizations that utilize kidnappings is to make financial profit. Other organizational interests similar to those described above may also be present, at least in terms of the message directed to group members. While the goal of gaining wide media coverage may be important in some cases, most profit-oriented organizations will prefer to extract a quick ransom payment without attracting too much attention – as the kidnapping becoming public knowledge the chances of being located by security forces increase.

When assessing the interests of kidnappers, a crucial factor to consider is the initial investment made into the operation. More than twenty years ago, an attempt was made to calculate the cost of a kidnapping operation in Italy (Clutterbuck 1978: 66). The study computed the costs associated with abducting the victim and laundering the payment, and found that the net gain of a million dollar ransom was only about US$250,000.[5] While the fact that most contemporary kidnappings occur in a territory friendly to the abductors presumably makes the costs of launching an operation significantly lower, this financial breakdown is still useful in demonstrating why it is in the kidnappers' best interest to keep the hostage alive in order to receive a ransom payment. As one kidnapping negotiator puts it "if you are running a china shop, you don't break the china" (Peter Dobbs quoted in Prochnau 1998). At the same time, it is important to keep in mind that if the kidnappers conclude that they cannot extract a large enough payment to make a sufficient profit, they may decide to kill the hostage as an "investment" – death of a hostage can set a precedent for other related negotiations and is likely to raise the willingness to comply in order to secure the release of other hostages held by the same group. In some cases, the bodies of murdered hostages have also been offered to their family for a payment (Prochnau 1998).

Another important concern of the kidnappers is to prevent other groups from extracting the ransom fee for their hostage. This explains why it is in the interest of kidnappers to provide "proof-of-life" and to establish a contact codename. As the expression suggests, "proof-of-life" is designed to provide evidence that the kidnappers actually hold the hostage and that he or she is alive. This can take the form of direct contact with the hostage, a tape recording of the hostage's voice reading a section of the morning newspaper, or a photograph of the hostage holding the newspaper. Another commonly used tool is proof-of-life questions, or questions to which only the hostage is able to provide the correct answer, such as the hostage's mother's birth date or the nickname of a childhood friend (Prochnau 1998). Unfortunately, proof-of-life can sometimes take a more gruesome form, as it did in the 1973 Gene Paul Getty II kidnapping, in which the perpetrators sent Getty's right ear to a Rome newspaper to establish proof that were actually holding the victim (Mickolus 1980: 393).

c) *Negotiators of Barricade Situations.* The primary concern of the negotiator is the safe release of hostages. A related interest is the minimization of danger to the hostages' physical or mental health during the negotiation process. For the negotiator, it is also important to ensure a peaceful surrender of the hostage-taker, while keeping substantive concessions to a minimum. Last but not least, the negotiator tries to preserve a good reputation by projecting confidence and control.

Some of the negotiator's interests differ sharply from those of the tactical unit, whose instinct is to go in and "take care of the hostage-taker". Other conflicts can occur between the negotiator and city officials, who press for a quick resolution to bring the city's life back to normal. Finally, the negotiator's interest in reaching a peaceful settlement through negotiation is usually in direct opposition to official government policy of "no negotiations with terrorists".[6]

d) *Negotiators of Kidnap Situations.* As in the case of barricade situations, the principal goal of preserving the life and health of the hostage applies to kidnapping negotiations as well. Another important goal is to lower substantive concessions, such as the ransom payment, to a minimum. Further noteworthy interests occur in relation to the constituency. The negotiator has an interest in retaining psychological balance and a professional image during the negotiations. He or she also needs to be honest with the constituency about the victim's chances of being released – nothing will hurt the victim's family as much as false hope. Despite the need to project confidence and control, the negotiator has to also be prepared for failure. Another concern worth mentioning is the avoidance of prosecution when negotiating in countries where ransom payments are illegal by keeping a low profile. Even though paid on a daily basis, the negotiator also has an interest in resolving the situation in the shortest possible amount of time, as being on the job means spending 24 hours per day with the victim's family (Auerbach 1998).

Options

a) *Perpetrators in Barricade Situations.* The options of barricade hostage-takers are rather limited. While the perceived position of power allows them to dictate demands and deadlines, very few tools are at hand for the hostage-takers to enforce the prompt fulfillment of these demands. Once the deadline approaches, the perpetrators have only two options: let the deadline pass or carry out their threat and kill a hostage. This is a no-win situation, as passing of the deadline weakens the perpetrators' negotiating position by exposing their reluctance to kill, while killing of a hostage is likely to trigger a forceful resolution of the incident. Another important factor to take into consideration is the nature of the demand. Politically motivated groups will most likely make demands such as publication of the group's manifestos in mainstream media or the release of imprisoned members of their group. Criminal hostage-takers are likely to demand money, a get-away vehicle, and free passage.

A possibly good strategy for the hostage-taker might be to release some hostages at the beginning of the standoff to demonstrate good will. This leaves the negotiator in a weakened position, based on the rule of reciprocity. This rule states that if someone does a favor for us, we feel obligated to repay it in the future (McMains and Mullins 2001: 207). The release of hostages on "humanitarian grounds" can also be a useful way of influencing public opinion. For instance, the 1974 Moslem International Guerillas who hijacked the Greek freighter *Vori* and threatened to explode it along with themselves and their hostages, later claimed that they would have "rather killed [themselves] then harm [the hostages]" (Mickolus 1980: 433). Such expressed "humanitarian concerns" are designed to portray the involved terrorists as resorting to hostage-taking with "good intentions" and only out of desperation, mitigating the public opinion backlash deriving from the fact that lives of civilians are at stake.

Barricade hostage-takers also have the option of countering the threat of a forceful resolution by employing deliberate deception tactics, either in the form of the aforementioned strategy of expressing desire to die, or by portraying themselves as stronger or more prepared to deal with the assault than they actually are. For instance, when David Protter seized hostages at the Israeli consulate in Johannesburg in April 1975, he used various voices and accents in his talks with the police in order to give the impression that he had many accomplices (Mickolus 1980: 520). Deception can also be employed for other purposes, such as in the example of the 1975 takeover of the Saudi Arabian embassy in Paris. At one point one of the Palestinian commandos, describing himself as a doctor, radioed for an ambulance, claiming that one of the hostages had been shot in the leg (Mickolus 1980: 407). This bluff was designed to put additional pressure on the authorities without the risk of a negative public reaction associated with deliberate harming of hostages.

Another option available to barricade hostage-takers is to attempt to relocate with the hostages to an unknown location. This alternative, however, leaves the perpetrators vulnerable to sniper fire. It is unadvisable for the security forces to allow the hostage-takers to change location, since the situation would change from a barricade scenario to a kidnapping, significantly weakening the bargaining position of the authorities. The final option is the BATNA, which in this case consists of a shootout with the security forces. The BATNA will be discussed later in more detail.

b) *Perpetrators of Kidnapping Incidents.* Like other hostage-takers, kidnappers can also put forward all sorts of demands. These can range anywhere from purely profit-oriented demands to altruistic claims designed to spread a positive image of the organization. For instance, many groups in South America and Africa in the 1970s have successfully demanded things like medication, rehire of laid-off workers, improvement of working conditions, and investments into poverty-ridden regions, in exchange for the release of kidnapped officials and business executives. In many instances the demands were of a combined nature, such as in the case in the 1974 kidnapping of a co-proprietor of the largest company in Argentina. In this instance, the Montoneros demanded US$60 million (the record for a political kidnapping at the time), as well as distribution of US$1.2 million worth of food and clothing to various parts of the country, in exchange for the safe release of their hostage (Mickolus 1980: 479).

The range of options available for the kidnappers to enforce the fulfillment of their demands is much broader due to the fact that they are not faced with an immediate threat of a forceful resolution of the incident. Kidnappers have the option of countering the negotiator's tactics through indirect communication. In the event of an impasse, the kidnappers can apply additional pressure by cutting off negotiations for an extended period of time or by sending the victim's finger or ear to his or her family. The abductors can also lower their demands in order to make the ransom payment more affordable. Alternatively, they can release the hostage on "humanitarian grounds", as the Armed Forces of Liberation (FAL) did in the 1970 kidnapping of the Paraguayan consul Joaquin Waldemar Sanchez when the Argentinean government became the first Latin American country to successfully refuse to deal in a political kidnapping case (Mickolus 1980: 166–167). Another option available to kidnappers is the BATNA, which in this case, is killing and abandoning the hostage.

c) *Negotiators of Barricade Situations.* The options of hostage negotiators are extensive, as the crisis negotiation practice for barricade situations has become very well developed over the past thirty years. The negotiators use a variety of tools that work to their advantage. Figure 2 summarizes the FBI guidelines for crisis negotiations.

Since the hostage-taker is surrounded by security forces and cannot escape, negotiators use time both to calm down the perpetrator and to wait for his primary needs, such as the need for food, water, and sleep to become more pressing, thereby drawing attention away from the original demands. The negotiator first has to develop an effective line of communication with the hostage-taker, and then use active listening skills to build rapport and gather intelligence. Through rapport, the negotiator tries to influence and later change the hostage-taker's behavior. It is the task of the negotiator to persuade the captor that he is in a no-win situation.

The challenge of negotiating with politically or religiously motivated organized hostage-takers is the fact that they have prepared their actions in advance and the individuals involved have actually chosen to be in the situation. Another factor working against the negotiator is the frequent availability of more than one individual to handle the communications, which makes the rapport-building process

Figure 2. FBI Guidelines for Crisis Negotiations

---

1. The use of time to increase basic needs, making it more likely that the subject will exchange a hostage for some basic need.
2. The use of time to collect intelligence on the subject that will help develop a trade.
3. The use of time to reduce the subject's expectation of getting what he wants.
4. Trades can be made for food, drink, transportation, and money.
5. Trades cannot be made for weapons or the exchange of hostages.
6. The boss does not negotiate.
7. Start bidding high to give yourself room to negotiate (ask for all the hostages).
8. *Quid pro quo*: get something for everything.
9. Never draw attention to the hostages; it gives the subject too much bargaining power.
10. Manipulate anxiety levels by cutting off power, gas, water, etc.

Source: McMains and Mullins. (2001) *Crisis Negotiations: Managing Critical Incidents and Hostage Situations in Law Enforcement and Corrections.* Anderson Publishing, 2nd edition: 37.

much more complex (Strentz 1991). A successful way to deal with politically motivated incidents has been for the negotiator to stress the attention that the perpetrators' cause has already received. Since publicity is usually one of the main goals in these incidents, the captors can sometimes be persuaded that they have succeeded in their mission, and that killing hostages will only hurt their cause in the eyes of the public (Fuselier and Noesner 1990). Since most organized movements use the rhetoric of liberation from oppression and inhumane treatment, the same language can be used in reference to the hostages to appeal to the moral beliefs of the captors. Other, more risky moral appeals can also be used, such as the following plea employed by the negotiators of the 1973 hijacking of Japan Airline Flight 404. At one point, the control tower at the Dubai airport relayed the following message: "If you intend to kill the passengers on board . . . do it at once. Otherwise be human enough to release them . . . Please give up your intentions. There are other means of unbloody possibilities to reach your political aims" (Mickolus 1980: 399). The use of this technique in combination with the guarantee of a free passage for the terrorists has historically been the most frequent formula for peaceful resolution of politically motivated barricade incidents. Such an outcome is sometimes labeled as the "Bangkok Solution", referring to the 1972 incident in which members of the Black September group took over the Israeli embassy in Thailand, but after 19 hours of negotiations agreed to release their hostages and drop all other demands in return for safe passage out of the country (Mickolus 1980: 367). Zartman notes that despite falling short of punishing the terrorists for their crime, such a solution is balanced – it uses a concession only to restore the original situation, which the government found acceptable but the terrorists did not (Zartman 1990: 164). This assertion seems to be supported by the fact that following the Bangkok incident Black September strongly criticized their operatives for backing down and losing face for the organization. At the same time, it should be pointed out that despite the factual return of the situation to the pre-incident status, the terrorists managed to gain publicity and therefore did succeed in fulfilling one of their main objectives.

Another useful tool in the negotiator's toolbox is the categorization of victims into groups (i.e. women, children, employees, injured, elderly etc.) and pressing for simultaneous release of a whole group of hostages. This technique enables the negotiator to use one, principle-based line of reasoning for the release of multiple hostages, which is more productive than negotiating by sheer numbers or having to develop persuasive justifications for the release of individual hostages.

The next important task for the negotiator is to humanize the victims to their captors as much as possible by promoting maximum interaction among them. The importance of this was demonstrated during a 1975 incident, in which the South Maluccan Independence Movement took over a train in the Netherlands. In order to prove their seriousness, the terrorists chose one of the passengers for execution. Just prior to the act, the victim was allowed to talk to his family on the phone to deliver his farewell message. After hearing the emotional conversation, the terrorists were no longer able to execute the man and chose another passenger, whom they killed on the spot (McMains and Mullins 2001: 18). The personalization of hostages to their captors also serves to activate the so-called Stockholm Syndrome, a positive relationship between the hostage-taker and the hostage. This phenomenon is named after a 1973 bank robbery incident that occurred in Sweden, in which the hostages protected their captor with their own bodies during surrender. One of the victims later even married the hostage-taker while he was in prison (Antokol and Nudell 1990). The importance of this phenomenon will be discussed later.

One of the negotiator's main tasks is to deal with the question of demands. It should be borne in mind that all demands have an *instrumental*, as well as an *expressive* value. In other words, each material-type demand, such as money, food, media attention, or a getaway vehicle (instrumental), also constitutes an expression of a certain type of emotion or a psychological need (expressive) (Antokol and Nudell 1990: 36). It is especially the expressive value of the demand that the negotiator should concentrate on, as this provides insight into the captor's hidden interests. The negotiator then should work to satisfy these interests in alternative ways, sometimes by recognizing the validity of the terrorists' grievance or, in the case of individuals, even by simply listening and showing that he or she cares.

The negotiator's position in hostage situations is strong, as he or she is backed up by security forces that can go in and attempt to rescue the hostages. This is the negotiator's BATNA.

d) *Negotiators of Kidnap Situations.* The options in kidnapping negotiations are limited due to the negotiator's much weaker bargaining position. It is possible to use the same type of moral appeal as mentioned in the previous case, but this has limited chances of success with abductors that have other goals than gaining publicity. Still, the negotiator is not completely helpless. He or she can work to humanize the victim to the captors and can use a wide scope of objective criteria to point out obstacles to meeting the ransom demand (discussed below). When facing an experienced counterpart, it is also important to demonstrate to the kidnappers an understanding of the game and to illustrate that they are not making all the rules (i.e. payment will only be made in local currency). It is also important to stall for time and to refrain from making a payment too quickly. Otherwise the captors are likely to respond by accepting the sum as a "fee" for the hostage's internment and by making another demand, as was the case in the 1995 kidnapping of Thomas R. Hardgrove by the Revolutionary Armed Forces of Colombia (FARC) (Hardgrove 1998). While stalling for time, the negotiator can also cooperate with local authorities and attempt to locate the hostage. This however has little chance of success, especially in Latin American countries where the hostages are usually held in areas militarily controlled by the abductors. Sometimes the location of the victim can be detected and a rescue operation can be launched, but this is an extremely risky proposition. It is advisable to lower the demand through negotiations and to make the ransom payment. Another option is to give up on the release of the victim, which is something that few families are willing to accept.

BATNA

The purpose of a BATNA is to formulate the likely outcome of the situation should negotiations fail. This should be done beforehand in order to determine whether it is advisable to even start negotiating. During the negotiations, it is desirable to strengthen one's own BATNA, while making the counterpart's BATNA appear as weak as possible (Fisher and Ury 1991).

a) *Perpetrators in Barricade Situations.* The obvious BATNA of a hostage-taker is to begin killing hostages. This, nevertheless, will in most cases trigger a rescue attempt by the tactical unit, which the hostage-takers are not likely to withstand. Historically, with the exception of a very few notable incidents, such as the 1995 hostage crises in Kizlyar and Budyonnovsk,[7] hostage-takers in general have not been able to withstand armed rescue operations. Few hostage-takers realize this; in the beginning of the standoff they hold a firm belief that they are the ones with the most power in the negotiations. After rapport with the captors has been established, it is the negotiator's task to point out the hostage-takers' weak BATNA in a non-threatening manner.

b) *Perpetrators of Kidnapping Incidents.* The BATNA of kidnappers is much stronger, due to the fact that their location is unknown. They can always kill the victim without sanction, should they decide that negotiations are no longer advantageous. It is important to keep in mind, however, that launching the kidnapping operation was not cheap and that the abductors are likely to settle for a much lower payment than the original demand. An alternative BATNA is to attempt to sell the victim's body back to his or her family, but as has been pointed out by some authors, "the discount is large" (Prochnau 1998).

c) *Negotiators of Hostage Situations.* The negotiator's BATNA in a barricade incident is a rescue operation. The longer the duration of the standoff, the more time the tactical team has to collect intelligence, study blueprints, and practice storming the location where the hostages are being held. While seemingly attractive, the BATNA is certainly not to be preferred over negotiations. Statistics show that an armed assault results in a 78 percent injury or death rate, sniper-fire in a 100 percent injury or death rate, while containment and negotiation have had a 95 percent success rate (McMains and Mullins 2001: 33). Furthermore, 75 percent of all casualties in hostage incidents arise from a rescue attempt (Poland and McCrystle 2000: 48).

d) *Negotiators of Kidnap Situations.* The negotiator's position in kidnapping situations is much weaker than in the case of a barricade incident, precisely because of the absence of a good BATNA. The negotiator can only work to bring down the ransom demand and make a payment, or to give up on the negotiations. Paying the ransom is usually the preferred option.

Objective Criteria

Objective criteria are a powerful tool in negotiations, as nothing facilitates an agreement better than the perception that a fair standard is being used. This is especially important in crisis negotiations, where developing trust with the hostage-taker is extremely challenging and can hardly be achieved without the use of neutral evidence to support the negotiator's claims. Objective criteria are defined as facts that are independent of the will of either party.

a) *Perpetrators in Hostage Situations.* Barricade hostage-takers are likely to point to a standard that could be described as "might makes right". In other words, the possession of hostages gives the captor the feeling of an absolute leverage. Organized groups are also likely to incorporate other objective criteria such as their previous record of killing hostages at deadlines to prove their seriousness or the government's record of making concessions in hostage incidents. Sometimes the terrorists will also attempt to reverse government rhetoric and use it as objective criteria, as the PFLP did during the 1968 hijacking of ElAl Boeing 707. When the organization's outrageous formula for the exchange of hostages for an unusually high number of imprisoned terrorists was challenged, the PFLP responded by arguing that because Israel had claimed that one Israeli life was worth one hundred Arab lives, the trade was fair (Mickolus 1980: 94).

Other, more appealing standards that can be used as objective criteria by the terrorists include factual evidence of the injustices that have been perpetrated against the people the group claims to represent, or the group's record of attempting to pursue their grievance by non-violent means. This has the power of giving the perpetrators an image of using violence only as a last resort. The hostage-takers can also point to previously successful terrorist campaigns, to explain why they have taken up arms. When demanding the release of their compatriots from prison, the hostage-takers might also point to the absence of a fair trial or to the mistreatment of the group's members while in prison.

b) *Perpetrators of Kidnapping Incidents.* Organized kidnappers with a political motivation are likely to use argumentation identical to the one described above. Groups whose only purpose is to extort money will probably use mainly the "might makes right" argument, in addition to the affected company's or family's financial capabilities and their past records of making concessions. Existence of a kidnap and ransom insurance premium could also be used, but it is unlikely that the kidnappers would have that kind of information; specialized insurance companies have very strict confidentiality standards, sometimes even including a clause that makes the policy invalid in the event of an information leak (Prochnau 1998). Extortionist groups also have the option of pointing to the poverty level of a particular region and stating that the money will go to the poor. While there have been numerous instances in Latin America and Africa in which hostages were exchanged for investments in a poverty-plagued region (Auerbach 1998), a political group can also use this argumentation to justify collecting money – an action otherwise harmful to the organization's popular image.

c) *Negotiators of Barricade Situations.* The hostage negotiator also has a wide range of objective criteria at which to point. The obvious ones are the innocence of the victim and the emotional suffering of his or her family. While these standards are likely to be deflected, it is still very important to pronounce them in order to enhance formation of the Stockholm Syndrome, which serves to humanize the victims to their captors, making cold-blooded execution of hostages psychologically more difficult (Poland and McCrystle 2000: 26). Objective criteria such as a bank holiday, heavy traffic, or unavailability of a key person can also be a useful tool in talking through deadlines. The difficulty of transporting the demanded amount of money can be illustrated using historical examples, such as the 1972 hijacking of United Airlines Flight 239, in which the hijacker received a ransom payment of US$200,000 but had to leave US$40,000 on board because he was unable to transport the full amount (Mickolus 1980). Pointing to the crisis response unit's history of peaceful resolution of similar incidents can also help calm the captor down. If, on the other hand, the hostage-taker is too relaxed, reminding him of the tactical team's presence can help make his or her approach more serious. Most hostage-takers also become very concerned with the consequences of their behavior as the incident progresses. A very powerful tool is for the negotiator to point to the objective fact that in similar instances, hostage-takers are charged only with misdemeanor (assuming no hostages are harmed and there is no other violation of the law). From a legal standpoint, hostage-taking is not a serious crime and the sentence is likely to be reduced due to overcrowded prisons (McMains and Mullins 2001: 128).

d) *Negotiators of Kidnap Situations.* The kidnap negotiator also has the option of appealing to the moral values of kidnappers by talking about the victim's family duties and the values that he or she holds. A standard that is more likely to have an impact, however, are the payee's financial difficulties to meet the demand. It is also possible to refer to deals negotiated with the same organization for the same type of hostage. The difficulty of assembling large sums of money to pay the ransom without raising suspicion and risking intervention of the authorities is another good objective criterion.

Other Contrasting Negotiation Dynamics

In this section, additional contrasting dynamics of kidnap and barricade situations will be discussed.

Time-Element

Time is an extremely important factor in crisis negotiations. It does, however, affect each of the two discussed scenarios in different ways. During barricade situations, time is clearly on the negotiators' side, since the hostage-taker is tied to his or her location. As time elapses, the abductor's primary needs such as hunger or thirst tend to replace other, hierarchically higher sets of needs (McMains and Mullins 2001: 108). This opens up a wide range of opportunities for the negotiator to trade items such as food, water or tobacco for the release of a hostage or some other "favor" on part of the hostage-taker. Elapsing time also helps in reducing the subject's expectations of having his or her demands fulfilled. From a tactical perspective, prolonging the incident also provides more time to gather intelligence and to prepare for an assault.

Most of these time-related factors are not present in the kidnapping scenario, for obvious reasons. One of the few aspects that does remain similar is the favorable role of time in intelligence gathering, as modern technology can be used to detect the kidnappers' location. This option, however, should not be overestimated, as most kidnappers are well aware of the possibility of being traced. Furthermore, since most of today's kidnappers hold their victims in an area under their direct military control, even locating the kidnappers may not be too helpful, as a rescue operation would risk too many additional lives.

Another important distinction related to the time element is the duration of the incident. While barricade situations last on average between 8 and 10 hours (Poland and McCrystle 2000: 59), about one half of all kidnapping victims are held for 1–10 days, about a quarter from 11 to 50 days, and the rest from 50 to over 100 days (Royal and Sun Alliance Insurance Group). The differences in duration of an incident have important implications in terms of moments of greatest danger to the hostages' lives. While in most barricade situations the killing of hostages occurs at the beginning of the standoff as a result of initial panic, kidnappers kill their victims in cold blood later in the incident, either to make a statement or to terminate the situation after concluding that their interests can no longer be satisfied through negotiations. The psychological processes on part of the hostage-taker that make barricade negotiations so effective are also absent in kidnapping situations. In the barricade scenario, the location of the hostage-taker is contained and it is only a matter of time before the subject is worn out. Also, the hostage-taker is under extreme stress, and his or her ability to think rationally is often severely impaired or completely disabled. The high level of adrenalin in the suspect's blood often results in a quick transition between a wide range of human passions. According to research conducted by the German elite counterterrorism unit *Grenzschutzgruppe-9* (GSG-9), most barricade situations begin with the hostage-taker experiencing rage and making the decision to take hostages. This feeling is later replaced by excitement, as the hostage-taker becomes accustomed to the perceived position of absolute power. When the suspect discovers that not everything is going according to his or her initial plan, he or she becomes increasingly frustrated. Frustration then increases the already high level of stress, resulting in a more rational approach to the situation. At this point, the level of the captor's adrenalin drops and he or she begins to feel the signs of fatigue, which later turn into complete exhaustion (Strentz 1995). It is vitally important to note, however, that this emotional decline is a cyclical, rather than a linear process. As a result, the gradual de-escalation usually appears in a very confusing pattern, which has many peaks and valleys, especially at the end when the hostage-taker is about to surrender (Strentz 1995). The key implication of this is that the frequent changes in mood are a natural and an incontrollable occurrence, and can be overcome only with passing time (See Figure 3).

In kidnapping incidents, the aforementioned psychological processes do not occur, as the abductors are not exposed to a long period of continuous stress, since they are not confined to a particular area and are not under the immediate threat of a tactical resolution. For this reason, kidnappers are able to think and act much more rationally than barricade hostage-takers, and consequently do not lower their demands as easily. This does not mean however, that no change in demands takes place. The longer the abductors hold their victim, the greater burden the victim becomes. Besides having to worry about the health of the hostage, prolonging the incident also increases the chance of being detected by the security forces. The willingness to lower demands with time is therefore usually present in kidnapping incidents as well, even though the hypothesis that the duration of the incident is positively correlated with chances for a successful resolution has yet to be conformed by statistical data analysis (Hayes 2001: 423).

Means of Communication

Effective means of communication are the precondition of any successful negotiation. In barricade incidents, establishment of a communication line is the first action that takes place after the perpetrator's location has been secured. In most incidents, negotiations are usually conducted through a direct phone line or via a field "throw telephone". The direct communication setting helps the negotiator in building rapport and is also useful in providing critical intelligence. In cases when the perpetrator refuses to communicate, prompt answering of the telephone is going to be the first concession the negotiator will seek in exchange for minor favors such as food, drink, or turning the air conditioner back on (McMains and Mullins 2001: 108).

In kidnapping situations, communication is much more problematic from the negotiator's standpoint. In the best case scenario negotiations take the form of radio transmissions. Frequently, communication is only one sided, taking the form of a short phone call stating demands. Such phone calls usually last no longer than two minutes in order to avoid detection of the caller's location (Clutterbuck 1978: 64). Alternatively, the abductors can communicate through letters, e-mail, audiotapes sent to radio stations, or newspaper advertisements. Such one sided communication puts kidnappers in a position of considerable advantage, as it eliminates the crisis negotiator's ability to employ appropriate negotiation tactics.

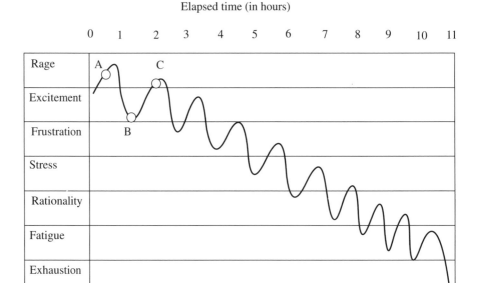

Figure 3. Psychological progression in barricade situations.

Source: Strentz, Thomas (1995). "The Cyclic Crisis Negotiations Time Line". *Law and Order*, March.

Demands and Deadlines

Demands are an indispensable part of any crisis negotiation. In barricade situations, the hostage-taker is likely to issue a set of extreme demands at the beginning of the incident. These should become more realistic throughout the course of negotiation, as the perpetrator's approach becomes more rational due to the cyclical psychological processes described earlier. The negotiator can help in reducing the quantity of demands by focusing on a particular demand and by asking clarifying questions. If, for example, the hostage-taker asks for a getaway vehicle, the negotiator can focus the discussion on the characteristics of the vehicle, such as model, make, color, interior design, etc. Such conversation has the potential of occupying the perpetrator's mind to the point that he or she simply forgets about the other demands made earlier (McMains and Mullins 2001: 142).

In kidnapping cases, demands are also typically extreme in the beginning and slowly become more realistic as the incident progresses. In this scenario, however, such adjustment is not caused by the psychological forces described above, but by the abductors' positional approach to negotiations – the demands are high because the hostage-taker aims to leave room for compromise. In Colombia, for instance, kidnapped businessmen are usually released for an average of about US$2 million, even though the initial demands are as high as US$100 million (Royal and Sun Alliance Insurance Group 2002).

In both barricade and kidnapping cases, a strict deadline will usually be attached to the fulfillment of demands, accompanied by a threat to start killing hostages. It is the negotiator's job to make these deadlines pass while keeping the hostages alive. This is usually achieved by introducing some of the "objective" obstacles to meeting the deadline that were described earlier, and by reminding abductors that if anyone is hurt the negotiations end and BATNA is employed. The key is to provide a credible justification for not being able to meet the time limit, helping the hostage-taker to save face. The nature of the demand that is attached to the deadline plays an important role in assessing its credibility and urgency. Some demands are simply too unrealistic to be credibly backed by the threat of killing hostages. Murdering someone in cold blood is an extreme measure that most hostage-takers are not eager to resort to, unless they feel that no other option exists. Based on the theory of cognitive dissonance, which states that we are more likely to accept arguments that support our position, the reluctance to kill enables the negotiators to talk through deadlines as long as they provide a believable explanation for not being able to fulfill them.

In kidnapping incidents, the absence of ongoing direct contact makes the passing of a deadline a much more volatile moment. Still, based on empirical evidence, meeting the opening demands at the initial deadline clearly is not an advisable option – as the aforementioned Hardgrove kidnapping case demonstrates, immediate compliance invites further claims (Hardgrove 1998). Since most contemporary kidnappings are conducted by organized groups experienced in negotiations, the "objective" explanations for not being able to meet a deadline are not likely to have much persuasive power. Still, it is probably better to provide some explanation for not meeting the deadline, than to simply ignore it. This point will allow the negotiator to make it clear that he or she understands the game, without unnecessarily provoking the kidnappers.

Non-Negotiable Demands

Some demands in crisis negotiations are referred to as non-negotiable, either because of official policy or because of the potential of making the situation more volatile.

In barricade situations for instance, additional weapons will not be given to the hostage-taker under any circumstances, as the suspect might be using a fake or a non-functional weapon. Satisfying his or her demand would only provide the tools necessary for a violent exchange. Another example of a non-negotiable demand is the exchange of hostages (McMains and Mullins 2001: 117–118). The desire to bring a specific person to the scene may indicate the hostage-taker's intent to hurt this person. Further, introducing new individuals to the situation disrupts the formation of the Stockholm Syndrome and raises overall tensions (Fuselier 1986). Other non-negotiable demands in a barricade situation also include supplying the hostage-taker with alcohol or drugs, as these substances have the potential of escalating the suspect's violent behavior (McMains and Mullins 2001: 117).

It is the negotiator's responsibility to handle non-negotiable demands. This is usually done by the deflection of the focus toward a different demand or by introducing issues pertaining to primary needs, such as hunger or thirst.[8] If these attempts fail and the hostage-taker is insistent, the negotiator should carefully explain why the demand is not going to be fulfilled. It will be crucial to emphasize in a non-threatening manner that the non-negotiability of the entire package does not mean that individual demands cannot be discussed (McMains and Mullins 2001: 107).

In politically motivated kidnapping incidents, most non-negotiable demands are related to government policy, such as exchange of prisoners, withdrawal of military forces, or an alteration of policies toward a certain country. In profit motivated incidents, non-negotiable demands are not likely to be an important part of the negotiation, with a possible exception of a demand for a particular person to handle negotiations. Such a demand provides an opportunity for the negotiator to swing momentum to his or her side by simply refusing – the issue of who does the talking is unlikely to be important enough for the kidnappers to actually carry out their threats of killing the hostage.

Deliberate Deception

Despite the existence of legal precedents in the US determining that promises made to hostage-takers during hostage negotiations are not legally binding contracts,[9] the use of deliberate deception during barricade negotiations is generally not a good idea. While Hayes' analysis shows that bluffing, even if detected, does not reduce the likelihood of a negotiated solution (Hayes 2001: 422), several other factors should be taken into consideration. First of all, the effort invested into building rapport with the hostage-taker could be jeopardized and the difficulties of reestablishing credibility with the suspect are usually not worth the risk. Secondly, the wide media coverage barricade situations receive can make bluffing costly in the long run, as public familiarity with deceptive police tactics will make establishing credibility in future hostage negotiations even more challenging. An exception to this general rule can be made in cases involving emotionally disturbed persons. In one case for instance, the negotiator was able to successfully resolve the incident by dressing in a white robe and a white headdress posing as God and instructing the hostage-taker to surrender (Poland and McCrystle 2000: 47). Still, deception should only be used after the traditional approaches have failed.

In kidnapping incidents, "bluffing" can be utilized more extensively for several reasons. First, fulfillment of the demands could be impossible and deceit may be the only chance left for saving the life of a hostage. Secondly, most kidnapping negotiations are covert, limiting the negative repercussions arising from wide media coverage. On the other hand, experienced kidnappers may monitor the location of the victim's family to detect any inconsistencies (Bolz, Dudonis and Schultz 2000: 120). In addition, the abductors are also likely to have developed sophisticated handover techniques that eliminate the possibility of a successful "con".

Face-Saving

Assisting the counterpart in developing an effective face-saving mechanism in order to help justify the concessions that have been made despite the original hard line position is an important element of most negotiations. This is especially true in barricade situations, since the standoff begins with the hostage-taker perceiving his or her position to be one of absolute power, but ends with the suspect's embarrassing surrender. In order to facilitate the hostage-taker's decision to capitulate, it is extremely important to prevent the feeling of humiliation by providing reasoning support and by stressing the hostage-taker's "admirable display of courage and humanity" by not hurting anyone and peacefully surrendering. This is going to be more difficult if the abductor has locked himself in his position by making public statements. It is therefore important to limit spectators of the standoff, especially during the concluding stage (McMains and Mullins 2001: 77).

Resulting from a lack of direct contact, kidnapping negotiations do not rely as heavily on face saving as barricade situations, even though this technique can still be useful. In this scenario it is the negotiator's task to supply feasible argumentation for his counterpart to use in "selling" the negotiated deal to his or her constituents, who may disagree with conditions of the settlement.

Role of Media

Media coverage of hostage crises has been the topic of many heated debates, with one side arguing for the right to free speech and the other drawing a link between media coverage and the contagion of hostage-taking tactics (Wardlaw 1982: 77).

In barricade situations, the sensational nature of the incident always succeeds in attracting wide media attention, which can have both positive and negative effects. On the negative side, an irresponsible approach by the media can directly affect the outcome of the incident. In several instances, the media has provided the hostage-takers with critical intelligence, putting the hostages in grave risk. During the 1977 hijacking of a Lufthansa aircraft to Mogadishu, for example, a radio report revealed that one of the pilots on the airplane was secretly passing information to the authorities during routine transitions to the ground. The hijackers heard the broadcast and reacted by executing the German Captain. In another incident in Cleveland, Ohio, the local television station transmitted footage showing police snipers moving into position just as the incident was about to conclude. Having seen the report, the perpetrator thought he was about to be attacked by the tactical team, resulting in prolongation of the incident by an additional 24 hours. Another possible damaging effect of media inquiry is the establishment of direct contact with the hostage-takers. During the 1977 Hanafi Muslim takeover of three buildings in Washington DC, a reporter asked one of the terrorists whether a deadline had been set. The police who saw the lack of a deadline as one of few positive aspects of the situation were outraged (Wardlaw 1982: 79).

Despite the great potential for making things more difficult for the responders, the media can also be very helpful. In politically motivated barricade situations, which are usually designed to attract wide attention in order to convey a message, it is not uncommon for the captors to demand media coverage or publication of a group manifesto. In such instances the cooperation of media is critical. For instance, the 1972 Frontier Airlines Fight 91 hijacking was successfully resolved after several television and radio stations agreed to air the hijacker's two and a half hour speech, in which he asked for world peace and better educational opportunities for poor Mexican children (Mickolus 1980: 309).

In kidnapping incidents, a possible negative effect of media inquiry consists of increasing the perceived importance of individual hostages as a result of wide media focus on the victims. Such perception by the kidnappers can result in increased demands, hindering the negotiator's efforts to make terms of the settlement more favorable. On the other hand, the media can also play a very positive role in kidnapping incidents as they can provide a platform for effective communication between the kidnappers and the negotiator.

Stockholm Syndrome

As mentioned earlier, the Stockholm Syndrome is an important factor in crisis negotiations. In most general terms, this phenomenon transpires by the formation of mutually positive feelings between the hostage-taker and the hostages. The Stockholm Syndrome provides another good example of the differing dynamics in various negotiation scenarios.

In barricade situations, the syndrome is comprised of a four way process. The first relationship is based on the dependency of the victim on the abductor – the latter decides when the former will eat, sleep, go to the bathroom, live, or die. The bond of dependency is not dissimilar to the relationship between a mother and a child (Poland and McCrystle 2000: 24). This dynamic is strengthened by the hostage's instinct to do everything necessary in order to survive. The victim's humbleness and obedience helps to reduce anger of the hostage-taker, who in turn reciprocates by a more humane treatment of the hostage. This reciprocation only reinforces the positive feelings on behalf of the victim. Another dependency bond is formed between the hostage-taker and the negotiator, who projects the image of someone who can hurt but desires to help (McMains and Mullins 2001: 167). The third relationship that helps to reinforce the positive mutual feelings between the hostage and the abductor is the perception of a common enemy: the tactical unit. The hostage-taker feels threatened by the police for obvious reasons. The victims also perceive the authorities negatively, as they feel that not enough is being done to secure their release. Moreover, the security forces represent an apparent threat to the hostages as well, due to their uncertain ability to distinguish between the hostage-takers and the hostages. The shared negative relationship toward a third party makes the Stockholm Syndrome even stronger. In the words of a released hostage of the PAL BAC 111, which was hijacked in 1976 by members of the Moro National Liberation Front (MNLF) in the Philippines: "We all became sort of one unit, the passengers, the hijackers, the pilot, against the outside world. We found ourselves wanting to explain the cause of the hijackers" (Mickolus 1980: 608–609).

Besides providing a more favorable environment for Stockholm Syndrome formation, barricade situations present the negotiator with an array of options for its encouragement. The negotiator can promote the positive relationship by forcing as much interaction between the hostage-taker and the victims as possible. Feasible techniques include the delivery of food in large portions requiring cooperation between the captor and the captives, asking the hostage-taker to check on the health of hostages, discussing family responsibilities and requesting information about the treatment of hostages, and asking to deliver messages from family members (Clutterbuck 1978: 62). Introduction of joint problem solving by referring to all parties involved as "us" is another strong tool.

In kidnapping incidents, formation of the Stockholm Syndrome is much more difficult. First, the mutual negative relationship toward a third party is absent. Second, kidnappers have the possibility of eliminating the factors that contribute to the syndrome's formation by rotating guards and by continual blindfolding and ear plugging of the victim. Hostages can also be harshly interrogated, humiliated by degradation, denied sleep or food, and be exposed to periods of noise and light alerted by periods of total silence and darkness. Since formation of the Stockholm Syndrome is dependent on absence of negative experiences with bad treatment, such measures can effectively eliminate its formation (Poland and McCrystle 2000: 25).

Encouragement of the syndrome's development is also a much more difficult task in kidnapping incidents. Similar techniques as those used in barricade situations can be employed, but their effect will be limited due to the absence of ongoing contact of the victims with their captors.

Conclusions

Negotiations in general are not possible unless there is an overlapping point of reference in the range of expectations of both parties (Zartman 1990: 173). At the initial phase of hostage incidents, such overlap rarely exists, and changing the hostage-takers' expectations is precisely the most important task facing the negotiator. At the same time, barricade and kidnapping situations differ significantly in most aspects of the negotiation process, resulting in the need to employ varying approaches. Nevertheless, the interest-based negotiation framework used in this article provides a useful analytical tool for identifying the key differences between the two scenarios. This type of analysis can then be used as a guide for modifying successful barricade-hostage negotiation strategies, in order to apply them to kidnapping incidents. By analyzing each hostage crisis with regard to the people, interests, options, BATNA's, and objective criteria involved, it is possible to identify opportunities for expanding the range of options and introducing alternative solutions that may succeed in bringing about a peaceful resolution. Further, the interest-based negotiation framework provides a helpful instrument to analyze the negotiability of each type of incident. This is especially important, as an understanding of the negotiating positions of all parties needs to precede the selection of an overall negotiation strategy. The negotiability guidelines for individual scenarios are presented below.

Contrary to popular belief, the negotiator's position in most barricade incidents is quite strong. In an absolute majority of barricade situations the hostage-takers do not place themselves into the situation voluntarily. Under the condition that the hostage-taker desires to live, the threat of force by the tactical unit in combination with the suspect's inexperience, reluctance to kill, and inability to depart freely, constitute a no-win situation for the hostage-taker. This scenario provides a framework in which the well-defined crisis negotiation strategies have the potential of reaching a peaceful resolution without granting substantive concessions.

In politically or religiously motivated barricade incidents, the dynamic changes significantly due to the premeditated nature of the act, along with the voluntary character of the perpetrators' involvement. In this relatively infrequent scenario, the negotiator's position is considerably weakened by the perpetrators' lack of authority to make any important decisions, including the decision to surrender without reaching all formulated objectives of the operation. For members of terrorist organizations, in which great emphasis is placed on discipline and commitment, the prospect of surviving and being labeled a traitor is far less attractive than an "honorable death for the cause". However, in most such incidents, the traditional crisis negotiation approach still applies, with the key difference that since the perpetrators' objectives have been formulated with some thought in advance, their expectations of the outcome will not be easily modifiable. Consequently, the duration of the incident may be significantly longer than in *ad hoc* hostage-taking cases, and patience is therefore imperative. The hostage-takers' behavior will sometimes be unbalanced and the demands and conditions are likely to change rapidly, especially as the incident progresses. This may lead many members of the hostage rescue team to the conclusion that the terrorists' approach is not serious and that the only option remaining is a rescue operation. However, the hostage-takers' erratic behavior should be understood as a sign that is essentially *positive* in nature – it signals a frustration associated with an unanticipated development of events, an important component in bringing about a change of expectations.

Another difficulty in politically motivated barricade incidents is the reluctance of most governments to grant any concessions, under the rationale that doing so would only invite further acts of terrorism. Since the negotiator's position in premeditated incidents is relatively weak, the lack of substantive incentives for the release of hostages reduces the chances of peaceful resolution. While Hayes presents evidence that governments with a history of substantive concessions during hostage incidents are likely to experience an increase in terrorist activity, he also documents that minor, instrumental concessions[10] are not associated with such an increase. Further, even if substantive concessions are made, their effect on future terrorist activities can be minimized by denial and secrecy (Hayes 2001: 425).

Unlike in the kidnapping scenario, where some concessions will be necessary, in barricade incidents the authorities at least have a strong BATNA in the form of a rescue operation. It is perhaps the historical frequency of using this option that has nearly erased barricade hostage-taking from the repertoire of most terrorist organizations. The probable non-compliance of future hostages resulting from the outcomes of the 11th September hijackings is likely to reinforce this trend.

As in the case of ideologically motivated barricade incidents, negotiations of kidnappings are also complicated by the pre-meditated and voluntary character of perpetrators' involvement. In addition, the hostages in kidnapping incidents are likely to be carefully selected from a larger pool of candidates, making it more difficult for the negotiator to plead for the release on humanitarian grounds or to convince the hostage-takers about insufficient availability of funds to pay the ransom. In criminally motivated cases, the negotiator's counterpart is also likely to be experienced, possibly gaining the ability to identify and eliminate many of the tricks the negotiator may attempt to employ. At the same time, the kidnappers' negotiating know-how has the potential of increasing the predictability of their actions while also reducing the volatile aspects of hostage negotiations resulting from inexperience and panic. Further, a business-like approach employed by the abductors paves the road for a negotiated settlement. Such an agreement, however, will inevitably include a ransom payment, the sum of which will be determined by the negotiator's ability to introduce a balanced combination of patience, firmness, and willingness to identify a "fair offer". In early stages of the incident, the negotiator should buy time by disputing the very principle of a ransom payment itself. During this stage, the negotiator should also introduce a firm position on minor demands that are unlikely to be important enough for the kidnappers to justify "breaking their goods", such as ignoring orders on who should represent the victim's family during negotiations. Firmness in this early stage is critical for reducing the kidnappers' hopes for extorting a quick and large ransom payment. In the second stage, which follows after the principle of a ransom payment has been established, the negotiators should use their experience from previous incidents to identify a reasonable counteroffer and then try to bring the final settlement as close to this number as possible. From the beginning of this second stage of negotiations, time is no longer purely on the side of the negotiator. He or she should bargain, but should also seek closure of the deal relatively soon after the "terms of trade" have been agreed upon.

Purely politically or religiously motivated kidnappings are by far the most difficult hostage crisis scenarios to resolve. The definition of demands will provide invaluable insight into the negotiability of the incident. In cases where the perpetrator's sole purpose is generating publicity, the demands are likely to be defined in a vague and declaratory manner, leaving room for any necessary adjustments that will "justify" the refusal to release the hostages. In such incidents, the perpetrators are not interested in a serious negotiation; the operation is rather designed to generate wide public attention, before killing the hostage and attempting to blame his or her death on government inaction. The options available to negotiators in such incidents are very limited; they can only attempt to prolong the talks in order to gain clues that might help in locating the victim, or at least in tracking down the perpetrators.

In political incidents where goals are defined more tangibly, negotiation is possible, but still extremely challenging. The kidnappers' negotiating position is so strong that it provides little incentive to settle for anything less than the original demand. At the same time, this demand is likely to be unacceptable for the government. However, unless the negotiator is given something to work with, the chances of the hostage's survival are minimal. The only way to negotiate such incidents is to provide something for the terrorists to gain. Since minor concessions such as food or safe passage are inapplicable to kidnapping scenarios, governments should be prepared to make some substantive concessions, with the option of mitigating the negative effects of the deal by secrecy or subsequent denial.

Overall, there are several important implications of the findings presented in this paper for government policy on international hostage-taking. First, an *a priori* exclusion of negotiations from the list of responses is not a useful idea, since such position eliminates the most effective resolution tool available. Further, since some form of negotiation is going to take place in barricade situations regardless of the official government policy, any benefit of the hard-line rhetoric in terms of deterring further acts of hostage-taking will be lost.

Secondly, an *a priori* exclusion of substantive concessions from the negotiators' arsenal effectively eliminates the possibility of a successful resolution of an absolute majority of kidnapping incidents. Even though the government's hard line approach of "no negotiations with terrorists" is based on logical argumentation, a policy of flexible response seems to be a more useful approach to international hostage-taking. Such policy would allow the evaluation of negotiability of each specific incident, and subsequent issuance of the appropriate response. This approach would enable an application of the hard-line policy in some cases while not being an obstacle to a negotiated settlement in others.

Acknowledgements

The author would like to thank William Monning J.D., Jason Pate, and the anonymous reviewers for their comments on earlier versions of this paper.

Notes

1. In fact, most crisis negotiation manuals say little about kidnappings except that they are different from barricade situations due to the fact that the location of the victim(s) as well as that of the perpetrator(s) is unknown in kidnappings.
2. According to Royal and Sun Alliance Insurance Group, 67 percent of victims are released with a ransom paid and 15 percent without a ransom paid. Up to 10 percent of kidnapping victims are killed and the remaining 7 percent are rescued.
3. Perpetrator interviews and victim debriefings show that most of the hostage-takers of the 1980s were provided with a list of demands, but only minimal instruction on how to proceed during the standoff with the security forces (Fuselier and Noesner 1990).
4. Parents will most likely use the legal process to gain custody of their children after fleeing to another country, while pedophiles and emotionally disturbed persons are not likely to initiate contact and issue demands, making any negotiation impossible.
5. The target study of a victim and the scouting costs were estimated to be around US$30,000; members of the snatch group received US$10,000–15,000 each adding up to about US$60,000 total; guards were paid roughly US$2000 per month plus a percentage of the final ransom payment. Money could be laundered at about a 30–40 percent charge (Clutterbuck 1978: 66).
6. This policy has sometimes been rephrased as "no concessions policy" – the refusal to make concessions does not eliminate the option of negotiations.

7. Both of these incidents, however, involved more than 100 very well armed and well organized Chechen terrorists.
8. McMains and Mullins describe how the negotiator can suggest taking a lunch break and continuing the discussion later. The mentioning of food has the potential of reminding the hostage-taker of his primary needs.
9. United States vs. Crosby, 1983; State vs. Sands, 1985.
10. For example, providing food, safe surrender or even safe passage when hostages are released unharmed.

References

Antokol, Nudell (1990) *No One a Neutral: Political Hostage Taking in the Modern World.* Alpha Publications.
Bandura, Albert (1998) "Mechanisms of Moral Disengagement". In Walter Reich (ed.), *Origins of Terrorism: Psychologies, Ideologies, Theologies, States of Mind.* Washington D.C.: Woodrow Wilson Center Press, 2nd edition.
Bolz, Frank, Jr., Dudonis, Kenneth and Schultz, David (2002) *The Counterterrorism Handbook: Tactics, Procedures and Techniques.* London: CRC Press, 2nd edition.
Clutterbuck, Richard (1978) *Kidnap and Ransom: The Response.* London: Faber and Faber.
Corsi, J.R. (1981) "Terrorism as a Desperate Game – Fear, Bargaining, and Communication in the Terrorist Event". *Journal of Conflict Resolution* 25,1: 47–85.
Fisher, Roger and Ury, W. (1991) *Getting to Yes.* New York: Penguin Books, 2nd edition.
Fuselier, Dwayne (1986) *What Every Negotiator Would Like his Chief to Know*, FBI Law Enforcement Bulletin.
Fuselier, Noesner (1990) *Confronting the Terrorist Hostage Taker-Hostage*, Internet, available at <http://www.emergency.com/host-tkr.htm> (accessed on 1/29/02).
Hardgrove, Thomas (1998) *Testimony at the House Committee on International Relations*, Internet, available at <www.g21.net/narco.html> (accessed on 1/30/02).
Hardgrove, Thomas (2001) *Reactions to Proof of Life*, Internet, available at <http://angelfire.com/nv/dmifc/media/hardgrove2.html> (accessed on 1/30/02).
Hayes, Richard (2002) "Negotiations with Terrorists". In Victor Kremenyuk (ed.), *International Negotiation.* San Francisco: Jossey-Bass.
Hoffman, Bruce (1998) *Inside Terrorism.* New York: Orion Publishing Co.
McMains, M.J., and Mullins, W.C. (2001) *Crisis negotiations: Managing critical incidents and hostage situations in law enforcement and corrections* (2nd ed.). Cincinnati, OH: Anderson.
Mickolus, Edward F. (1980) *Transnational Terrorism: A Chronology of Events, 1968–1979.* Westport: Greenwood Press.
Miller, Judith (2002) "U.S. Plans to Act More Rigorously in Hostage Cases". *New York Times* 18 February 2002.
Prochnau, William (1998) "Adventures in the Ransom Trade". *Vanity Fair.*
Poland, J.M. and McCrystle, M.J. (1999) *Practical, Tactical, and Legal Perspectives of Terrorism and Hostage-taking.* Lewiston, NY: E. Mellon Press.
Royal and Sun Alliance Insurance Group. *Statistics on Kidnap and Ransom.* Internet, available at <http://www.rsa-profin.co.uk/KR/statistics.htm> accessed on 1/15/02.

Strentz, Thomas (1991) "13 Indicators of Volatile Negotiations". *Law and Order*.
Strentz, Thomas (1995) "The Cyclic Crisis Negotiations Time Line". *Law and Order*.
Wardlaw, Grant (1982) *Political Terrorism*. London: Cambridge University Press.
Zartman, I. William (1990) "Negotiating Effectively With Terrorists". In Barry Rubin (ed.), *The Politics of Counterterrorism*. Washington, DC: The Johns Hopkins Foreign Policy Institute.

Testing the Role Effect in Terrorist Negotiations

WILLIAM A. DONOHUE and PAUL J. TAYLOR

In a recent paper, Donohue and Taylor (2003) reviewed seven lines of research that provided data about the effects of role on strategy use in negotiations. Central to each line of work was evidence for a one-down effect. Specifically, negotiators who saw themselves as having fewer options than their opponents were more likely to resort to aggressive strategies as a way of seeking change in the power structure. The emphasis of these negotiators' dialogue was on defending a personal position by attacking the other party's social legitimacy and attempting to force the other into unnecessarily yielding on critical issues. In contrast, negotiators who perceived themselves as having a greater number of options were less threatened by the power structure of the situation and, consequently, were more likely to risk their social identity with affiliative and conciliatory dialogue. In other words, the role associated with the less powerful, "one-down" position typically fostered use of competitive, aggressive messages as a means of shifting power, even though that strategy can be least effective in reaching agreement (Levine and Boster 2001).

The purpose of this article is to explore this effect in the context of terrorist hostage-taking and negotiation. Data used to examine the role effect were derived from 186 descriptive accounts of terrorist incidents collected from the chronologies compiled by Mickolus and his colleagues (Mickolus 1980, 1993; Mickolus, Sandler, and Murdock 1989; Mickolus and Simmons 1997). The accounts selected contained sufficient descriptive material to enable a coding of the power and affiliative behaviors that occurred during the incidents as well as a coding of the way in which the incident ended. Of greatest interest are role differences exhibited by the various kinds of terrorists involved in these incidents. To understand these role differences, this article begins with a review of the literature that is perhaps most informative about the terrorist negotiation context. The article then considers these findings in the theoretical framework of the one-down effect, and uses this review to form hypotheses about the effect of role on terrorists' behavior and incident outcome.

International Negotiation Series 1:
I.W. Zartman (ed.) Negotiating with Terrorists, 83–102
© 2006 *Koninklijke Brill NV. Printed in the Netherlands.*

Hostage Negotiation Research

Early research into terrorist hostage-taking highlighted the interdependence between parties' cooperative and aggressive behavior and how this influences the dynamics of incidents. For example, Corsi (1981) used decision trees to show that acts of force by both terrorists and authorities can influence the response of the other party, as well as shape how the incident unfolds. By systematically modeling these relationships, other researchers (e.g. Sandler and Scott 1987) have noted the importance of complementary and reciprocal dynamics in the bargaining process between terrorists and authorities. As might be expected, these dynamics also associate differently with the possible outcomes of terrorist incidents. For example, in their descriptive analysis of politically motivated attacks, Friedland and Merari (1992) found relationships between factors such as the degree terrorists were armed and their subsequent commitment to the act. Finally, in developing this research from a psychological script perspective, Wilson (2000) highlighted the importance of negotiators' identity, as measured by differences in terrorist group, on the type of behaviors terrorists are prepared to use and the outcomes that they achieve.

More direct evidence of how role influences these behavioral relations comes from research that focuses on the various language strategies used in hostage negotiation. For example, Donohue and Roberto (1993) studied communication strategies across 10 actual incidents in which police negotiators talked to hostage-takers with a variety of different role backgrounds (i.e. experienced criminals, mentally disturbed, domestic problems). The results indicated that the police negotiators controlled the amount and pace of the discussions and the topics that were considered. The police were also more likely than the hostage-takers to use collaborative relational messages that show support and provide information, whereas the hostage-takers were significantly more likely to use power strategies such as threats, demands, and language containing negative affect. Thus, while police negotiators sought to control interactions by controlling the emphasis on dialogue, they also recognized the need for affiliative messages to manage the disparity in power between the two parties.

Rogan and Hammer (1994) used another set of hostage negotiations to explore the importance of identity or facework in negotiations. Facework focuses on the issue of controlling one's identity and threatening the others' identity in an attempt to alter the individual's view of him or herself as being competent and in control of the situation. Rogan and Hammer discovered that the police negotiators relied heavily on trying to restore the hostage-taker's face (i.e. used language to portray the hostage-taker in positive terms) while the hostage-takers relied more on restoring their own face or making themselves look strong and in control. Thus, the perpetrators were much more focused on defending their own identities than the police negotiators, who showed little concern for personal identity and concentrated more on trying to support the perpetrators' identities.

In further exploring the importance of identity within role differences, Donohue and Roberto (1996) found that the hostage-takers in authentic contexts used more distributive or power-seeking strategies, made more demands, and proposed fewer integrative or win-win options than the hostage-takers or police negotiators in simulated contexts. Although these simulations were conducted by actual police negotiators, the role effect was not as significant as that found with actual hostage-takers, presumably because negotiators in simulated sessions have a lower commitment to their identity. The actual hostage-takers were significantly more interested in protecting their identities than individuals in any other category of negotiation.

The possibility of role orientations influencing negotiators' language choices is also evident in Taylor (2002a), who showed that messages typically orient around avoidance (withdrawn), distributive (competitive) and integrative (cooperative) approaches to interaction. Taylor argued that these broad orientations emerge from negotiators' interpersonal predispositions and personal role expectations in the conflict, and showed that their characteristic behaviors formed a single dimension running from extreme crisis to normative problem solving. Consistent with Donohue and Roberto (1993), Taylor demonstrated that those negotiators holding firm to specific orientations tend to use communication behaviors that seek to aggressively increase power or concede power to open dialogue to more normative problem solving. Moreover, Taylor found that negotiators generally adopt consistent orientations to instrumental (task-focused), relational (trust and liking-focused), and identity (identity or face-focused) concerns at any one time, reasserting the central importance of roles to many aspects of negotiation dynamics (Wilson and Putnam 1990).

Theoretical Explanations for the One-Down Role Effect

Based on this hostage negotiation research and findings from other contexts reviewed by Donohue and Taylor (2003), it appears that negotiators who see themselves as having fewer options in comparison to their opponents often seek to regain power through competitive, attacking dialogue, even though that strategy can be least effective in reaching agreement (Levine and Boster 2001). Hostage-takers, buyers, union negotiators, low-power political groups and husbands in a divorce negotiation rely on more power-oriented messages to promote a more competitive and more power-focused negotiation context. The emphasis of their dialogue is on gaining control in the interaction by attacking the other party's social legitimacy and attempting to force the other into unnecessarily yielding on critical issues. In contrast, the hostage negotiators, sellers, management negotiators, high power international negotiators, and wives use a broader range of communication choices including more affiliative and interest-focused messages. Because these negotiators have more options available that do not impinge on their overall position, they feel able to risk their social identity with more open and conciliatory dialogue.

The regulation of control and its attendant focus on power is an often used theoretical tool for explaining negotiation processes (Bacharach and Lawler 1986) as well as behavior in other interpersonal contexts (Bales 1970; Leary 1957; Mahalik 2000; Schmidt, Wagner, and Kiesler 1999). For example, the concept of losing control is the most widely accepted explanation for domestic violence in which violence emerges as a strategy for regulating control that has been threatened in some way (Eisikovits, Goldblatt, and Winstok 1999). According to this perspective, the extent to which the regulation of control becomes necessary depends on the prominence of identity. For violence to emerge there needs to be a high degree of concern and commitment to the social and personal identity that underlies an individual's position. Individuals must value their identities, integrate them into all aspects of their social life, and work to defend them often. In order to defend their identity, individuals must also recognize norms and values in the social context that sanction violence as an acceptable and appropriate means of restoring one's identity. Being competitive and power-focused, or integrative and affiliation-focused, must be viewed as a normatively-sanctioned strategy for identity management. Finally, individuals need to frame situations in a way that calls for the use of violence or power strategies. That is, they must work to actively structure the situation so that power, threats, or violence are viewed as a legitimate response to that situation. Thus, for negotiators whose personal or professional lives grow from their identity as competent negotiators, situations that threaten control need to be perceived in such a way that power messages are seen as a legitimate way of responding to restore identity. The focus is on the identity and on the legitimization of force to restore it.

The importance of regulating control and power suggests that achieving symmetrical power may reduce the magnitude of the one-down effect. Pfetsch and Landau (2000) focus on the effect of power symmetry in international conflict. They contend symmetry is a necessary but not sufficient condition for successful negotiations. Properties of symmetry/asymmetry largely describe the relative potential power and strength of parties and thus power-role status. Patterns of role behavior along these dimensions are seen in the process of negotiation – lower-power parties will seek to negotiate on equal terms as the stronger party by cultivating non-material resources (e.g. actor, joint, procedural, issue-related techniques, etc.). Again, the lower-power party is likely to concentrate more on non-substantive issues as a means of equalizing power and reestablishing identity. In this context, police negotiators often talk about the need to quickly restore the hostage-taker's identity as a means of focusing on substantive issues (Donohue, Kaufmann, Smith, and Ramesh 1991).

However, role differences can also emerge from non-identity based biases (see Putnam and Holmer 1992 for a review). For example, Neale, Huber and Northcraft (1987) found that the assignment of negotiator roles, such as seller or buyer, was sufficient to cue gain and loss frames. Negotiators playing the role of sellers tend to view an outcome as a potential gain (i.e. those in an offensive role), and typically make more concessions and engage in more information seeking behaviors than buyers who tend to hold a negative frame. Negative frames are linked to escalation of conflict, potential impasse, strikes, and third party intervention. Negotiators entering interactions with negative frames are somewhat more likely to engage in defensive facework and somewhat less likely to engage in protective facework than are people entering negotiations with cooperative frames. For example, research indicates that buyers are more likely to have a negative frame than sellers, which is consistent with evidence suggesting that buyers typically use more distributive behaviors than sellers (Drake 2001; Morley and Stephenson 1977).

The notion that power and expectations interact is evident in Olekalns and Frey's (1994) study of buyer-seller negotiations, in which framing was shown to be exaggerated by differences in power. High power positively framed and negatively framed negotiators are significantly advantaged by an imbalanced negotiation market in their favor. The interaction between expectations and perceptions of power may also account for the longer term oscillation between integrative and distributive behavior use reported by Druckman (1986). Evidence suggests that expressions of positive affect reverse the one-down phenomenon, prompting bargainers with positive frames to take advantage and engage in more risk seeking, more non-agreement, and less concession making than negotiators with negative frames. In other words, when a negotiator in a powerful offensive role perceives significant benefits to using the power, they may well use their advantage. This prompts an aggressive counter-response from the low-powered defender, which in turn forces the offensive negotiator to adopt more cooperative strategies to avoid a crisis or breakdown of the interaction. This pattern of interdependence may presumably continue indefinitely, so long as interactions do not cross a threshold of extreme hostility that leads to a breakdown irrespective of any subsequent cooperation (Taylor 2002b).

Using the Role Effect to Understand Terrorist Negotiations

This review suggests that the one-down role effect of increased aggression during negotiation revolves around three key issues. First is the issue of *power complementarity*. In comparison to the other party, terrorists find themselves in a role that imposes more constraints on their ability to control the negotiation process and attain their desired outcomes. This reduced power places the terrorist in a one-down position that becomes more prominent over time as authorities develop tactical and negotiation positions. The response of many terrorists is to adopt this one-down position and threaten or actually use violence to generate fear, coercion, or intimidation in an effort to realign the balance in power (Russell, Banker, and Miller 1979). However, not only is the power structured differently, but also the strategic responses to the discrepancy are typically complementary. That is, the one-up party (e.g. the authorities) generally responds to this discrepancy with less aggression and more affiliative strategies.

However, associated with the one-down effect is a limit to power complementarity that comes in the form of attenuated outcomes. If terrorists adopt a cooperative orientation to interaction, then the parties are able to develop normative dialogue that retains power complementarity and achieves better outcomes. In contrast, terrorists that adopt the one-down position are less likely to secure their desired outcomes because the increased aggression discourages the one-up party (i.e. authorities) from helping the other maximize gains. In particular, when the one-down party's behavior becomes extreme, then the one-up party often withdraws affiliation in favor of more aggression (Alexandroff 1979).

Second is the *prominence of identity*. For individuals more committed to sustaining their role identities for their professional or personal pursuits, such as terrorist and police negotiators, a key goal is to vigorously defend that public identity. Central to the beliefs and attitudes that form the terrorists' identity is an ideology (Crenshaw 1988; Hoffman 1999). A terrorist's ideological perspective provides a set of beliefs about the external world that not only fosters an identity around commitment to a cause, but also shapes expectations about the rewards of terrorism and dictates the extent to which the terrorists' goals are dependent on the cooperation of the authorities.

Although every terrorist has an individual identity, researchers have identified three major ideological perspectives (Hoffman 1999; Post, et al. 2002). The *nationalist-separatist* seeks to establish a geographically separate political state based on either ethnic or political criteria (e.g. Irish Republican Army, Popular Front for the Liberation of Palestine). These terrorists are often accountable to a developed criminal organization and are both trained and experienced in the terrorist role. The ideology itself is generally an extreme example of the beliefs and backgrounds of the immediate social group, such that these communities treat the role of terrorist with respect and importance (Silke 2003). However, because the community's beliefs also dictate the legitimacy of the terrorism, violence is typically planned, only used as necessary, and more likely to be directed away from harming innocents.

The *social revolutionist* uses terrorism as a way of drawing attention and applying pressure on the authorities to promise changes in social or economic order (e.g. Japanese Red Army). These terrorists necessarily possess a degree of interdependence with the authorities because their goals focus on fighting for improvement or change in a system of which they are already part. By using the threat of killing hostages as a bargaining tool, these terrorists expect to force authorities to compromise on a position or make concessions in support of their cause. However, since one of their aims is to gain support for the revolution, they are likely to avoid levels of aggression that would serve to reduce the publics' sympathy (Wilson 2000).

Radically different from the two secular groups is *religious fundamentalist* terrorism, which is viewed as a "sacramental act" carried out in fulfillment of some theological order (Hoffman 1999). While the focus of secular terrorists is on using terrorism to change some aspect of the current political or social order, the religious terrorist seeks to cause damage directly to a society. Their role is one of an extreme martyr figure who, in making an honorable sacrifice, would expect to receive both social recognition and rewards in the afterlife (Silke 2003). This set of goals means that religious terrorists have a clear out-group mentality and are likely to show little interdependence with authorities or hostages. They consider themselves as being at "total war", such that greater use of violence is not only morally justified but a necessary expedient for the attainment of their goals (Hoffman 1999).

The third issue is *individual bias* from situational, task, and frame perspectives. The one-down role effect appears most likely to emerge when a number of individual biases start to develop. For example, when individuals define the task as revolving around a single issue they remove options for more collaborative trade-offs and more nuanced views of the conflict. Also, more aggressive strategies emerge when individuals perceive that violent means of addressing the issues are socially sanctioned, and they enter the conflict with a fixed sum bias and a negative frame. As noted by Corsi (1981), the propensity for these dynamics to emerge will vary across the types of terrorist incidents, since each type differs in terms of its setting, the available possibilities, and the way in which the interaction is played out. In this study, where the data are aerial hijackings and barricade siege incidents, these differences are likely to affect the degree terrorists use power-gaining and affiliative strategies. Specifically, the mobile nature of some aerial hijackings means that they are associated with extreme time-critical interactions, where the traditional attrition approach to negotiation is not necessarily appropriate or possible. In such contexts, negotiators often focus on the prominent alternative and take a more aggressive approach to interaction in an effort to reach a conclusion

(Donohue et al. 1991). Moreover, the confined context of the aerial hijacking may lead hostage-takers to perceive themselves as being under greater threat from tactical strategies. Again, the response is to use power strategies that make overt threats in an attempt to discourage such actions.

Hypotheses

To test the role effect in the terrorist negotiation context it is useful to focus on the power and affiliation negotiation strategies displayed by terrorists and their negotiation counterparts. These strategies are coded in the incident reports used as the dataset for this study. Power moves are defined as aggressive attempts to gain leverage in the incident. Affiliation moves are defined as direct attempts to cooperate and bargain for suitable outcomes.

Based on these concepts and the issues that drive the one-down effect we put forward the following hypotheses:

- H1: Terrorists who reject the one-down role effect and rely more on affiliation moves by spending more time negotiating and showing a willingness to make concessions are more likely to secure their desired outcomes.
- H2: Terrorists who respond with the one-down effect will resort to power strategies as a way of seeking change in the power structure and are less likely to secure their desired outcomes.
- H3: Religious fundamentalist-oriented terrorists who are more personally committed to their identities are more likely than the other two terrorist groups to resort to power strategies as a means of seeking change in the power.
- H4: Aerial hijackings are more likely to involve overt power strategies compared to barricade-siege incidents, which are more likely to involve bargaining for certain outcomes.

Method

Data Sample

Data were 186 descriptive accounts of terrorist incidents collected from the chronologies compiled by Mickolus and his colleagues (Mickolus 1980, 1993; Mickolus, Sandler, and Murdock 1989; Mickolus and Simmons 1997). The accounts selected contained sufficient descriptive material to enable a coding of behaviors that occurred during the incidents as well as a coding of the way in which the incident ended. 100 of these accounts were aerial hijackings in which the perpetrators took control of an airplane or helicopter for a sustained period of time. The remaining 86 accounts were barricade-siege incidents in which the perpetrators took control of a public building (e.g. embassy) or a private location (e.g. bank). The selected incidents took place between 1968 and 1991, and were located in over 50 different countries. The incidents were reportedly committed by both autonomous perpetrators and perpetrators affiliating themselves with known terrorist organizations including the Black Panther Party, Islamic Jihad, the Irish Republican Army, and the Popular Front for the Liberation of Palestine. These affiliations allowed the incidents to be grouped according to whether they were associated with a nationalist-separatist, social revolutionary, or religious fundamentalist ideology (Post et al. 2002).

A content analysis of the descriptive accounts revealed a number of variables that reflected overt power moves and affiliative acts within the terrorist incidents. These behaviors were identified through a grounded approach to categorizing descriptions in which the coding scheme was continually expanded and refined until it effectively reflected the behavior of both terrorists and authorities (Glaser and Strauss 1967; Holsti 1969; Krippendorff 1980). The behavioral variables were scored in a dichotomous format as either absent (or information missing) or present across all of the 186 incidents. This method of analyzing the data was adopted following previous research findings (Taylor, Bennell, and Snook 2002; Wilson 2000) that show a dichotomous approach as effective in producing interpretable results from descriptive material whilst minimizing the opportunity for subjective and unreliable coding of the data.

The behavioral variables were found to form eight scales on which the terrorist incidents could differ. These scales focused on differences in negotiation behavior, but also reflected the other actions used by parties within the broader context of the terrorist attack. Table 1 reports the final eight scales with a definition of the categories that constitute each scale. Four of the scales depict power moves and were scored such that higher scores reflect more aggressive attempts to gain leverage in the incident. For example, the Control scale depicts terrorists' treatment of their hostages during the incident and runs from no attempt to control to killing of a hostage. Two of the scales depict the degree of affiliation shown by the terrorist and are scored with higher scores reflecting more direct attempts to cooperate and bargain for a suitable outcome. For example, the Negotiate scale runs from no dialogue to conciliation and so captures the extent to which terrorists are prepared to engage in substantive problem-solving. The remaining two outcome scales reflect the actions of the authorities in response to the terrorists. The Force scale measures the extent to which authorities carried out tactical behaviors beyond negotiation, with higher scores representing the use of more aggressive strategies during the incident. The Capitulation scale depicts the extent to which authorities complied with terrorists' demands and goals and was calculated so that higher scores reflect larger concessions.

Table 1. Definitions and scoring methods for power, affiliation, and outcome scales.

Behavioral Scale	Description	Scores
Power Scales		
Control	Extent to which the terrorists controlled or mistreated their hostages during captivity.	0 = No control 2 = Tied or gagged 1 = Threatened 3 = Physically harmed 4 = Killed
Damage	Extent to which the terrorists damaged the infrastructure of the plane or building being used.	0 = No damage 1 = Threaten damage 2 = Non-deliberate damage 3 = Deliberate damage
Demands	Number of the following demanded by the terrorists: asylum, general and specific release of prisoner, money, publicity, travel, or other.	0 = No demands 1 = One demand 2 = Two demands 3 = Three demands 4 = Four demands 5 = Five demands
Weapon use	Conditions in which the terrorists used their weapons.	0 = No use 1 = In response 2 = Spontaneously
Affiliation Scales		
Negotiate	Extent to which terrorists interacted with Authorities to reach a resolution.	0 = No dialogue 1 = Dialogue 2 = Negotiation 3 = Suggest alternative 4 = Conciliation
Release	Extent to which terrorists released hostages during the incident.	0 = Retention 1 = Release Women / Children 2 = Release some passengers 3 = Release All passengers
Outcome Scales		
Capitulation	Extent to which Authorities conciliated with terrorists to reach a resolution.	0 = Attrition 1 = Offers 2 = Concessions 3 = Allowed escape

Table 1. (cont.)

Behavioral Scale	Description	Scores
Power Scales		
Force	Extent to which Authorities use aggressive strategies to resolve the incident.	0 = No strategy 1 = Containment 2 = Tactical raid 3 = Terrorists killed

Reliability of the transcript coding was assessed by having one independent coder apply the coding dictionary to descriptions of the aerial hijackings and a second coder apply the scheme to the barricade-siege incidents. The reliability of coding, measured at the individual behavior level with Cohen's Kappa (Cohen 1960), was .64 with 75 percent agreement for the Control scale (Range = .52 – .82); .87 with 92 percent agreement for the Damage scale (Range = .76 – .94); .74 with 76 percent agreement for the Demands scale (Range = .55 – .85); and .84 with 91 percent agreement for the Use of weapons scale (Range = .83 – .87). The two affiliation scales showed similar levels of reliability with Kappa equaling .97 with 98 percent agreement for the Conciliate scale (Range = .80 – 1.00) and .69 with 75 percent agreement for Negotiation scale (Range = .62 – .76). Finally, the reliabilities of the outcome scales were .79 with 88 percent agreement for the Capitulation scale (Range = .62 – .95) and .67 with 83 percent agreement for the Force scale (Range = .60 – .76). According to Fleiss (1981), a Cohen's Kappa of .40 to .60 is fair, .60 to .75 is good, and greater than .75 is excellent. Thus, these results indicate that the scales developed from the coded descriptions of the incidents are reliable.

Results

A preliminary analysis of the interdependence among the scales revealed a positive correlation for power (Mean r = .23) and a positive correlation for affiliation (Mean r = .30), but no relationship between power and affiliation (Mean r = .03). The small correlation between the power and affiliation measures was principally due to the power-orientated Demand scale, which correlated positively with both of the affiliation scales (Mean r = .30). Recalculating the correlation between the power and affiliation scales with the Demand scale removed revealed a negative relationship between the two dynamics (r = −0.37).

To test Hypotheses 1 and 2 that examine the impact of the terrorists' behavior on the incident resolution, we correlated the power and affiliation scales with the two

Table 2. Pearson's distribution free correlation (rho) for behavioral scales by Authority's behavior.

	Authority's Behavior	
Behavioral Scale	*Capitulation*	*Force*
Power		
Control	−.43*	.26*
Damage	−.49*	−.08
Demands	.23*	−.11
Weapon use	−.56*	.20
Affiliation		
Negotiate	.47*	−.36*
Release	.28*	−.52*

NOTE: * $p < .05$ (two-tailed).

outcome measures. Table 2 presents non-parametric correlations (Spearman's rho) that were calculated without taking into account cases in which both scale scores were zero (i.e. no behavior occurred). This modification is a common approach to dealing with accounts where the absence of a given behavior may not be taken as a definite indication that the behavior did not occur but only that it was not reported as having occurred. By ignoring joint non-occurrences, the correlations minimize the possible error created by this ambiguity and so are likely to provide a more accurate picture of the interrelationships among behaviors (e.g. Bennell and Canter 2002; Taylor, Bennell, and Snook 2002).

Consistent with predictions, the data presented in Table 2 indicate that the use of power and affiliation behaviors by terrorists have quite different associations with the degree that authorities capitulate. Of the power-orientated strategies, violently controlling hostages, damaging the building or aircraft, and extensively using weapons were all associated with lower levels of concessions from the authorities. The exception to this trend was the correlation for the Demand scale, which suggested a positive relationship between making more demands and concessions by the authorities. In contrast to the overall negative correlations associated with the power scales, terrorists' use of affiliation strategies correlated positively with authorities' behavior. Both increases in terrorists' willingness to negotiate and their willingness to give up hostages were significantly associated with more concession-making by the authorities. Thus, consistent with Hypothesis 1, negotiators who take a more problem-orientated approach to the negotiation achieved better outcomes.

Correlations in the second column of Table 2 test the hypothesis that terrorists' use of aggressive behavior will influence the way authorities respond (Hypothesis 2). The correlations indicate that terrorists' use of aggressive strategies had a mixed effect on whether or not the authorities reciprocated with force. Specifically, higher levels of controlling behavior and weapon use were both related to greater use of force by the authorities, but the opposite was the case for the Damage and Demand scales. This suggests that the authorities may respond to attempts to gain power with personal aggression, but only after the occurrence of certain types of behavior, and not to a significant degree. In particular, only scores on the Control scale showed a significant correlation with the Force scale, which is consistent with the view that authorities will resort to aggressive tactics if hostages are being physically harmed or killed (McMains and Mullins 2001). This is a key exception to the role effect. The effect generally reveals a complementary behavioral pattern with the one-down participant demonstrating increased aggression while the one-up respondent is generally more affiliative. In the case of response to extreme terrorist power strategies, respondents appear to engage in reciprocal rather than complementary behavior.

Consistent with the expected complementary behavioral pattern of the role effect, the relationship between terrorists' use of affiliative behaviors and authorities' use of force was overwhelmingly negative. Both a greater willingness to negotiate and a greater willingness to release hostages showed a significant negative association with the Force scale, suggesting that the authorities were unlikely to use aggressive strategies when terrorists' were not acting to change the power structure of the situation.

Examining Hypothesis 3, Table 3 reports the mean score for each of the power and affiliation scales as a function of ideology, where the highest mean score is shown in bold. Consistent with Hypothesis 3, religious fundamentalists showed greater levels of aggressive strategies than both nationalist-separatist and social revolutionary terrorists on all but the Demand scale. Specifically, non-parametric one-way ANOVA's (Kruskal-Wallis 1952) reveled significant differences among the three groups in the degree of violence towards hostages, $H(2,183) = 9.59, p < .05$, the degree of damage during the incident, $H(2,183) = 7.49, p < .05$, and the use of weapons during the incidents, $H(2,183) = 13.17, p < .05$. For all three scales, post-hoc comparisons (Marascuilo and McSweeney 1977) revealed that religious fundamentalists used significantly higher levels of aggression than social-revolutionists (respectively, $\psi = 37.8, 30.5,$ and $40.6, p < .05$) and higher but non-significant levels of aggression compared to nationalist-separatists (respectively, $\psi = 20.9, 15.5,$ and $21.3, p > .05$). In terms of affiliative behavior, there was a significant difference among terrorist groups in their willingness to conciliate, $H(2,183) = 11.21, p < .05$, with religious fundamentalists being significantly less likely to release hostages compared to nationalist-separatists ($\psi = \square 41.0, p < .05$) and social revolutionists ($\psi = \square 21.7, p < .10$). There were no significant differences across the three ideologies in the willingness to use negotiation ($H < 1, ns$).

Table 3. Mean scale scores as a function of terrorist ideology.

Terrorist ideology			
Behavioral scale	*Nationalist-separatist*	*Social revolutionary*	*Religious fundamentalist*
Power			
Control	1.84	1.27	**2.47**
	(1.69)	(1.60)	(1.73)
Damage	0.86	0.52	**1.27**
	(1.08)	(0.83)	(1.28)
Demands	1.60	**1.87**	1.53
	(0.78)	(1.11)	(0.92)
Weapon use	0.78	0.46	**1.13**
	(0.85)	(0.75)	(0.83)
Affiliation			
Negotiate	**1.68**	**1.68**	1.60
	(1.49)	(1.54)	(1.40)
Release	**1.89**	1.43	0.93
	(1.22)	(1.24)	(1.10)

NOTE: Standard deviations in parentheses.

Finally, the predicted differences (Hypothesis 4) among aerial-hijackings and barricade-siege incidents were examined by calculating the mean score for each of the power and affiliation scales as a function of incident type. Table 3 gives these means and reports in bold the larger of the scores between barricade-siege and hijacking incidents. A series of Mann-Whitney U tests across incident type revealed that aerial hijackers were significantly more likely to inflict damage to the incident location compared to perpetrators of barricade-sieges (U = 3441.0, z = $-$2.63, p < .05) and that hijackers had a non-significant tendency to make greater use of their weapons than barricade-siege perpetrators (U = 4035.0, z = $-$0.82, p > .05). In con-

Table 4. Mean scale scores as a function of incident type.

	Type of incident	
Behavioral scale	Aerial hijacking	Barricade siege
Power		
Control	1.48	**1.71**
	(1.64)	(1.72)
Damage	**0.86**	0.55
	(1.03)	(0.94)
Demands	1.60	**1.90**
	(0.95)	(0.99)
Weapon use	**1.69**	1.58
	(0.85)	(0.79)
Affiliation		
Negotiate	1.50	**1.88**
	(1.60)	(1.36)
Release	1.31	**1.87**
	(1.27)	(1.16)

NOTE: Standard deviations in parentheses.

trast to the hijackers focus on violence, perpetrators of barricade-siege incidents typically asserted power through verbal demands ($U = 3546.0$, $z = 2.19$, $p < .05$). They also showed a non-significant tendency to support these demands by threatening and carrying out threats on the hostages compared to hijackers ($U = 3894.0$, $z = 1.17$, $p > .05$). Consistent with this focus, barricade-sieges involved significantly more negotiation than aerial hijackings ($U = 3545.0$, $z = 2.15$, $p < .05$) and were significantly more likely to involve the release of hostages than aerial hijackings ($U = 3291.5$, $z = 2.92$, $p < .05$).

Discussion

The data generally provide support for the three key dimensions of the one-down effect in the context of terrorist negotiation: a) complementary strategy use with the one-down party behaving more aggressively and, as a result, achieving attenuated outcomes, b) the prominence of identity that can magnify the role effect, and c) the impact of situation on individual biases that affect the degree and type of behavior.

Specifically, the first dimension of the effect holds that those who define themselves in the one-down role and resort to aggressive strategies as a way of seeking change in the power structure are less likely to obtain the outcome they desire. In contrast, terrorists who spend more time negotiating and showing a willingness to make concessions are more likely to secure their desired outcomes. Interestingly, in the context of terrorist attacks, the behaviors that increase affiliation between the parties and led to better outcomes included making excessive demands. Although this contradicts our expectations from other forms of negotiation where making excessive demands is considered an aggressive strategy, authorities in intense conflict situations may conceivably view any form of dialogue as cooperative and a helpful inroad to resolving the incident.

Regarding the prominence of role identity, when compared to nationalist-separatists and social-revolutionaries, the terrorists with a religious ideology typically used more aggressive strategies. This use was pervasive across the different kinds of aggressive strategies, which is consistent with the idea that these terrorists aim to maximize fear and threat rather than use these dynamics to achieve some other goal. Consistent with this notion, religious terrorists engaged in very little affiliative behavior compared to nationalist-separatists and social-revolutionaries. This unwillingness to engage in normative interaction illustrates the religious terrorist's lack of interdependence with the system they are attacking and their determination to achieve a set of goals without giving consideration to alternatives (Silke 2003). These findings suggest that identity plays a significant role in the evolution of terrorist negotiations and, consequently, that it is important to understand the cultural and social background of those terrorists authorities engage in negotiation.

However, it is important to note that there were some important variations across the hijacker and barricade-siege roles. Compared to barricade-siege incidents, hijackers typically i) used more overt aggression as a means of shifting power; ii) tended not to engage in negotiation; iii) tended not to use threats to the hostages as a way of gaining leverage in the incident or negotiation, and iv) were less likely to make concessions, presumably because they were less prepared to engage in any form of bargaining to obtain a certain outcome. The focus of aerial hijacks was on overt aggression to maximize the threat of the situation and force the authorities into capitulating. In contrast, the barricade-siege incidents were focused on more indirect attempts to change the power structure combined with normative bargaining for a resolution.

Perhaps the most significant implication of these findings is that in extreme circumstances the role effect takes some interesting twists. In less extreme conditions, such as buyer-seller negotiations, the one down effect generally reveals more conciliatory behavior from the higher-power party. The higher-power party experiments with reaching out to propose more negotiated options while focusing on the substantive nature of the conflict. However, in the current findings, when the lower-power party (i.e. the terrorist) engaged in extreme aggression, the higher-powered authorities quickly reciprocated with tactical attempts to resolve the dispute.

One explanation for this role-effect twist comes from research in game theory. Some studies in this area have explored the relative impact of small and large discrepancies in initial power between subjects. Research supports an "inverted U-shaped" relationship between relative threat capacity (how much each side can harm the other's position) within a bargaining game and indexes of contending (e.g. counterthreats, penalty use, unwillingness to yield to a threat). Hornstein (1965) and Vitz and Kite (1970) found that contending was more prominent when there was mild discrepancy in threat capacity than when there was equal or highly unequal threat capacity. Hornstein, in particular, provided evidence that the low-power negotiator was unwilling to accept lower status in the mild discrepancy condition, and fought for equal treatment (i.e., followed threats with aggressive behavior) to a much greater extent than when confronted with a highly unequal discrepancy.

This discrepancy-size explanation would predict that terrorists who perceive mild discrepancies in power levels would be more willing to use highly contentious and deadly strategies to equal power whereas those who perceive highly unequal threat capacity would be more willing to negotiate. Does this finding suggest that an important strategy for fighting terrorism is continuous muscle-flexing by the higher-power party to discourage terrorist aggression? There is considerable debate about the appropriateness of using force in general to combat terrorism, with critics highlighting that such action can confirm the terrorists' self image as heroic martyrs, increase the demand for revenge, and potentially add to those who identify with the cause (Enders, Sandler, and Cauley 1990; Seger 2003). However, within the context of negotiating with terrorists, it may prove a useful strategic complement to traditional attrition-focused techniques.

Future research examining the role effect in a terrorist context ought to extend into more in-depth analyses of actual terrorist incidents. For example, in the current analysis we implicitly viewed the behaviors of terrorists as leading to certain "responses" by the authorities. However, the actions of authorities and terrorists are necessarily intertwined, such that an authority's actions are likely to have an equally significant effect on the strategies terrorists' perceive as useful to pursue and the way they expect the authorities to react. The result is that certain actions by the authorities will work to lower the aggression used by terrorists, while others may shift the focus of aggression away from afflicting damage and towards attempts to control the bargaining process. Extending this line of argument to the longer-term, we might also consider the possibility that terrorists' initial behaviors are shaped by expectations derived from authority's responses to previous incidents.

Understanding how negotiators influence one another during the bargaining process could be addressed by obtaining actual interactions between terrorists and authorities to gain a more refined understanding of how these negotiations evolve. The data set examined here offers only secondhand accounts of activities in these incidents, and the utility of the analysis hinges on whether the behavioral scales adequately capture the complex dynamics of the interaction (Mickolus 1987). Actual interactions would provide a far more detailed picture of how terrorists and authorities define and implement their roles. Far from being a mere academic exercise, the development of such a body of knowledge can be of direct use to negotiators and policymakers attempting to save lives in terrorist crisis negotiations.

References

Alexandroff, A. (1979) *Symmetry in international relations*. Ithaca, NY: Cornell University Press.

Bacharach, S.B., and Lawler, E.J. (1986) "Power dependence and power paradoxes in bargaining". *Negotiation Journal* 86: 167–174.

Bales, R.F. (1970) *Personality and interpersonal behavior.* New York: Holt, Rinehart, and Winston.

Bennell, C., and Canter, D.V. (2002) "Linking commercial burglaries by modus operandi: Tests using regression and ROC analysis". *Science and Justice* 42: 153–164.

Cohen, J.A. (1960) "A coefficient of agreement for nominal scales". *Educational and Psychological Measurement* 20: 37–46.

Corsi, J.R. (1981) "Terrorism as a desperate game: Fear, bargaining, and communication in the terrorist event". *Journal of Conflict Resolution* 25: 47–85.

Crenshaw, M. (1988) "The subjective reality of the terrorist: Ideological and psychological factors in terrorism". In R.O. Slater and M. Stohl (eds.), *Current perspectives on international terrorism*. London: Macmillan Press.

Donohue, W.A., and Roberto, A.J. (1993) "Relational development as negotiated order in hostage negotiation". *Human Communication Research* 20: 175–198.

Donohue, W.A., and Roberto, A.J. (1996) "An empirical examination of three models of integrative and distributive bargaining". *International Journal of Conflict Management* 7: 209–229.

Donohue, W.A., and Taylor, P.J. (2003) "Role effects in negotiation: The one-down effect". Unpublished manuscript, Michigan State University.

Donohue, W.A., Kaufmann, G., Smith, R. and Ramesh, C. (1991) "Crisis bargaining: A framework for understanding intense conflict". *International Journal of Group Tensions* 21: 133–154.

Drake, L.E. (2001) "The cultural-negotiation link: Integrative and distributive bargaining through an intercultural lens". *Human Communication Research* 27: 317–349.

Druckman, D. (1986) "Stages, turning points, and crises: Negotiating military base rights, Spain and the United States". *Journal of Conflict Resolution* 30: 327–360.

Eisikovits, Z., Goldblatt, H., and Winstok, Z. (1999) "Partner accounts of intimate violence: Towards a theoretical model". *Families in Society: The Journal of Contemporary Human Services* 80: 606–619.

Enders, W., Sandler, T., and Cauley, J. (1990) "UN conventions, technology and retaliation in the fight against terrorism: An econometric evaluation". *Terrorism and Political Violence* 2: 83–105.

Fleiss, J.L. (1981) *Statistical methods for rates and proportions.* New York: Wiley.

Friedland, N., and Merari, A. (1992) "Hostage events: Descriptive profile and analysis of outcomes". *Journal of Applied Social Psychology* 22: 134–156.

Glaser, B.G. and Strauss, A.L. (1967) *The discovery of grounded theory: Strategies for qualitative research.* Chicago: Aldine.

Hoffman, B. (1999) *Inside Terrorism.* New York: Columbia University Press.

Holsti, O.R. (1969) *Content analysis for the social sciences and humanities.* Reading, MA: Addison-Wesley.

Horstein, H.A. (1965) "Effects of different magnitudes of threat upon interpersonal bargaining". *Journal of Experimental Social Psychology* 1: 282–293.

Krippendorff, K. (1980) *Content analysis: An introduction to its methodology.* Beverly Hills, CA: Sage.

Kruskal, W.H., and Wallis, W.A. (1952) "Use of ranks in one-criterion variance analysis". *Journal of the American Statistical Association* 47: 583–621.

Leary, T. (1957) *Interpersonal diagnosis of personality.* New York: The Ronald Press.

Levine, T.R., and Boster, F.J. (2001) "The effects of power and message variables on compliance". *Communication Monographs* 68: 28–48.

Mahalik, J.R. (2000) "Gender role conflict in men as a predictor of self-ratings of behavior on the interpersonal circle". *Journal of Social and Clinical Psychology* 19: 276–292.

Marascuilo, L.A., and McSweeney, M. (1977) *Nonparametric and distribution-free methods for the social sciences.* Belmont, CA: Wadsworth.

McMains, M.J., and Mullins, W.C. (2001) *Crisis negotiations: Managing critical incidents and hostage situations in law enforcement and corrections* (2nd ed.). Cincinnati, OH: Anderson.

Mickolus, E.F. (1980) *Transnational Terrorism: A Chronology of Events, 1968–1979.* London: Aldwych Press.

Mickolus, E.F. (1987) "Comment – Terrorists, governments, and numbers: Counting things versus things that count". *Journal of Conflict Resolution* 31: 54–62.

Mickolus, E.F. (1993) *Terrorism 1988–1991: A Chronology of events and a selectively annotated bibliography.* Westport, CT: Greenwood Press.

Mickolus, E.F., and Simmons, S.L. (1997) *Terrorism 1992–1995: A chronology of events and a selectively annotated bibliography.* Westport, CT: Greenwood Press.

Mickolus, E.F., Sandler, T., and Murdock, J.M. (1989) *International Terrorism in the 1980s (vol. 2, 1984–1987).* Ames, IO: Iowa State University Press.

Morley, I., and Stephenson, G. (1977) *The social psychology of bargaining.* Cambridge, MA: Harvard University Press.

Neale, M.A., Huber, V.L., and Northcraft, G.B. (1987) "The framing of negotiations: Contextual versus task frames". *Organizational Behavior and Human Decision Processes* 39: 228–241.

Olekalns, M., and Frey, B.F. (1994) "Market forces, negotiator frames and transaction outcomes". *European Journal of Social Psychology* 24: 403–416.

Pfetsch, F.R., and Landau, A. (2000) "Symmetry and asymmetry in international negotiation". *International Negotiation* 5: 21–40.

Post, J.M., Ruby, K.G., and Shaw, E.D. (2002) "The radical group in context 2: Identification of critical elements in the analysis of risk for terrorism by radical group type". *Studies in Conflict and Terrorism* 25: 101–126.

Putnam, L.L., and Holmer, M. (1992) "Framing, reframing, and issue development". In L. Putnam and M. Roloff (eds.), *Communication and negotiation* (pp. 128–155). Newbury Park, CA: Sage Publications.

Rogan, R.G., and Hammer, M.R. (1994) "Crisis negotiations: A preliminary investigation of facework in naturalistic conflict discourse". *Journal of Applied Communication Research* 22: 216–231.

Russell, C.A., Banker, L.J., and Miller, B.H. (1979) "Out-inventing the terrorist". In Y. Alexander, D. Carlton, and P. Wilkinson (eds.), *Terrorism: Theory and Practice.* Boulder, CO: Westview.

Sandler, T., and Scott, J.L. (1987) "Terrorist success in hostage taking incidents: An empirical study". *Journal of Conflict Resolution* 31: 35–53.

Schmidt, J.A., Wagner, C.C., and Kiesler, D.J. (1999) "Covert reactions to big five personality traits: The impact message inventory and the NEO-PI-R". *European Journal of Psychological Assessment* 15: 221–232.

Seger, K.L. (2003) "Deterring terrorists". In A. Silke (ed.), *Terrorists, victims and society: Psychological perspectives on terrorism and its consequences.* Chichester, UK: Wiley.

Silke, A. (2003) "Becoming a terrorist". In A. Silke (ed.), *Terrorists, victims and society: Psychological perspectives on terrorism and its consequences.* Chichester, UK: Wiley.

Taylor, P.J. (2002a) "A cylindrical model of communication behavior in crisis negotiations". *Human Communication Research* 28: 7–48.

Taylor, P.J. (2002b) "A partial order scalogram analysis of communication behavior in crisis negotiation with the prediction of outcome". *International Journal of Conflict Management* 13: 4–37.

Taylor, P.J., Bennell, C., and Snook, B. (2002) "Problems of classification in investigative psychology". In K. Jajuga, A. Sokolowski, and H.H. Bock (eds.), *Classification, clustering, and data analysis: Recent Advances and applications.* Heidelberg: Springer.

Vitz, P.C., and Kite, W.R. (1970) "Factors affecting conflict and negotiation within an alliance". *Journal of Experimental Social Psychology* 5: 223–247.

Wilson, M.A. (2000) "Toward a model of terrorist behavior in hostage-taking incidents". *Journal of Conflict Resolution* 44: 403–424.

Wilson, S.R., and Putnam, L.L. (1990) "Interaction goals in negotiation". In J. Anderson (Ed.). *Communication yearbook* 13: 374–406. Newbury Park, CA: Sage.

Negotiating under the Cross: The Story of the Forty Day Siege of the Church of Nativity

MOTY CRISTAL

Introduction

Terror is a global phenomenon, but to define it is a challenging task. Within the context of negotiating with terrorists, I will use the US Government definition: terrorism is premeditated, politically motivated violence perpetrated against non-combatant targets by subnational groups or clandestine agents, usually intended to influence an audience. This article is a practitioner's account that seeks to contribute to the emerging research field of negotiating with terrorists by integrating the case narrative with existing analytical frameworks and theories.

Modern urban warfare, as an extension of the global fight against terrorism, requires the development of new tools and techniques that combine the power of language with the language of power. Through intensive field experience, Israel and its military forces have developed several insights and lessons that are strongly linked to the global concern of how to negotiate with terrorists.

Despite the common motto to "never negotiate with terrorists", or the argument that negotiations themselves are perceived as an achievement for terrorists, the complexity and comprehensiveness of the current fight against terrorism cannot afford to rule out the use of negotiations. Based on the experience at the Church of Nativity, I take the view that *negotiations* must be developed as an operative tool within the context of fighting terrorism.

The following describes my unique experience, as a team member of the Israeli military Crisis Negotiation Unit (CNU), in negotiating a peaceful resolution to the crisis over the Church of Nativity in Bethlehem, during April and May 2002 (see timeline of events in Figure 1). As such, it is an *Israeli* professional perspective, and in order to put this personal experience in an accurate context, it is useful to give some biographical background. Since 1994, I have been engaged in the Israeli-Arab peace process in different official and non-official negotiation capacities. I have witnessed Israeli-Arab negotiations both in peacetime and during armed conflicts.

International Negotiation Series 1:
I.W. Zartman (ed.) Negotiating with Terrorists, 103–129
© 2006 *Koninklijke Brill NV. Printed in the Netherlands.*

Background

The failure to reach an agreement at the July 2000 Israeli-Palestinian Camp David summit marked a shift in the direction of the protracted Israeli-Palestinian conflict – a shift from conflict resolution to conflict management. Conflict management is typically conceptualized as a mediating step in the path to conflict resolution. The peacekeeping literature defines conflict resolution as an end state that removes the causes, as well as the manifestations, of a conflict between parties. In so doing, it eliminates the sources of incompatibility in their positions. In contrast, the goal of conflict management is to eliminate violence and violence-related means of pursuing the conflict by shifting to a purely political level (Zartman and Rasmussen 1997). Returning from Camp David without reaching a framework agreement proved – for both sides – that either "there is no partner for peace" (Israeli perspective), or "the maximum they offered does not meet the minimum we need" (Palestinian perspective). From this point on, the parties once again faced the need to manage their conflict, as they had in the past, but under worsening conditions. In September 2000, an unprecedented cycle of violence involving both sides began.

Palestinian suicide bombers penetrated Israel's towns while Israel retaliated against terrorist networks within Palestinian cities. Furthermore, this spiral into greater violence occurred in a more volatile global context. For many in Israel and in the world, the Palestinian armed struggle since September 11th has been framed within the context of global terrorism, as suspected links between the Palestinian Islamic movements and Osama Bin Laden's terrorism network have multiplied.

During the first three months of 2002, the number of Israeli casualties increased from a monthly average of 15 to 100, reaching its peak when a Palestinian suicide bomber blew himself up in the middle of a public traditional Jewish Passover dinner at the Park Hotel in Netanya. The following night, two Palestinian terrorists broke into a house in one of the major West Bank settlements, murdering five people before being killed by IDF troops.

This served as the immediate trigger for operation "Defense Shield", which was carried out by the IDF in April 2002, with the aim to destroy the Palestinian terrorist infrastructure and the "suicide bombing" industry. Operation "Defense Shield" garnered overwhelming support from the Israeli public. Despite the traditional political division between the "peace camp" and the right wing in Israel, the repeated suicide attacks from the Palestinian controlled areas in the West Bank even led the Labor party, traditionally identified with the "peace camp", to back the Sharon government in this military campaign.

As part of the military operation, the IDF took over Bethlehem, a major Palestinian town, five miles south of Jerusalem. On 2 April, the IDF launched an

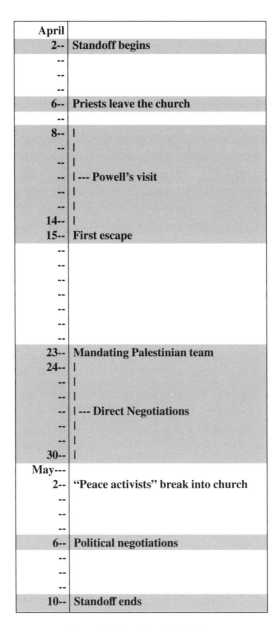

April	
2--	**Standoff begins**
--	
--	
--	
6--	**Priests leave the church**
--	
8--	|
--	|
--	|
--	| --- Powell's visit
--	|
--	|
14--	|
15--	**First escape**
--	
--	
--	
--	
--	
--	
--	
23--	**Mandating Palestinian team**
24--	|
--	|
--	|
--	| --- Direct Negotiations
--	|
--	|
30--	|
May---	
2--	**"Peace activists" break into church**
--	
--	
--	
6--	**Political negotiations**
--	
--	
--	
10--	**Standoff ends**

Figure 1. Timeline of the Siege

attack on the city. Heavy fighting broke out in the streets of the Old City behind "Manger Square", the plaza leading to the Church of Nativity, while the IDF was searching for suspects, ammunition, and explosives. A group of about 60 armed men, most of them wanted by Israel for terrorist attacks, broke into the Church of Nativity, knowing that the Church could provide them with a safe shelter; an additional 160 Palestinian civilians and security forces who were not participants in the fighting sought refuge in the holy compound as well. With this development, the IDF Crisis Negotiation Unit (CNU) was called to manage the emerging crisis.

The CNU is comprised of reserve personnel with military backgrounds, experts in various fields including strategy, psychology, social and political science, Middle East studies, negotiation, counter-terrorism, and special operations. The CNU's primary training is to jointly manage crisis situations involving hostage-taking with special operation teams.

In the early days of the military operations, the CNU was involved in "talking out" dozens of armed Palestinians from refugee camps without use of force. Equipped with brief, though significant, experience in handling and resolving military crises situations involving besieged Palestinians, the CNU was called to Bethlehem and led the military deployment around the Church, comprised of infantry and armored units, intelligence and special technical capabilities, and military-civilian liaisons.

The Church and the Priests

A clear picture of the scene must be provided in order to better understand the negotiations. The Church of Nativity is located in the heart of Bethlehem. The town of Bethlehem was built around the place where Christians believe Jesus was born. The Church was originally erected around the year 900 AD and in its current structure around 1200 AD. In a region that has faced wars and atrocities, and which continuously has been encircled by diverse ruling powers, including the Romans, Byzantines, Crusaders, Ottomans, British, Jordanians, Israelis and Palestinians, the Church of Nativity always has provided a haven for those who seek peaceful refuge.

The Church compound, ringed by ancient fortress walls, includes the Basilica – the holiest place in Christianity where Jesus Christ was believed to have been born, and three different Christian monasteries: the Franciscan order of Roman Catholicism which also holds the *Casa Nova* hotel considered part of the holy compound, as well as the Greek Orthodox monastery and the Armenian monastery, which are separated from the main compound by a wall (see Figure 2).

The priests serving the Church of Nativity belong to all three orders and come from dozens of countries in Latin America, Europe, the Middle East, Russia, and

Figure 2. The Church of Nativity

Asia. They perceive themselves to be the protectors of the holy places, and are anxious to maintain the centuries' old balance among the three orders.

During the first weeks of the siege, it was unclear whether the armed Palestinians were holding the priests hostage or whether the clerics were free to leave the Church. Upon establishing contact, the CNU learned that the priests were in an ambivalent position: they were both forced to *and* chose to stay. They were coerced into staying not only because of the armed threat but also for three additional reasons. First among these was religious compulsion. Protecting the Church is their religious mission. Leaving the compound in the hands of armed Muslims was considered a betrayal of their religious and moral duties. Second was their concern for the "day after". The priests knew that when the crisis was over and regardless of its outcome, they would have to remain among the Palestinian population of Bethlehem. They knew that in the eyes of these people, "collaborating" with the IDF would bring a death sentence and therefore they chose to stay and serve as significant players in the crisis. Last but not least was their determination to preserve the religious *status quo* among the different orders. Each group was concerned that being evacuated or leaving the Church could result in a change in the centuries' old *status quo* among the three orders.

However, beyond these constraints lay a potential facilitative and mediating role for the priests. Four days after the standoff began, through direct negotiations *with the priests* and with implicit agreement of the armed men inside, some of the priests left the church. This move set a precedent for the whole crisis: clerics were allowed, both by the IDF and by the armed men inside, to freely exit the Church, but if they chose to stay, they took it upon themselves to serve as interlocutors between the besieged and the IDF.

Reflecting on the conceptualization of the multi-stage negotiation process presented by Zartman and Berman (1982), the release of priests at that early stage could have been considered the beginning of the *diagnostic* phase, followed by *formula construction* and a *detailed agreement*. At this initial point of the crisis, it was evident that both sides approached the situation from a bargaining paradigm, and were unlikely to shift to a more "problem-solving" orientation. The parties perceived these early negotiations as win-lose rather than win-win, and each side sought to gain a larger share of whatever benefits might be derived through manipulation of the bargaining process (Hopmann 1998). However, the release of several priests at this early stage also indicated the presence of a fragile commitment by the parties to negotiate for the resolution of the crisis. That said, the release also served other interests of the two sides. For the armed men inside, allowing the priests to leave the church undermined Israel's attempts to portray present them as hostages; and for Israel, creating valid communication channels with the priests, supplying the needs of the clerics despite the strategy of withholding food and basic needs from the Palestinian terrorists, and allowing the clerics to safely leave the Church contributed to being able to successfully manage possible future international and legal pressure to lift the siege.

The Terrorists and Organizational Structure

Resolving the crisis through negotiations required a sharp understanding of the social and organizational structure of the different groups assembled in the Church. Zartman has defined negotiation as a basic process of decision-making (cited in Hayes 2002), and the siege definitely entailed a situation of interdependent decision-making where the outcome was not exclusively in the control of any of the parties, but rather was a result of their joint decisions (Hopmann 1998).

Two hundred and twenty Palestinians found refuge inside the Church, among them a fair number of civilians, including people who were near the Church when the IDF surrounded the compound, employees of government agencies operating in the area, and workers of different Christian orders. The groups of civilians were the most vulnerable. Israel's position was that they were free to leave the Church at any moment and safely return to their homes. However, fear of their peers, the strong cultural sense of hierarchy, and the fear of the stigma they would face if they would leave turned the civilians into *de facto* hostages held by an armed and besieged group.

The actual power inside the Church was split among individuals with three main affiliations. The first were the Tanzim groups. The Tanzim is the armed wing of the Fateh movement, the largest political power in the Palestinian arena and Yaser Arafat's main power base. In the Christian-dominated area of Bethlehem, the Tanzim was the main perpetrator of terrorist activities. The second group was composed of Palestinian officials. A few of the local commanders of Palestinian Security Forces who were inside the Church were wanted by Israel for conducting and supporting terrorist activities. These commanders had direct contacts and access to Chairman Arafat who was, at that time, besieged in his presidential compound in Ramallah. The third group was Hamas, a small, strong, and extremist group of terrorists, whose leader, wounded in the exchanges of fire while breaking into the Church, assumed a significant role in the late stages of the siege.

From the early stages of the crisis, it was evident that any decision taken by people inside would depend on its implications for the balance of power among these organizations inside the Church and, more importantly, within the Palestinian political arena. Therefore, understanding the internal balance of power among these groups was fundamental for peaceful resolution.

In terms of the negotiation process, the lack of clear leadership among the Palestinians was a major disadvantage. However, during the siege, Israel explored ways to turn this deficiency into a tactical advantage. Hayes (2002) explains this idea and cites research done on hostage situations where "operational groups from more than one terrorist organization may have trouble negotiating successfully because they lack a common worldview, the demands are greater, and coalition leadership is weak". This observation initially was correct for Bethlehem, but the situation changed over time. A barricade situation is usually unplanned and therefore entails no organized leadership, no clear demands, and no clear strategic goals. However, if the crisis is prolonged, as was the case in Bethlehem, each of these elements actually develops during the siege.

Moreover, the basic concept of power, which becomes the fundamental factor in every hostage negotiation (Hayes 2002), is different in siege situations. In a siege, as this case indicates, the *perceived* power and the psychological "safe zone" that the besieged might sense has equal standing to any *real* power one of the parties has, bringing an additional dimension to Hopmann's (1998) observation that the outcome of the bargaining process is no longer predetermined by the structure of the game, but rather is directly influenced by the ability to manipulate the position of other parties with reference to the potential application of force.

The External Factors

While understanding the crisis as a volatile and fluid event, the CNU had to carefully analyze the external factors bearing on the situation. Many of these factors varied during the 40 day siege, but several major elements were under constant examination. In particular, the response of the international community was monitored at various levels such as the reactions of states, religious organizations, non-state actors, and individuals, in particular within the Christian world. Furthermore, media and public opinion were taken into account.

Almost every development wherein there was international involvement immediately affected the negotiation setting. For example, the failed mediation attempt of US Secretary of State Colin Powell to end both the Bethlehem and Ramallah/Arafat siege undermined the armed mens' belief that the international community, led by the US, would force Israel to withdraw. Powell's failure also shifted US efforts from public diplomacy to more tacit intervention through its CIA representatives in Tel Aviv. While international mediation efforts by EU countries and others were handled at the political level, and while the Ministry of Foreign Affairs maintained open dialogue with embassies and foreign representatives, the scene on the ground in Bethlehem was left to the military. This strategic decision aimed to prevent the Palestinians' attempts to shift the crisis from a military operational one to an issue of international politics, a shift that would have resulted in heavy pressure on Israel to withdraw without completing the mission of uprooting the terrorist threat from Bethlehem. This distinction between political and military responsibilities served as a cornerstone for the CNU in managing the crisis and in enabling the CNU to conduct crisis negotiations on the ground.

The Christian world served as a central point of reference for the crisis management. It was evident that neither the Vatican nor any other religious Christian actor had real influence on the armed Palestinians. Israel, through political channels and the developing relationships between the CNU and the priests, managed to mitigate the possibility that these Christian actors would make calls for immediate lifting of the siege.

The relationships maintained with the international media played an important role among the external factors influencing the scene and the negotiations. Before Bethlehem, the CNU had never operated in a "live" media environment. Media experts, as well as professional spokespersons from the IDF and the Ministry of Foreign Affairs, joined the CNU and provided an important professional analysis. Using Gilboa's taxonomy (2000) of media coverage in international negotiations, the Bethlehem case suggests a model midway between the "closed door" and the open diplomacy models; despite the extensive and direct media coverage characteristic of the open diplomacy model, media coverage in Bethlehem still left the public unaware of the actual agendas, goals, and party positions involved.

The CNU's main challenge was how to efficiently work with the media in a way that supports a peaceful resolution. The basic assumption was that the media would empower the men inside: international coverage would force Israel to withdraw. This psychological conviction had to be matched by an Israeli effort to present more objective media coverage, which would report both the complexity of the situation and the likelihood that the crisis could be resolved in a peaceful manner. Furthermore, working with the media served as a communication channel with the men inside. However, despite the immediate temptation to *directly* address the besieged men through the media, the CNU worked *indirectly*, addressing the Palestinian leadership, encouraging the Palestinian negotiators, and presenting clear, positive alternatives to the Palestinian public and to the families of the besieged. The messages were not intended to threaten but rather to psychologically persuade the men inside and those within their supportive environments.

The third major external element was the daily assessment of Israeli and Palestinian public opinions. Both sides heavily relied on public support throughout the siege. However, a massive attack on the Israeli forces or changing circumstances in the Bethlehem area could have strategically changed the course of the negotiations. The daily assessment, which analyzed factors such as the number of Israeli casualties in other battlefields across the West Bank and the easing of the curfew over Bethlehem, greatly affected that day's negotiation plan.

In trying to manage this complex system, the CNU realized that external factors, while beyond the unit's immediate control, ought to be considered or incorporated into the making of negotiation strategy. An instinctive attempt to ignore, control, or minimize their significance would likely have resulted in a negative consequence. The challenge the CNU faced was to understand how these factors affected the scene and then plan accordingly.

Core Analysis of the Situation

One possible starting point for analyzing the scene is to cast it as "an international crisis where besieged Muslims were surrounded by Jewish soldiers in the most holy place to Christianity". The CNU defused this high stakes context by reframing the situation as a local military crisis caused by a group of armed "terrorists" in Israeli eyes and national heroes in the eyes of the immediate public and the Arab world. These men were blockaded in a closed compound seeking a *dignified* way out. Experience had taught the CNU that it would be possible to identify such a way. The challenge was to either find it or create it.

Classic negotiation literature stresses reconciling interests, not positions. This is because the basic problem in negotiation lies not in the conflicting positions, but in the conflict between each sides' needs, desires, concerns, and fears (Fisher, Ury and Patton 1991). Consistent with this concept, the CNU identified several goals or interests held by the armed men. It should be noted that each one of those interests carried a different weight at different times by different individuals and therefore the attempt to present these as a coherent structured "interests map" is solely for the purpose of this analytical discussion.

The main Palestinian interest was to force Israel to withdraw from Bethlehem by withstanding the siege. Achieving this goal would have transformed them – as individuals and as a group – into the "new liberators" of Bethlehem, granting significant social and political status. Their strong belief and their rationale was, most likely, that they had supportive media coverage, that the international community would force Israel to withdraw, and that time was on their side.

Another interest, shared by many inside the Church, was to strengthen the organization to which they belonged. As earlier stated, various groups and terrorist organizations were represented in the Church. The overall context of the crisis demonstrated an interest in building organizational political capacity, which would serve internal political discourse within the Palestinian armed struggle when the crisis was over.

The more steadfast the Tanzim would be against the IDF, the more political power it would have in the Palestinian arena. The greater the leadership role taken by Hamas, the more it would gain from this crisis, and thus the more influence it would have in the Christian areas of Bethlehem. Obviously, "collaborating" with the IDF, not to mention surrender to it, would result in irreversible organizational damage and irrecoverable social and tribal stigma. The concepts of "*Sharaf*" or "*Karame*" in Arabic mean much more than when they are translated as "honor" or "dignity". They define fundamental elements of personal and social life in the Muslim context, Arab society, and the Palestinian armed conflict, in particular.

As a result, they held an interest to either freely leave the Church (to live) or honorably sacrifice their life (to die – *Istish'had*). Like most humans, the men inside would have preferred to live and continue their lives among their families and within their communities. However, for many of them, the religious commandment and Islamic high moral of sacrifice of life for *Allah* was worth more than life. It is the highest fulfillment of life. It is the *right* life.

Hayes (2002) indicates that ideologue terrorists are less likely to negotiate and that the continuing problem of terrorists (referring to suicide bombers) acting in the name of religion provides more evidence that bargaining leverage with such groups is almost nonexistent. While this religious and cultural mindset obviously posed a significant challenge to the CNU, *almost* is the key word. Negotiating a peaceful resolution with a terrorist who considers his death a religious commandment requires a tremendous intellectual and moral effort, but experience shows it *is* possible.

In the context of this siege, the challenge was greater than that which the CNU faced in previous situations of peacefully "talking out" besieged terrorists. The particular setting of the Church of Nativity provided the terrorists with a "psychological safe zone", a sense of security that the physical and international protection of the Church provided.

Security was physical due to the Church's fortress structure, with thick walls, a maze of rooms, corridors and tunnels. The building was, in fact, built hundreds of years ago for the express purpose of providing shelter from enemies. The international protection was sensed because Israel could not ignore the tremendous political pressure exercised by the international community, mainly the Christian world, to peacefully ending this crisis, either by reaching an agreement or simply by leaving Bethlehem and lifting the siege.

A second tier in the terrorists' sense of psychological protection stemmed from the religious, cultural, and social cohesion the situation created for the men inside, a mentality of "we are all facing the enemy, and we will stick together". This psychological tier strengthened the group identity through positive identification with other group members, shared concerns about their future, and a willingness to incur certain costs (Hayes 2002). The CNU therefore faced the challenge of how to engage this emerging collective identity and to steer it toward a constructive direction, not a suicidal one.

The last, but definitely not least, dimension was the issue of responsibility. It is a well-known phenomenon in these situations that people under siege tend to defer the decision to surrender to higher authorities. This goes beyond Hayes' (2002) indications that terrorists involved in hostage-barricade situations are following their training and standard operating procedures rather than making independent decisions and that terrorist leaders are reluctant to enter legitimate politics. It involves the wider concept of accepting responsibility in siege situation. This tendency is familiar from Israeli military history, when besieged soldiers have asked their commanding forces' "permission" to surrender. In the strict, hierarchical structure of Palestinian society, this pattern of "it's not our decision – it's for the leadership to decide" posed an additional challenge to reaching any agreement with the terrorists inside the Church.

In sum, the CNU analyzed the interests of the besieged Palestinians by taking into consideration these three elements. First, the Palestinians' interests were understood to be a desire to become the "new liberators" of Bethlehem – either by forcing Israel to leave or by dying in the name of *Allah*, as well as to strengthen their organization within the framework of the Palestinian armed struggle. Second, there was a need to understand their "psychological safe zone". Third, to reconstruct the challenge of the terrorists' responsibility toward resolving the crisis.

This article portrays an Israeli perspective that is confined to the negotiation aspects of a militarily managed crisis. As a result, the range of Israeli considerations will be limited, leaving aside what Mnookin, Peppet and Tulumello (2000) define as "behind the table negotiations" – the negotiator's relationship with the client, in this case, with the internal Israeli organizational and inter-agency decision-making processes. On the Israeli side, the main interest was to try the terrorists in court. This was the purpose of the military campaign in the West Bank, including Bethlehem. Failing to realize this objective – due to the sense of a "safe zone" which the terrorists experienced in Bethlehem – would have significantly undermined Israel's deterrence policy. However, this interest was situated within an overall "cost-benefit" analysis. Capturing the terrorists who were inside the Church was not defined as an "at all costs" goal. The interests of not damaging the Church, carefully managing foreign relations, and not causing civilian casualties in Bethlehem were defined as equally important.

Fisher, Ury and Patton (1991) use the term "BATNA" (Best Alternative To a Negotiated Agreement) to frame the negotiation setting. However, using the term "best" to describe selecting among alternatives to the negotiated agreement is not always feasible. In the Israeli-Palestinian conflict (as well as other international conflicts) the alternative to a negotiated agreement is continuation of the occupation for Israel and resort to armed conflict for the Palestinians. Neither of those alternatives is "better" than an agreement.

Therefore, in certain settings it is suggested that we identify not only the BATNA, but also the "WATNA" – a Worst Alternative To a Negotiated Agreement. Based on the experience gained from the Israeli-Arab negotiations, it can be argued that "WATNA" is a general term for the consequences of not reaching an agreement. Fisher, Ury and Patton (1991) suggest that having a better BATNA improves one's bargaining position. The same logic applies to WATNA – the worse the alternative, the weaker one's bargaining position.

With regard to the situation in Bethlehem, the WATNA logic indicates that the Palestinian side was in a much better negotiation position. Its BATNA was better than the Israeli BATNA, and the Israeli WATNA was worse than that of the Palestinians. There was only one scenario for Israel that would have been a better alternative to negotiated resolution: unconditional surrender of the Palestinian terrorists. Based on the CNU analysis, this outcome was unlikely. The Palestinians had two better alternatives that *they believed* were likely to occur: either Israel would be forced to leave Bethlehem or, when the moment came, they would all die. The religious and cultural background of the Palestinians meant that they were prepared to die for *Allah*. As such, suicide becomes a better alternative than reaching an agreement, which would be perceived as surrender. For Western cultures, there might be a difficult conclusion, however in the Middle East and the Muslim tradition it is a reasonable choice, especially during times of conflict and war.

Therefore, in trying to evaluate the alternatives available to both sides, the terrorists had the better set of alternatives with a greater likelihood of their occurrence than did Israel. For the Palestinians, "walking" to their BATNA (Fisher, Ury and Patton 1991) was easier and more likely to happen than for the Israelis to arrive at theirs.

With regard to a WATNA analysis, the conclusion is the opposite of what has been described above. For the Palestinians, there was only one worse alternative to an agreement – surrender. As mentioned, based on the CNU's analysis, this was very unlikely. Israel, on the other hand, faced several potential scenarios that could have jeopardized its interests. The four undesirable alternatives were i) being forced to leave Bethlehem under international pressure, ii) death of Israeli soldiers while maintaining the siege, iii) damage to the Church, or iv) Palestinian civilian casualties.

The Negotiation Strategy

Israel's negotiation strategy on the ground was based on three pillars: to undermine the psychological safe zone; to restructure responsibility of all local players – inside the Church and on the scene – who had influence on the outcome of the crisis; and, to create, through negotiations, a legitimate resolution of the crisis.

Each of these three strategic goals was situated in and derived from the Islamic setting overshadowing the negotiations and the crisis in general. Negotiation in an Islamic setting, in particular in war zones or during armed conflicts, is a complex task the exposition of which is beyond the scope of this article. Nevertheless, the key idea that motivated the CNU negotiators during the crisis and which was learned from previous experiences was the need to breach the differences in value sets between the opposing sides.

Every negotiation is carried out between parties with distinct values. In recent years, academic attention towards the area of "cross cultural negotiations" has grown (Thompson 2001, Faure 2002). Consideration of cultural values can enable parties to understand what issues are more or less important and to influence nego-tiators' interests and priorities (Brett 2000).

Understanding Arab Muslim culture, and especially modes of negotiation, requires transcending the differing sets of sacred values held by the parties (Thompson 2001). It is especially important to comprehend the significant role of language and of the speaker for Arab negotiators, since Arab culture is high-con-text (Brett 2000, Faure 2001). Language is important and communicating in Arabic creates a certain relationship that is crucial to crisis management. It also entails ana-lyzing and exploiting the blend of emotions that the situation creates: hate, scorn, and moral superiority together with feelings of inferiority. Finally, it requires respecting the meaning of honor and an honorable solution.

The Direct Negotiation Process

In response to heavy pressure after 21 days of siege, Arafat agreed to nominate Salah Ta'amri as the head of the negotiation team. Ta'amri, a charismatic political leader in the Bethlehem area and a member of the Palestinian Legislative Council belonged to the dominant Muslim *Ta'amra* tribe in the area. He already had a unique experience negotiating with the IDF. In 1982, during the Lebanon war, he was the senior POW held by Israel. A well-known colonel in the Palestinian armed forces operating against Israel, he became the leader of the Palestinian POWs, negotiating with the military prison's authorities as to the terms and conditions of daily life. During this period, he established a fine reputation not only among his peers, but also among the Israeli security establishment. The two other main polit-ical figures were Christians: Hanna Nasser, the long time Mayor of Bethlehem, and Matri Abu Itta, the Palestinian Minister of Tourism.

The Israeli assessment was that each of these three individuals represented dif-ferent Palestinian interests, and had different personal and organizational points of view. This assessment served as a leading factor in the way the Israeli negotiation team addressed issues during the negotiations. It also further underscored the complexity of the negotiation process.

Another important participant was Anton Salman, a Christian Palestinian lawyer who managed the legal affairs of the Franciscan order. On the day the armed terrorists stormed the Church, he voluntarily entered to stay and remain with his clients and colleagues. After three weeks, through a fascinating socio-psychological process, he became the only person who was allowed – both by Israel and the terrorist leaders – to go in and out of the siege compound. The fifth member of the Palestinian negotiation team was a Palestinian liaison officer, a veteran of Israeli-Palestinian security cooperation. The Israeli negotiation team, as part of the CNU, was comprised of experts in crisis negotiation, the Middle East, political scientists, and psychologists. It was headed by the CNU commander, "Col. L".

From the beginning, Israel refused international requests to facilitate, participate, and even escort the Palestinian negotiation team to the meeting point. Moreover, in an attempt to frame the crisis as a local and not as an international one, the Israeli government insisted on conducting the negotiations at the scene. Negotiating in this localized setting served another important goal. It allowed a mutual (Israeli-Palestinian) understanding of realities on the ground to emerge, which is a necessary element for reaching a satisfactory agreement. On the other hand, Israel respected the Palestinian delegation's request (read "interest") to control the flow of information, and agreed to the keep the media outside the negotiation space.

Of the 39 days of the crisis, direct negotiations took place over five days between April 23 and April 28. At this juncture, the Israeli and the Palestinian negotiation teams agreed upon and drafted the guidelines for the agreement, which was executed on the political level ten days later. Furthermore, a direct non-official channel was established at one point between the negotiators and EU security officers, which served to clarify and guarantee messages across the negotiation table.

Due to the unique nature of the situation and the special circumstances in which the negotiators found themselves, the spirit of the negotiations was different than the common pattern of Israeli-Palestinian negotiations of all kinds, be they political, military, economic, security liaison, or of any other variety. Within the political arena, the alleged power asymmetry inherent in the Israeli-Palestinian dialogue[1] is addressed through wording, gestures, and nuances. Even if their efforts do not fully succeed, at least both sides seek to address the imbalance and put their delegations on an even playing field. In my experience, most negotiators believe this is the right thing to do to facilitate negotiation progress and increase the likelihood of a positive outcome. On the scene at Bethlehem, the power asymmetry was apparent and straightforward. It was an integral part of both the reality and perceived reality.

The first meeting was structured to include the opening statements, procedural understandings, and an attempt to identify if any "Zone of Possible Agreement", (ZOPA) or "Bargaining Zone" existed (Raiffa 1982). Israel's opening statement emphasized the military nature of the crisis. In light of the common perception of Israeli-Palestinian dialogue, Ta'amri's counter-statement was surprising, as it indicated the same interest, acknowledging the power asymmetry and trying to reduce the likelihood of military intervention. Furthermore, Ta'amri stated that he expected no humanitarian gestures from Israel and therefore would ask for none. He said, "I came to negotiate the future of the heavily wanted men".

Using the Zartman and Berman (1982) definition, the opening statements could have been indicative of the beginning of the "formula construction" phase of the negotiation, as it reflected Ta'amri's strong interest in demonstrating local and national leadership in resolving this crisis through a negotiated agreement based on professional and political judgment.

The second element of the first session was to establish procedural understandings or the "rules of the game". When negotiations commenced, the dynamics of the military siege already existed: fierce military rules of engagement, several casualties, supplying food to the priests, several escapes from the Church, international efforts such as the failed visit of Secretary Powell, live media coverage, Israel's military withdrawal from Palestinian towns, and the continuous curfew of the Bethlehem area. Israel offered, and the Palestinians agreed, that as long as there were negotiation sessions in progress there would be no firing on the scene. For the IDF it meant changing the "rules of engagement". A second rule understood by the parties was that people – the injured or ill, civilians, priests and security forces – would be freely allowed to leave the Church, while Israel would allow no food, water, or electricity to be supplied to the Church, in order to prevent prolonging the crisis. The Palestinian team accepted this rigid rule, knowing that later exceptions could be negotiated. This "outbound and not inbound" rule was adhered to even when "peace activists" managed to break into the Church. The terrorist leaders, in compliance with this rule, isolated the activists, suspecting that some of them were Israeli intelligence agents.

The third and most important "rule of game" was the joint understanding regarding their mandates. Both teams knew that despite the fact that they were negotiating within a military setting, the content of these negotiations – that is, the future of the heavily wanted terrorists – remained the sole mandate of the political leadership. In other words, both teams realized that they were negotiating with a limited and unclear mandate regarding the principles of any final deal.

The issue of mandate and of principal-agent relationship is an emerging research field in negotiation theory (Thompson 2001). Within the Israeli-Palestinian context, it is often used as a negotiating tactic to shrink the bargaining zone (Thompson, 2001). However, in the given siege circumstances, giving up this bargaining tactic was a common interest of both negotiation teams. To deal with the mandate issue, we agreed that whatever is brought to the table and is *beyond* the mandate of either of the teams would be stated as such. There would be no use of such common phrases as "I'm authorized to offer (or to accept)", since there was no mandate to do so. Instead, a clear and honest statement was to be used: "this is beyond my mandate and I will have to check it and respond accordingly". This simple understanding between the negotiation teams rarely existed in other Israeli-Palestinian negotiations. In Bethlehem, it served not only as a procedural basis but also as a powerful confidence building measure.

The third structured element was identifying the bargaining zone. The teams agreed that the negotiations would concentrate on the future of the heavily wanted terrorists in order to resolve the crisis, free the church, enable a secure withdrawal of the IDF forces from Bethlehem, as well as to lift the curfew imposed on the town. In trying to identify if a bargaining zone existed, each side stated its "taboos", or its political and military "red lines". Israel indicated, both across the table and publicly in the statements of Prime Minister Sharon, that the crisis would not be resolved (that is, Israel would not leave the town) unless the heavily wanted terrorists were either jailed in Israel or deported. This *position* reflected Israel's initial agenda of uprooting terrorist networks in the West Bank. The Palestinians, in a long and deliberative argument, stated that the Palestinian national narrative could not accept any agreement to deport a Palestinian from his land or to hand him to the occupier's prison. This Palestinian taboo to any agreement on deportation or prison was rooted in the strong nationalistic, cultural, and even religious senses of belonging to the land and to the villages (*sumud*). These taboos, defined as "sacred values", were of the genre of values and beliefs that people regard to be so fundamental that they cannot be discussed or debated (Thompson 2001). In this particular case then, these values left no bargaining zone for negotiating an agreement.

The first negotiation meeting was concluded with a clear gap between the Israeli and Palestinian positions. However, despite the fact that at this stage no zone of possible agreement was identified, there was a sense that the spirit of mutual respect sensed by the parties could led the teams towards engagement in a joint problem-solving approach (Thompson 2001; Watkins and Rosegrant 2001). The situation was one in which the differences among negotiators constituted the raw material for creating value (Sebenius 2001).

The next three meetings went beyond these positions, empowering the teams to better investigate and understand their reservations and considerations. Progress was achieved by using the tool of procedural agreement on the components of any future resolution. As Watkins and Rosegrant (2001) argue that control of the process yields control over the outcome, the negotiators agreed that the people inside the Church would be divided into four different categories that would be treated differently: civilians that would be free to go directly home; Palestinian

Security Forces personnel that, subject to an honorable identification process, would be free to return home; and two groups of suspected terrorists, those wanted for minor offenses and the heavily wanted terrorists. These four categories served as the procedural platform for the negotiations to progress based on the understanding that the only gap between the two sides' positions existed over the fourth group: the heavily wanted terrorists. This procedural "division of value" surfaced a dilemma that accompanied the negotiation teams until the last day of the siege: it was labeled the "90–10 dilemma".

If the key to ending the siege is linked to the future of only 10 percent of the besieged, why not allow the 90 percent to leave? The answer lies with the interests of both sides. The Palestinian considerations involved the public interpretation of an act that would leave the warriors in the hands of the IDF, challenging the ethos of human shields. For Israel, leaving the heavily wanted terrorists inside without a complete resolution had the potential of increasing international pressure and prolonging the crisis. However, in a later stage of the negotiations, the teams developed some creative ideas – based on this "90–10 dilemma" – to overcome a last minute crisis in the negotiations.

The procedural understanding about the groups paved the way to a more substantial understanding leading to the guidelines of the agreement. The understanding was that every agreement reached would deal with the terrorists as individuals and not as a group. In other words, there would be a tailor-made solution for each terrorist on the most wanted list, differentiating him from his peers. From this point, the challenge was to brainstorm options (Fisher, Ury and Patton, 1991) that were acceptable to both sides and tailor them accordingly.

During the second and third negotiation meetings, the two teams explored options while not associating any particular solution with any specific individual. Options, such as time-limited deportation, voluntarily exile, a national mission abroad, transfer to a Palestinian prison with or without international supervision, and transfer to Gaza, were considered. These options had two strengths. They did not challenge either Palestinian or Israeli taboos (as introduced at the first meeting), and they were jointly developed and brainstormed and, thus, had a certain degree of legitimacy.

The third negotiation session ended with an understanding that subject to political re-examination of these options, the final association of names to options would be done directly by Ta'amri, Palestinian officials, and the terrorist leaders inside the Church.

The fourth negotiation meeting aimed to move the process forward and to finalize the first implementation of the understandings reached. Based on the progress made, Israel and the terrorists (through the negotiation team, and mainly Anton Salman who went in and out of the Church) agreed that the first group of youth (ages 15 to 17) would be allowed to leave the Church freely and that Israel would allow them to carry out two bodies that were temporarily buried in the Church courtyard. A successful implementation of this first deal could have been a benchmark in the positive progress of the negotiations. The following implementation steps were already agreed: release of 26 Palestinian Security Forces personnel and the entrance of Ta'amri into the Church, with food, to present the terrorist leaders with the guidelines of the agreement.

This negotiation process took place in a hostile war zone, under clear power asymmetry, but at the same time with a strong commitment of both teams to reach an agreement and prevent further escalation. This process was a unique example of a complex negotiation. It was complex in terms of the various factors affected by the actions, and the varied and sometimes conflicting interests that were represented around the negotiation table (Zartman 2003). These factors included the required inter-agency coordination on the Israeli side and the diverse personal, organizational, and national agendas of the Palestinian negotiators. This process of breaking the negotiated challenge into pieces, clearly and frankly underlining interests and taboos, setting procedural frames, and then agreeing to key substantial guidelines, was essential for identifying and understanding the critical obstacles and finding the path that would enable to resolve the crisis.

Upon completion of the fourth meeting and agreeing on the implementation sequence, Ta'amri asked Israel to grant him a special permit to travel to Ramallah to meet the besieged Arafat in the *Mukata* compound. Permission was given. The purpose of the Arafat-Ta'amri meeting was to officially approve the governing principles of the negotiated deal and through this approval to gain national legitimacy for its implementation. Despite Israel's low expectations for clear results from this meeting, due to Chairman Arafat's record of ambiguity and lack of clarity in his decisions, it nevertheless agreed to the meeting and acknowledged its importance to the negotiation process as a whole.

However, while these negotiations were developing, the scene itself was evolving in potentially destabilizing directions. There was a need to accelerate the implementation process. The first incident was the heavy fire exchange during the second negotiation session. In what was perceived by the participants as an attempt to undermine Ta'amri's authority, heavy shooting came from the Church and was answered by IDF fire. The following night, five youths who could not handle the terrorist regime inside the Church, escaped and surrendered. This escape encouraged the negotiation teams to accelerate the implementation process and to release, as soon as possible, the rest of the young people.

The night of April 24–25 marked another significant development. Hearing rumors and indications on progress in the negotiations, and as a result of psychological, social and structural pressure, several gunmen broke into the Armenian compound, which until then was unharmed, breaking clerics' utensils, stealing the charity coin boxes, the gold and diamond-made holy cross, and physically attacking the Armenian priests. In the early morning, the IDF forces noticed a priest carrying a cloth sign on which was written "HELP" standing in the center of the Armenian order. The IDF contacted the man and rescued him, together with two of his elder colleagues.

This incident was condemned by the Palestinian negotiators and added a sense of urgency for concluding an agreement. The next night, in an unprecedented act, two Palestinian Security personnel contacted the CNU asking for protection to flee from the Church. They were rescued from a hidden gate at the back of the Church. It was evident that the men inside were facing a "hurting stalemate" (Touval and Zartman 1985), when one side realizes that it is unable to achieve its aims, resolve the problem or win the conflict by itself. The hurting stalemate is "mutual" when the other side reaches the same conclusion while getting the word that an enticing opportunity exists and they must catch it. Together with the opportunity embodied in the Ta'amri-Arafat meeting, it looked as though the two sides faced a ripe moment composed of a mutually hurting stalemate, marked by a recent or looming catastrophe (sticks), a way out (carrots), and a valid spokesperson for both parties (Zartman 2000).

Ta'amri met Arafat on Saturday, April 27. The same morning two armed Palestinians broke into a house in a Jewish settlement 30 km south of Bethlehem, murdering a baby and her parents. At the same time, on the political level, the negotiations to lift the siege of Arafat in Ramallah made progress. Meanwhile, in Bethlehem the preparations for the first deal – "youth for bodies" – were completed. On Sunday afternoon, April 28, the first deal was implemented. Nine youth and two bodies in wooden coffins left the Church. This marked a significant development. There was no longer stalemate: progress towards resolution had been made.

Under the surface, this development had even greater significance. The Palestinian negotiation team, and Ta'amri himself, earned the official and unofficial *legitimacy* to resolve the crisis. The armed men inside, by allowing the deal to be completed, took upon themselves the *responsibility* to peacefully resolve the crisis. A mutual acceptance of the agreed "rules of the game" was proved, and above all, the deal served as a significant trust-building measure, cementing the commitment of both teams to securely bring the crisis to an end.

Setbacks and Change in Mandate

However, upon completion of the first deal, the scene on the ground experienced an enormous setback. In a routine identification procedure, one of the nine young men who left the Church was identified as wanted for links to a terrorist cell in Bethlehem. He was arrested for further interrogation. This arrest jeopardized the understandings reached between the negotiation teams. The young man was released after several hours; however, the Palestinians perceived it as a major breach of trust. Ta'amri was proven, in his peers' eyes, to be wrong in trusting the Israelis.

The following day, while attempts were made to resume negotiations, the IDF – following the existing rules of engagement – killed Nidal Abayat, one of the terrorist leaders in the Church. Abayat was killed while firing at the Israeli troops. With these events, the fragile trust that had been built between the negotiation teams and the terrorists inside the Church collapsed. At this unstable point, news arrived regarding the siege of Arafat in Ramallah. On April 29, high political level negotiations led to an agreement to lift the siege of Arafat. According to the agreement, the heavily wanted terrorists who sought refuge in Arafat's compound and who were wanted by Israel for more severe allegations than the men inside the Church, specifically for the murder of the Israeli minister of tourism, Rahavam Zeevi, would be transferred to a Palestinian prison under British and American supervision.

This deal and the publicity surrounding it had three negative effects on the scene at the Church. First, it undermined the guidelines reached between the negotiation teams. According to the understandings reached in Bethlehem a tailor-made solution for each one of the terrorists would be applied. Among these options was that several terrorists would be leaving the country. When "higher ranked" terrorists were allowed by Israel to go to a Palestinian prison with international supervision (under the Arafat deal), it set a precedent for the option of Palestinian prisons under international supervision for Bethlehem's terrorists as well. Second, it negatively impacted the process. The negotiations regarding Arafat's compound were conducted at the political level with direct involvement of the CIA. In the Ramallah negotiations, political issues were involved that were hardly applicable to Bethlehem but now were threatening to break the already deteriorating Israeli-Palestinian "negotiation dance" at the Church. Third, now that Arafat was granted free access to the media, it could harm Israel's attempts to gain support in the international arena. Despite these severe setbacks, the fragile ground built by the negotiation teams in Bethlehem proved strong enough to absorb the shocks and sustain the momentum provided that rapid progress could be made.

Both teams in Bethlehem realized that to overcome the setbacks, the next implementation move must be carried out immediately. Building on this understanding, the negotiation teams reconvened in the absence of Ta'amri, who registered his disappointment with the arrest of the young man by staying away from the meeting. While the fifth session was conducted in his absence, his virtual presence in the room was noticeable.

This fifth meeting was devoted to finalizing the procedural details of the next reciprocal moves. These were the release of 26 Palestinian Security Forces personnel, and facilitating the entrance of Ta'amri into the Church (again with food) to present the terrorist leaders with the proposed personal solutions for each one. Regardless of the changed circumstances, Ta'amri agreed to abide by this arrangement, aware that Arafat's emissaries would soon become involved in the Bethlehem scene.

The next afternoon, the first step in the second deal was implemented. Twenty-six Palestinian Security Forces personnel left the Church and returned to their homes. This time no one was arrested and the preparations to bring the food in were completed. Despite the fact that supplying food and water to the besieged terrorists was against the Israeli negotiation strategy, the CNU approved the move on a tactical level, because it bolstered the overarching goal of the negotiations. Meanwhile, as Ta'amri felt that his mandate was weakening due to Arafat's increased involvement, a parallel process occurred on the Israeli side.

At this crucial point in the negotiations, the level of external intervention became noticeable. As previously stated, both teams knew that despite the fact that they were negotiating within a military setting, ultimate control over the content of any settlement reached was at the political level. Both teams knew that they were negotiating with a limited mandate and that political intervention would become visible at the last stages of the negotiations.

On May 3, the mandate of the Israeli negotiation team officially changed, from negotiating an agreement to blockading the area and utilizing increased pressure as a primary strategy. As the next scheduled negotiation meeting was headed by a new representative who had not participated in the early negotiations, and upon realizing that neither of the teams had a mandate to further negotiate or implement, Ta'amri called off the meeting. The negotiations had been moved to the political level.

On the ground, the situation continued to deteriorate. A group of peace activists managed to enter the compound further complicating the situation. Exchange of gunfire, as a direct result of the terrorist leadership's dissatisfaction with the latest development, caused a fire inside the Church bringing international media coverage to a peak.

During the next three days, representatives of Israel, Arafat, and the CIA negotiated a resolution for the crisis and presented it for approval at the political level. The "new deal" was exactly along the guidelines agreed by the negotiation teams ten days before. On May 6, Palestinian officials, without Ta'amri, went into the Church to obtain the agreement of the terrorist leaders and assign "voluntarily exile destinations" for 13 heavily wanted terrorists, while another group was deported to Gaza. It took four more days to finalize the implementation procedures and on

Friday, May 10, after obtaining confirmed approval from European countries, the standoff ended.

In a surreal final scene of the crisis, dozens of Palestinians lined up in front of the Church, quietly approaching the CNU team, which was in charge of the closing operation, shaking hands and saluting each other. Jihad Jua'ra, one of the most wanted terrorists, a Hamas leader who was injured during the fighting, was carried out on a stretcher by two CNU officers who had negotiated with him during the previous days. This gesture was important. It was a visible, international sign of an honorable solution. In a continuation of this surreal ending, after searching the Church and finding a fair amount of ammunition, rifles, and explosive devices hidden inside the holy compound, the CNU had to mediate among representatives of the three Christian orders as to who would be the first to enter the liberated Church.

The crisis was over, the Israeli forces withdrew from Bethlehem, the majority of Palestinians who were inside the Church returned home, several dozen were deported to the Palestinian-controlled Gaza Strip and some were sent to European countries. Both Israeli and Palestinian newspapers, as a reflection of public opinion, criticized the outcome. The Israelis headlines were along the lines of "Prize for terror – vacation in Europe", falling short of understanding the meaning of exile or deportation in the Palestinian national context. The Palestinians headlines claimed, "Bad agreement ended in exile", indicating the general dissatisfaction with an agreed deportation. These public reactions indicate the significant gap between reality and perceived reality. Given the high stakes, the complex interests, and the limited flexibility both sides had in exercising strategic alternatives, it is evident that the 39 day experience of crisis management was a combination of art and luck.

The Church of Nativity siege was an international crisis, carefully managed and peacefully resolved. It is not difficult to imagine a different scenario that could have led the whole region to a catastrophe. A scenario in which Israel breaks into the Church, or the Palestinians inside blow themselves up along with the civilians was just a matter of one wrong move made by any of the parties – Israel, the terrorist leadership inside the Church, the Palestinian leadership in Ramallah, the priests, or any other actor in this complex system.

Lessons Learned

The experience Israel gained from these negotiations and from previous siege or barricade incidents during operation "Defense Shield" has led to the development of a "manual" of experience which is valuable in handling urban warfare situations or other confrontations characterized by extreme limitations – operational, political or moral – on the use of force.

The first lesson is that there is *no general blueprint*. Each event has its unique characteristics. A different system is generated by each event. Therefore careful analysis is needed to identify the situation as one that requires crisis management, that is, as a situation that cannot be solved solely by tactical or operational moves. The analysis phase must be followed by a precise implementation process carried out by trained people with field experience combining the language of power with the power of language.

The second lesson is the need for a *thorough analysis of alternatives* to a negotiated deal. Alternatives can be either better or worse and should be considered for all stakeholders involved in the crisis. Alternatives should be analyzed in the specific context with consideration of the relevant cultural or religious values. Some alternatives that may be deemed reasonable or rational from one point of view may not be acceptable from another point of reference. Alternatives do not carry objective values. They are always subjective and depend on personal, organizational, national, cultural, and religious variables.

The third lesson for negotiating with terrorists is to present a *gradual process of establishing or creating the conditions that will enable the terrorists to peacefully conclude the crisis*. This process, as detailed above, is comprised of three major elements. The first is to understand the psychological state of mind. Very often, terrorists act in a psychological safe-zone that was "constructed" in their perceptions during an earlier training period. Undermining this psychological safe-zone is a necessary condition for moving terrorists toward non-violent acts. It can be accomplished either through psychological warfare or by a psychological build-up toward a positive outcome or end game that the terrorists can accept. The second element in creating conditions that will enable terrorists to peacefully conclude a crisis is to strengthen the legitimacy of the future resolution. This is a necessary, though not sufficient, condition for a successful conclusion. Legitimacy is created through various methods, including past precedents, senior approval, public opinion, and religious directives, among others.

The third and complementary condition is the ability to build independent decision-making capabilities. An agreement reached with terrorists would probably be different than what they had foreseen. This gap requires a decision to compromise, which is seldom in their hands. A common phrase used by terrorists is "it's not our decision". While in non-crisis "agent-principal" situations, it is common to ask for clarification or approval for certain offers made across the negotiation table (Thompson 2001), in crisis situations the goal is to bring the terrorists *themselves* to make decisions, starting from simple decisions such as allowing the terrorists to connect to a land-line phone, to their ability to approve the final deal independently.

Conclusion

In the midst of operation "Defense Shield", a military negotiation team managed to "talk out" more than 200 Palestinians who were besieged in the Church of Nativity in Bethlehem. This was a successful act of crisis management that involved significant negotiations with terrorists who were among and controlled the besieged. The sanctity of the Church as well as the international circumstances meant that for Israel to storm the Church and capture the armed terrorists was not a feasible option. For almost 40 days, the Israeli negotiation team worked with individuals representing an array of groups and interests. The main lessons from these complex negotiations are threefold. First, as there is no blueprint for action in these negotiations, a constant flexible analysis of the situation is required, Second, alternatives to a negotiated agreement ought to be analyzed within a subjective context (cultural, religious, etc.). Third, there is a need to engage in a gradual process of creating conditions that will enable the terrorists to securely conclude the crisis. This process is comprised of (a) undermining the terrorists psychological safe-zone, (b) constructing legitimacy for the negotiated agreement, and (c) building the terrorists' independent decision-making capabilities.

These lessons are subject to the general analytical observation that the negotiation scene acts as a *system* where a set of units or elements is interconnected so that changes in some elements or their relations produce changes in other parts of the system, and the entire system exhibits properties and behaviors that are different from those of the parts (Jervis 1997). The negotiated outcome of the "system" in Bethlehem was significantly different than the outcome reached a week earlier in Ramallah. I believe that it is due to the process orchestrated by the CNU. Critics claimed that the agreement reached in Bethlehem was the only possible outcome, taking into consideration the balance of power and the parties' WATNAs. However, this agreement, unlike many others reached during armed conflicts, was an outcome that resulted from sincere efforts made by the parties to engage in a joint problem-solving effort. Such an effort is not common in the context of negotiating with terrorists.

On a last and personal note, having interacted with Israelis and Arabs in times of peace, and during armed fights, I strongly believe that negotiation and conflict resolution skills are necessary to bring an end to this conflict. I am confident that our generation will achieve this goal.

Acknowledgements

This article is based on the CNU's joint understanding of the events and I wish to thank my colleagues at the CNU without whom I could not present the ideas incorporated herein, and to I. William Zartman, who introduced me to the basic ideas of international negotiation and encouraged me to combine theory with practice.

Note

1. The author disagrees with this common perception of power asymmetry and instead believes that power asymmetry has two dimensions: real and perceived. The Palestinians' strong sense of goal and purpose as well as ability to control the negotiation set (Lax and Sebenius 1986) provide them with a significant source of power that is absent on the Israeli side. For a summary of sources of power in negotiation, see Brett (2000).

References

Brett, Jean M. (2001) *Negotiating Globally*. San Francisco, CA: Jossey-Bass.
Dupont, Christophe and Faure, Guy-Olivier (2002) "The Negotiation Process", in V.A. Kremenyuk (ed.), *International Negotiation: Analysis, Approaches, Issues*. 2nd ed. San Francisco, CA: Jossey-Bass, pp. 39–63.
Faure, Guy-Olivier (2002) "Negotiation: The Cultural Dimension", in V.A. Kremenyuk (ed.), *International Negotiation: Analysis, Approaches, Issues*. 2nd ed. San Francisco, CA: Jossey-Bass, pp. 392–415.
Fisher, Roger, Ury, William, and Patton, Bruce (1991) *Getting To Yes*. New York, NY: Penguin Books.
Hayes, Richard E. (2002) "Negotiations with Terrorists", in V.A. Kremenyuk (ed.), *International Negotiation: Analysis, Approaches, Issues*. 2nd ed. San Francisco, CA: Jossey-Bass, pp. 416–430.
Hopmann, Terrence P. (1998) *The Negotiation Process and the Resolution of International Conflicts*. Columbia, SC: University of South Carolina Press.
Jervis, Robert (1997) *System Effects: Complexity in Political and Social Life*. Princeton, NJ: Princeton University Press.
Lax, David A. and Sebenius, James K. (1986) *The Manager as a Negotiator*. New York, NY: The Free Press.
Mnookin, Robert, Peppet, R. Scott and Tulumello, Andrew S. (2000) *Beyond Winning: Negotiating to Create Value in Deals and Disputes*. Cambridge, MA and London, England: The Belknap Press of Harvard University Press.
Raiffa, Howard (1982) *The Art and Science of Negotiation*. Cambridge, MA and London, England: The Belknap Press of Harvard University Press.
Regan, Geoffrey (1998) *Lionhearts: Saladin, Richard I, and the Era of the Third Crusade*. NY: Walker and Company.
Sebenius, James K. (2002) "Negotiation Analysis", in V.A. Kremenyuk (ed.), *International Negotiation: Analysis, Approaches, Issues*. 2nd ed. San Francisco, CA: Jossey-Bass, pp. 229–255.
Thompson, Leigh, L. (2001) *The Mind and Heart of the Negotiator*. 2nd ed. Upper Saddle River, NJ: Prentice Hall.
Watkins, Michael and Rosegrant, Susan (2001) *Breakthrough International Negotiations*. San Francisco, CA: Jossey-Bass.
Zartman, I. William and Berman, Maureen (1982) *The Practical Negotiator*. New Haven, CT: Yale University Press.
Zartman, I. William and Rasmussen, J. Lewis (1997) *Peacemaking in International Conflict: Method and Techniques*. Washington DC: US Institute of Peace Press.

Zartman, I. William (2000) "Ripeness: The Hurting Stalemate and Beyond". In Paul C. Stern and Daniel Druckman (eds.), *International Conflict Resolution After the Cold War. Committee on International Conflict Resolution.* Washington DC: National Academy Press.

Zartman, I. William (2003) "Conclusion: Managing Complexity" *International Negotiations* 8(1): 179–186.

The Moscow Theater Hostage Crisis: The Perpetrators, their Tactics, and the Russian Response

ADAM DOLNIK and RICHARD PILCH

Introduction

On 23 October 2002 at 21:00 hours, a white minibus[1] carrying a group of 53 armed men and women arrived at the Dubrovka Theater on Melnikova Street in Moscow. Within 30 minutes, the armed group had entered the theater during the performance of the popular "Nord-Ost" musical, swiftly taking 979 people hostage. It would prove to be a 58-hour ordeal that ultimately, would end with a controversial rescue operation that resulted in 128 dead hostages (Feifer 2003).

The Dubrovka hostage crisis was a spectacular media event, which immediately sparked a wide domestic and international debate concerning the appropriateness of the Russian response. This article attempts to reconstruct and assess the events that took place in terms of negotiability, and seeks to provide an analytical perspective on the possible alternatives that were available to the Russian authorities as the incident progressed. Central focus is devoted to the Russian response, namely the crisis negotiation approach and management of the tactical assault. A critical inquiry into the incident is especially important, as lessons learned from past hostage crises are an invaluable tool in developing future response frameworks. Further, the unprecedented use of a deadly chemical agent during the rescue mission may have far-reaching consequences for the resolution of future hostage events, as well as international chemical weapons treaties and developments in the Russian-Chechen conflict.

The reconstruction of the standoff presented in this account is based on open-source literature, such as Russian and international media coverage of the incident, interviews with various actors involved in the incident, and official press releases from the Russian government and the Chechen rebels. A traditional law-enforcement framework for negotiating barricade-hostage incidents is used to analyze the crisis negotiation approach. The analysis of the chemical agent and the implications of its use draws primarily on medical literature and historical precedents.

The greatest limitation of this article stems from the fact that most available accounts of the hostage crisis differ significantly in their description of virtually every aspect of the incident. This is further complicated by media self-censorship

International Negotiation Series 1:
I.W. Zartman (ed.) Negotiating with Terrorists, 131–164
© 2006 *Koninklijke Brill NV. Printed in the Netherlands.*

and by the fact that even eyewitness accounts are often contradictory. In order to compensate for these deficiencies, the authors have chosen to use only information that could be corroborated by at least three sources. At the same time, the authors realize that even such precautions do not ensure 100 percent accuracy. For the sake of completeness, alternative interpretations of the discussed events are included as endnotes.

Another possible shortcoming may be the authors' bias in using a crisis negotiation framework developed in the West. While it is true that this method has been strikingly successful in resolving barricade-hostage incidents, political and cultural circumstances, such as the traditional Russian inclination towards sledgehammer solutions, may render the nuanced Western negotiation approaches less applicable to the Russian context. Nevertheless, the authors believe that an analysis of possible alternative courses of action in the Moscow theater hostage crisis provides a useful tool for resolving similar incidents in the future.

Part I of this article provides a brief overview of the events that unfolded. This section also places the Chechen motivations behind the incident into perspective with regard to past Chechen operations and to their overall strategy. Part II focuses on the details of the attack itself, particularly the Russian response. Special attention is devoted to analyzing the successes and failures of both the negotiations and the tactical assault. The conclusion discusses the implications of the Moscow theater incident for the future, including its potential impact on the likelihood of success of certain crisis negotiation strategies and the future tactics of the Chechen rebels.

I. Overview of the Events

Chechens and Hostage-Taking

Since 11 December 1994, when Russian troops invaded Chechnya in an attempt to reassert control over the part of the country that had declared independence in 1991, Chechen rebels and the Russian army have engaged in an off-and-on reciprocal armed conflict. Before any meaningful analysis of the Moscow hostage crisis can be presented, it is essential to discuss several strikingly similar incidents that Chechen commandos had perpetrated in the past.

In addition to their guerilla warfare efforts in Chechnya, militant Chechens began terrorist attacks against civilian targets in 1995. On 14 June 1995, Field Commander Shamil Basayev's 100-strong commando unit simultaneously attacked the post office, the communications center, the market, and the hospital in the Russian town of Budyonnovsk, seizing some 1,500 hostages in the hospital and demanding that Russian forces pull out of Chechnya. The Chechen fighters were heavily armed, with each individual reportedly carrying 1,700 AKS cartridges, 11 hand grenades, five kilograms of TNT, three Mukha grenade throwers, and 152 Stechkin pistol cartridges (Arquila and Karasik 1999). Even several months before the attack, the Chechens reportedly rented basement rooms in the hospital and stored additional weapons there, including large-caliber machine guns, bazookas, and a heavy grenade launcher.[2] Overall, the operation carried signs of meticulous planning and execution.

To resolve the crisis that unfolded, the responding Russian forces led by the elite Alpha commando unit assaulted the Chechen positions but were forced to retreat, partially due to the terrorists' use of hostages as human shields. The standoff continued for another five days, after which Basayev's men, along with 150 "voluntary safe-passage hostages", evacuated Budyonnovsk and returned home to a hero's welcome. The hostages were than released. The Budyonnovsk incident was a humiliating experience for the Russians, who were publicly blamed for the deaths of the 50 hostages that were killed during the initial rescue attempt. Even more significantly, the Russian leadership was also forced to announce a temporary cease-fire and declare their commitment to serious negotiations with Chechen representatives in order to resolve the crisis.

Six months after the Budyonnovsk incident, another crucial hostage event took place in Dagestan. On 9 January 1996, Salman Rudayev's[3] 250-strong Chechen commando unit took more than 2,000 hostages at a hospital in the city of Kizlyar, and again demanded the unconditional withdrawal of Russian forces from Chechnya. Somewhat unexpectedly, the rebels were again granted free passage, and an 11 bus convoy carrying the commandos plus 143 hostages evacuated the area (Arquila and Karasik 1999). As the convoy approached the Dagestani-Chechen border, Russian forces unsuccessfully attempted a surprise attack aimed at freeing the hostages and punishing the terrorists. The rebels, however, were able to fight off the initial attack and retreated to a small nearby village of Pervomayskoe, seizing 25 additional hostages in the process. There, another long standoff began. Patience wore thin on the part of the Russians, and on 15 January 1996 they launched a furious assault on the village. Outnumbered 10 to 1, the Chechens were still able to hold off the Russian troops, though a good portion of luck was involved.[4] On 16 January 1996, while the rebels at Pervomayskoe continued to hold off the assault, another commando unit sympathetic to the Chechen cause hijacked a Black Sea ferry, the *Euroasia*, and threatened to blow it up – along with the 255 hostages on board – unless the Russian army stopped the siege (BBC October 24, 2002). In addition, yet another group of rebels kidnapped 30 employees of a Russian power plant in Grozny and issued similar demands. Finally, the Pervomayskoe siege ended when the rebels, aided by a complete breakdown of

Russian morale and by reinforcements smuggled in from Chechnya, managed to escape the village. The next day, after the Russian forces finally took control over Pervomayskoe, the hijackers of the *Euroasia* called off their plan to blow up the ship and surrendered to Turkish authorities. The exact number of casualties of the Pervomayskoe siege remains unreported, although it is known that at least 82 hostages were rescued, and 46 were released later.

Both of these incidents are critical to understanding the 2002 standoff in Moscow for several reasons. First, they provide insight into the Chechen approach to hostage-taking. While the Chechen rebels should by no means be understood as a homogenous entity, all of their organized hostage-taking operations have been extremely daring and well-planned, and all involved an unusually high number of ready-to-die commandos, some of whom were women. At the same time, none of the Chechen barricade-hostage incidents involved mass executions of hostages, and despite their preparedness to die, the perpetrators chose to live and evacuate the location when an opportunity presented itself. It is also clear that in all of these incidents the Chechens succeeded in attracting wide international attention and then attempted to deflect responsibility for the death of the hostages onto the Russian troops. If the goal of these operations was indeed to provoke a fierce military response that would demonstrate to the world the "ruthless and indiscriminate" Russian approach to the conflict with the Chechens, each of these incidents was a considerable success. Strengthened by such successes, the Chechens have demonstrated increasing optimism with regard to the outcome of their operations.

Second, these incidents provide insight into the Russian *modus operandi* in responding to hostage incidents. Whenever even the slightest probability of success exists, the Russians can be expected to attempt a rescue operation. Significantly, the chronology of Russian responses to Chechen hostage incidents shows signs of increased frustration. After Budyonnovsk, then-president Boris Yeltsin was heavily criticized for allowing the hostage-takers to get away. By the time the events in Kizlyar unfolded, there was strong resolve on behalf of the Russian leadership not only to avoid appearing weak by granting concessions, but also to teach the Chechens a lesson they would never forget. It seems that this instinct carried over to the Moscow incident as well.

Finally, both events fatally shattered the morale of Russia's elite Alpha unit, many members of which reportedly bought their own train tickets to leave the Pervomayskoe siege while it was still in progress (Arquila and Karasik 1999). The same unit was called on in 2002 to respond to the hostage crisis in Moscow.

Basic Timeline of the Dubrovka Incident

On 23 October 2002 (Day 1) at 21:45, a group of armed men and women dressed in plain clothes arrived at the Dubrovka Theater in Melnikova Street in Moscow.

In the lobby of the complex, the commandos changed quickly into military fatigues and covered their faces (Abdullaev 2002). Minutes later, shouting slogans and firing into the air, the gunmen stepped on the stage during the second act of the "Nord-Ost" musical. At this point, few spectators realized that their emergence was not a part of the show, which was set during World War II and was filled with special effects. When the terrorists fired more shots and commanded the actors to leave the stage and join the spectators as hostages, however, it became clear that the assault was real. As soon as the audience and staff were subdued, the rebels wired explosives and booby traps around the building. The terrorists then declared that they would blow up the structure if Russian forces attempted a rescue mission, a point that was reiterated in phone calls of the hostages that were able to contact their relatives via mobile phones. According to the Russian press agency INTERFAX, the Chechens installed about 30 different explosive charges around the theater, the largest of which was equivalent to roughly 110 pounds of TNT. Made out of two metal containers filled with ball bearings and containing an artillery shell as the main charge, the bomb was divided into two parts, one placed in row 15 of the main auditorium and the other in the balcony area. The detonator was guarded by one of the female terrorists. The remaining explosive charges consisted of 6–8 pound hexogen-based bombs placed throughout the theater and 1.75–4.5 pound plastid suicide belts with detonators worn by eighteen female terrorists.

At 23:00, the hostage-takers claimed the operation on behalf of the Chechen people and threatened to kill all of the hostages unless Russian troops pulled out of Chechnya within a week. In a prerecorded videotape delivered to the Moscow office of the Arabic news channel *Al-Jazeera*, the leader of the militants, Movsar Barayev, announced, "Each one of us is willing to sacrifice himself for the sake of God and the independence of Chechnya. I swear by God that we are more keen on dying than you are on living" (Singh 2002). Shortly thereafter, over 200 hostages were released, mainly children and Chechen and Georgian nationals who were able to produce proof of their nationality.

In the early morning hours of 24 October 2002 (Day 2), twenty additional hostages were released, following face-to-face talks between the terrorists and two Chechen politicians, Aslanbek Aslachanov and Ruslan Khasbulatov. Subsequently, the Russian leadership issued a public announcement that the theater would not be assaulted unless the rebels started killing hostages. Only one hour later, however, the first volatile moment since the beginning of the crisis erupted when the terrorists announced that they had killed a drunken policeman who attempted to enter the theater despite repeated warnings to stay away. This claim was not confirmed by the authorities at the time, and even today it is not clear what really happened.

At 10:20, much to the relief of foreign ambassadors who had by this time gathered in the operations command center located at the War Veterans Hospital No. 1 in direct view of the front of the theater, the rebels agreed to the release of all foreign nationals. This positive development was seemingly solidified an hour later, when Russian officials reciprocated the gesture by offering the rebels free passage to a third country under the single condition that all hostages were safely released. This offer apparently offended the terrorists, however, who responded by announcing that they would execute 10 hostages each hour if their demands were not fulfilled. Following a period of escalating tensions during which the anticipated release of foreign hostages never materialized, the Chechens finally agreed to resume communications with Red Cross representatives. About twenty minutes later, the tensions seemed to have been defused completely, as five additional hostages walked out of the theater.

At 18:45 hours, another volatile moment occurred when several gunshots were suddenly fired inside the theater. Minutes later it became clear that the gunshots did not signal the beginning of the threatened hostage executions but rather were an unsuccessful attempt by the rebels to stop two women hostages from escaping the location. This high-pressure moment was followed by a relatively calm afternoon highlighted only by an announcement from Grozny in which Chechen President Aslan Maskhadov denounced the attack.[5]

During the morning of 25 October 2002 (Day 3), 15 hostages were released, and the hostage-takers renewed their promise to free all 75 foreign nationals. The release of all remaining teenagers was also offered in exchange for Russian consent to a pro-Chechen demonstration on the Red Square. At 14:00, top Russian politician Dimitri Rogozin announced that the release of foreign nationals was only a matter of another three to four hours. Two hours later, in an apparent attempt to speed up the release of all foreigners, the Russians made another public promise to spare the lives of the terrorists if all hostages were released unharmed. The Chechens, again angered by this proposal, renewed their threat to initiate hostage executions on the following morning if their demands were not met. Despite the escalating tensions, however, four additional hostages, a man and three women, were released at 22:44.

Less than an hour into Saturday, 26 October 2002 (Day 4), a restricted message began to circulate among officials and reporters on the scene of the crisis. The Spetsnaz, Russia's elite counterterrorism force, was planning to raid the theater at 06:00, the Chechens' deadline for the initiation of hostage executions (FBIS ID# CEP20021028000333). In the early morning hours, however, a series of events within the theater significantly truncated the raid's timeline.[6] Witness accounts state that shortly after Spetsnaz forces arrived on the scene, the situation inside the theater grew tense. Apparently aware of the new developments outside, leader Barayev and another rebel named Yasser rushed into the main hall of the theater, shouting to their compatriots that an assault was about to begin. Emotions mounted in silence for some 20 minutes as both the rebels and hostages waited for something to happen. Suddenly, an overwrought male hostage leapt to his feet and charged toward the Chechen woman guarding the primary explosive, throwing a bottle at her in stride. She fired into the air and yelled for him to sit down, but he continued on. Another rebel then fired at the man. The bullet missed its target but pierced the eye of another male hostage seated in the vicinity, and a bullet penetrated the chest of a nearby woman as well.[7] The hostage-takers were reportedly distraught, and told the hostages to call the Red Cross (BBC, October 26, 2002). When the phone call came into the command center requesting medical assistance, the callers apparently did not describe the circumstances of the shooting, and those on the other end of the line neglected to ask.[8] According to Kremlin spokesman Alexander Machevsky, who spent the entire crisis at the command center, the general feeling was that the terrorists had begun carrying out their threats of executing hostages. At this time, the decision was made to storm the theater as soon as possible. The command center notified the city's ambulance service, and the Spetsnaz quietly moved into place (BBC, October 29, 2002).

The forces apparently approached the theater in three small teams. The first team took cover outside, while the second and third teams entered the "Central Station" gay nightclub that shared a wall with the theater (FBIS ID# CEP20021028000333). Once inside the club, one team paused and made preparations to blast through this wall. The other team proceeded into the club's basement and entered a tunnel system beneath the theater, then advanced to a set of iron doors marking the orchestra pit and forced these doors open using an explosive charge.

It seems that the Russians' intent to use gas in the raid, though discussed for days prior to the actual assault, only became apparent when team members entering the nightclub were spotted carrying gas cylinders (Politkovskaya 2002). Reports conflict regarding when and where the gas was released, but the consensus is that the gas was released into the air conditioning system sometime between 05:00 and 05:15, approximately fifteen minutes before the assault (Soldatov interview 2003).

Meanwhile, tensions had largely subsided within the theater. While many hostages and rebels alike reportedly sprawled out over the theater seats and slept, Barayev and other prominent members of the Chechen team spent their time in the theater's sound and lighting room, editing a videotape of the raid recorded by the hostage-takers themselves and by the theater's security cameras (*Moscow Times*, October 28, 2002). Alternatively, some sources state that these individuals were actually at the theater's bar, also located in the balcony area, celebrating a secret arrangement that had been made with the Federal Security Service (FSB) to exchange hostages for free passage (Soldatov interview 2003). Regardless, it is clear that Barayev and his senior staff were situated in the balcony area at the time of the assault.

As the gas crept into the theater, it drew the attention of both the rebels and the hostages.[9] Judging by a phone call from one of the hostages to a local radio station, the people inside the auditorium knew about the assault for at least two minutes before being overwhelmed by the gas. Rebels rushed about the theater screaming "Gas! Gas!" and "Turn on the air conditioning!"[10] While some succumbed to the effects of the gas before any defensive action could be taken, others successfully donned respirators that had been brought along for the attack.[11] In addition, those terrorists situated in areas far enough removed from the point(s) of release[12] were not exposed to the gas in large enough quantities to be overwhelmed. Thus, it is certain that a significant number of rebels remained conscious long enough that the explosive charges could have been detonated had such an end been desired, and had the necessary order been given.[13]

Entry by the three Spetsnaz teams appears to have been in phases. By almost all accounts and as best reconstructed in "temporal associations",[14] it was the team outside the theater that struck first, engaging the unaffected rebels in the corridor either from the outside or from within the corridor itself (FBIS ID# CEP20021114000199).[15] The sound of gunfire, possibly return fire from the Chechens (Spetsnaz reportedly use almost exclusively silenced weapons), apparently drew a number of those rebels not incapacitated by the gas out of the auditorium and toward the exchange (Myers 2002).[16] At the raid's outset, Barayev was immediately located in the upstairs kitchen and killed along with the other rebel leaders, either by a subunit of this initial assault team or by members of the team blasting through the wall of the bordering nightclub (FBIS ID# CEP20021030000064). The timing of this team's entry through the nightclub wall remains unclear but is thought to have occurred in concert with or slightly before that of the underground team (FBIS ID# CEP20021028000333). As the engagement in the corridor continued, the underground team entered directly into the auditorium from the orchestra pit and began to evacuate hostages immediately, wary of the fact that the explosives could be detonated at any time (FBIS ID# CEP20021114000199).

Spetsnaz forces ultimately converged on the auditorium and were successful in eliminating the primary threat (Glasser 2002). By approximately 07:00, only three rebels remained alive within the theater. They surrendered and were escorted away, while a fourth, apparently trying to blend in with a crowd of journalists, was apprehended outside. Several others were thought to have escaped in the chaos (McGeary 2002). At 07:20, the siege was over and the building was declared secure (BBC, October 29, 2002).

The casualties resulting from the assault were significant: 128 hostages died, 126 of them from gas poisoning and two others from gunshot wounds. Hundreds of people were treated for the effects of gas exposure, and 67 individuals who were supposed to be at the theater at the time of the siege allegedly remain missing.[17]

II. Details of the Attack

The Chechen Team

Although presented to the world as Movsar Barayev, the Chechen commando unit was actually led by one Movsar Suleimanov (Kline and Franchietti 2002), the 26 year-old nephew of Arbi Barayev, infamous leader of the Chechen Islamic Special Units who was allegedly personally responsible for the deaths of some 170 people.[18] It was precisely Arbi Barayev's reputation as a ruthless bandit and murderer that authorities were seeking to exploit when they referred to Movsar as "Barayev", with the apparent goal of evoking resentment and condemnation by association (Politkovskaya interview 2003).

After Arbi Barayev was killed in June 2001 in an eight-day Russian operation in Alkhan-Kala, his head was handed to his family in front of television cameras. Movsar then assumed leadership of the Chechen Islamic Special Units, along with control of the main highway in Chechnya and the kidnap-for-ransom industry dominated by Barayev's group at the time. Besides Arbi, Movsar also had a famous aunt, Khava, who became the first Chechen suicide bomber when she drove an explosives-laden truck into a military base at Alkhan-Kala in June 2000, killing 17 soldiers. Yet another prominent woman from the Barayev clan was Arbi's wife Zura, who was one of the women fighters accompanying Movsar in the Moscow operation (Tsvetkova 2002).

Despite the fact that Movsar Barayev was consistently portrayed as the leader of the group, it should be noted that the operational command and negotiations were actually in the hands of a man who called himself Abu Bakar.[19] In fact, according to some accounts, Movsar – a known drug addict with a very short attention span – spent most of the incident sleeping in the kitchen area of the second floor lobby (Politkovskaya interview 2002). Abu Bakar's leadership role was evident during the crisis when he categorically overruled Barayev's consent to a journalist seeking permission to take pictures inside the auditorium (FBIS ID# CEP20021030000064).

The composition of Movsar Barayev's commando unit, which called itself the Kamikaze of Islam,[20] was well thought out. 18 out of the 53 armed commandos were women, all in their early twenties and most of them widows of the conflict in Chechnya. Female operatives are ideal for such high profile operations, as they are generally more focused and dedicated, and thus much more result-oriented than males, who are often driven by the love for action and the machismo element. While one might expect that women would be softer on hostages because of their motherly instinct, women terrorists actually tend to be more ruthless precisely because of this instinct – once they decide that their violent actions will benefit their children and future generations, they will not hesitate to do what they feel is necessary for the success of the operation (Hudson 1999: 90). This was confirmed in Moscow, where many hostages reported that the women terrorists practiced much more merciless physical and psychological treatment of hostages then the men. The proportion of women to men in the commando unit was of further significance. Enough women were present to form a large and powerful unit of dedicated suicide bombers, but they were still a minority, allowing the exploitation of their desire to prove their worth to their male colleagues. It is by no means a surprise that the suicide explosive belts were attached to the bodies of female rather than male terrorists, who assumed different roles. According to an Alpha unit leader who observed the terrorists throughout the incident, at least five or six of the men were highly trained and experienced professionals (FBIS ID# CEP20021024000569).

Planning

The planning and organization of the Moscow operation were quite impressive. According to the Chechens' own account, preparations took between two and three months and involved the recruitment of the best commandos of the "Riyadus-Salikhin Reconnaissance and Sabotage Battalion of Chechen Martyrs"[21] from the Vedensky district, individuals not only capable of carrying out the operation but also willing to die in Moscow (Johnson's Russian List, 2 November 2002). The group then trained extensively for the operation in Chechnya. Six weeks before the actual raid, some of the team's members traveled to Moscow and found jobs as construction workers at the Central Station nightclub neighboring the theater (Venzke and Aimee 2003). During those six weeks, the "workers" conducted detailed casing of the location, and reportedly stored explosives and arms in the club's back rooms (Abdullaev 2002). On several occasions, some operatives also attended the "Nord-Ost" musical in order to familiarize themselves with the environment. The rebels did not leave anything to chance; they even smuggled battle-proven weapons for the operation from Chechnya in order to minimize the risk of malfunction associated with buying new weapons in Russia. The commando unit was well armed, carrying 15 semi-automatic AKMS740 rifles and 3000 cartridges, 11 Makarov pistols, 114 grenades (89 of them RGDs and the remaining 25 homemade), and even a homemade grenade launcher. The overall cost of the operation was estimated to be approximately $60,000, according to Chechens with first-hand knowledge of guerilla operations (Quinn-Judge 2002).

When preparations were complete, the rest of the commandos traveled via ground transportation to Moscow from various parts of the country. For instance, Movsar Barayev traveled by train from the southern city of Mineralniye Vody, while at least one female terrorist used a bus line from the

Dagestani town of Khasavyurt. Air transportation was apparently avoided for security reasons, as anyone who flies from the North Caucasus is run through an FSB database (Abdullaev 2002).

During the raid itself, the terrorists were highly professional. According to the Spetsnaz, the terrorists were optimally placed around the theater, "not having a single person at an unnecessary place" (FBIS ID# CEP20021114000199). Every member of the commando unit had a sector to watch over, and this was uniformly practiced with great caution and discipline. All of the key entry routes were wired with explosives, including the underground sewer passage beneath the orchestra pit, and several snipers closely monitored areas around the building. The terrorists moved from place to place within the theater via purposely complicated routes, having mined all of the intuitively more accessible pathways. Also, any outside view into the auditorium was obstructed to prevent sniper fire and reconnaissance. In the hallways, the terrorists moved in combat order, with one person covering blind areas while others passed. In addition the terrorists placed those actors of the musical costumed in military uniforms around the perimeter of the auditorium with the apparent intent of drawing fire to them in the event of an assault by security forces (FBIS ID# CEP20021114000199). The Chechens also allegedly changed the position of the explosives inside the theater after every release of hostages or every visit from the outside (FBIS ID# CEP20021024000569). Finally, according to Russian authorities, the terrorists placed several operatives outside the theater, whose task was to inform them about the events and reactions outside (McGeary and Quinn 2002). Overall, both preparation and execution of the attack showed a great amount of sophistication, expertise, and meticulous planning.

Goals of the Operation

In order to analyze the potential of negotiations in resolving the incident, it is essential to assess the motivations and goals behind it. There are several important components to this process, namely the selection of target, timing, tactic used, and overall strategy.

The selection of a theater as a target is significant for several reasons.[22] In their own words, the terrorists selected the Dubrovka theater because it was "in the center of the city and there were a lot of people there" (Abu Bakar interview for NTV, October 24, 2002). By attacking a target that was only some five kilometers away from the Kremlin, the terrorists intended to demonstrate that they could strike in the heart of enemy territory at any time. Also, seizing a Moscow theater during a popular performance furnishes a large number of middle to upper class hostages,[23] reinforcing the perception among ordinary Russians that they, too, could become targets. Moreover, there was an expressive element in attacking the theater, which had to do with the perception that Chechen children are dying while the "heartless Russians" are having fun. The theatergoers were thus seen as guilty by association, which was strengthened even more by the highly patriotic content of the show.

The timing of the attack is also important. During the year leading up the incident, the Russian media had consistently contributed to a false sense of security by treating the issue of the war in Chechnya as long over. Also, with Russia actively aligning itself with the US-led "war on terror", international sympathy for the Chechen rebels had faded significantly. A high profile incident was needed to bring Chechnya back into the spotlight.

The suicidal tactic selected for the operation is significant as well. The seeming irrationality of such an operation is useful in attracting extensive media coverage. This is followed by attempts to comprehend the motivations of such an act, leading to worldwide debates about the systemic foundations of the enormous dedication and hatred demonstrated by the attackers. In the eyes of many people, the group then gains the image of committed believers willing to do anything to reach their goals, also implying that the present environment is so humiliating that death is preferable to life under such conditions (Dolnik 2003). This is especially true in cases where suicide attackers are women, as in Moscow. The message conveyed by this operation is also directed inward. The willingness to die for the cause has been used by Chechen radicals as evidence of their fighters' moral superiority over the Russians, who are portrayed as pleasure-seekers, essentially weak despite their military dominance. The resulting perception among many Chechens has been that due to superior determination, their final victory is inevitable (Dolnik 2003).[24]

Overall, the selection of target and tactic reveals the possible scope of goals of the operation. Barricade hostage-taking is essentially an instrumental as well as an expressive act. The possession of hostages creates a "good" that hostage-takers can use to trade for specific measures the group seeks to achieve. In this instance, the possession of hostages was an instrumental means for achieving the pronounced demand of the pullout of Russian forces from Chechnya. However, the *expressive* nature of the Dubrovka incident seems to have been much more important. Through high profile incidents such as this one, the Chechen rebel groups try to draw wide media attention to their cause, which then serves as a platform for sending declared or tacit messages. Above all, the attackers wanted to express and explain their disagreement with and resentment towards Russian military operations in Chechnya. Second, the attack was designed to remind the world of the Chechen issue, as well as to express frustration with the inaction of the international community regarding the human rights situation in the region. Third, the apparent goal was to embarrass president Putin, who two years before the incident had announced that the war in Chechnya had been won. The Moscow operation was designed to demonstrate that the war is very much alive and that it will affect everyone, not just the Chechens and families of the soldiers fighting in the region. Fourth, based on previous experiences in similar incidents, the Chechens were sure that the Russian forces would storm the theater at some point. Steps were therefore taken to make the assault as difficult as possible, ensuring that many hostages would die as a result. The message that the rebels were hoping to send was that even though they were the ones to take the hostages, they only did so out of desperation, and that it was the Russian government that was responsible for the hostages' deaths. This goal seems to have been confirmed by the alleged mastermind of the operation, field commander Shamil Basayev. In a statement published at the rebels' website, Basayev acknowledged the failure of the attack in terms of forcing the Russians to pull out of Chechnya, but also praised the success of "showing to the whole world that Russian leadership will without mercy slaughter its own citizens in the middle of Moscow". If this was indeed the goal, then the operation was a success. The Chechens can now claim that throughout the incident their commandos had released a number of hostages as a sign of good faith and can point to the fact that all but four of the overall 132 fatalities of the incident were victims of the rescue operation.

Assessment of Volatility

From a crisis negotiation standpoint, the Dubrovka hostage crisis carried several signs of high volatility from the beginning. First, the incident was apparently premeditated and carefully planned; the hostage-takers knew well in advance what type of situation they were getting into. Such a premeditated incident is naturally quite difficult to negotiate, and the process is likely to last significantly longer than in the case of spontaneous hostage incidents. Further, the presence of multiple hostage-takers available to handle the negotiations made the situation even more unpredictable: building a rapport with hostage-takers is much more challenging if they are under direct pressure from their peers and if they can effectively negate the formation of a personal relationship with the negotiator simply by switching representatives. Moreover, the psychological process known as "groupthink" puts the hostages in increased danger, as group hostage-takers in general have the ability to be more decisive then individuals when it comes to killing hostages.

The second major volatile element of the Dubrovka theater crisis was the fact that the hostage-takers were well armed and heavily brutalized. Security precautions taken by the rebels made an assault on the location much more challenging, and the history of ruthlessness on the part of other Chechens made this group's claims of preparedness to kill the hostages in cold blood quite persuasive. In addition, the fact that the terrorists at one point separated the hostages into groups by gender and nationality was very disturbing. According to some reports, the female hostages were taken upstairs to the balcony while the rest of the hostages remained in the main auditorium (BBC, 25 October 2002). This filtering process not only signaled the anticipation of a tactical assault – holding hostages at different locations makes an assault more difficult, as multiple tactical teams must attack all locations simultaneously in order to limit the vulnerability of hostages held at other locations – but also allowed for a quick but "discriminate" execution of hostages if needed. The slaying of Russian males, perceived to be "involved" in the war against Chechnya, would have been psychologically easier and also less politically dangerous for the Chechens than killing women and foreign nationals.

The third possible volatile element was the reported absence of change in the terrorists' demands over time. In negotiable situations, hostage-takers start bidding high but reduce their demands as the incident progresses and as their exhaustion triggers a regression to a hierarchically higher set of needs such as hunger, thirst, and sleep. If such a process does not occur over a growing period of time, the chances of a negotiated solution decrease considerably (Strentz 1991). At the same time, the presence of multiple hostage-takers prolongs this process significantly, as the hostage-takers not only have the option of resting some of their crew by working in shifts but also are able to feed from the energy and determination of their counterparts. Particularly when the hostage-takers widely publicize their original demands and thus publicly lock themselves in their position, it becomes more difficult to negotiate a peaceful solution, as the one thing the image-conscious terrorists fear the most is failure. Yet despite the fact that the Chechens in Moscow showed little willingness to give up their sole original demand – the pull out of Russian forces from Chechnya – the abstract and expressive nature of this demand provided plenty of room for bargaining. Further, the claim that no change in the terrorists' demands occurred is not entirely true – the demands did become more specific throughout the incident. During their talks with Russian journalist Anna Politkovskaya, the rebels made clear what exact actions had to be taken and who would have to verify the initiation of these actions in order for the hostages to be freed. The first specific demand was that president Putin comment in some way on the issue of ending the war in Chechnya. The terrorists did not demand any written document or decree, just an oral statement (Politkovskaya interview 2003). Second, it was to be confirmed with the help of an international mediator that the withdrawal of troops from Chechnya would begin the next day. Even more significantly, Movsar Barayev, in his interview with the Russian television station NTV, voiced the possibility of releasing the hostages if the Russian leadership agreed to the commencement of negotiations with Chechen president Maskhadov. This point was again reiterated in the negotiations between Abu Bakar and Boris Nemtsov. While the specificity of these demands may not seem significant, it was in fact a vitally important indicator of changing expectations on the part of the hostage-takers. Such change is the first major step toward a negotiated solution, and its presence was therefore encouraging (Strentz 1995).

Finally, and perhaps most importantly, the declared desire on the part of the terrorists to die and become martyrs suggested a high level of volatility. The desire to live is a basic precondition of a negotiated settlement in barricade situations – if the hostage-takers are indifferent to staying alive, it is difficult to make them focus on personal safety and thus draw their attention away from their original demands. Also, the threat of force posed by the hostage rescue unit becomes much less powerful as a bargaining tool when survival plays no part in the hostage-takers' calculation of the outcome (Zartman 1990). Under circumstances in which the captors see it as their primary objective to kill themselves and take as many of their victims with them as possible, negotiation has very little chance of success. However, such situations are extremely infrequent. After all, the whole point of taking hostages is to protect ones own safety during the standoff.

Terrorist operations in which the perpetrator's death is the preferred outcome usually take the form of suicide bombings or *fidayeen* shooting attacks with no planned escape routes. In contrast, operations that involve hostages are usually designed to use the captives as leverage to get something – killing them is *not* the objective. At the same time, since the boom of airplane hijackings in the 1960s, hostage-takers have consistently threatened to blow themselves up along with the hostages. In fact, by the mid-1970s the majority of skyjacking or barricade hostage incidents involved such threats. In most instances, these had a rational basis – downplaying the role of one's own survival strengthened the terrorists' bargaining position, and the threat of a rescue operation became a much less powerful pressure tool for the responders (Zartman 1990). In incidents involving airplanes, this threat can be made credible even with a relatively small amount of real or fake explosive material, because blowing a hole in the aircraft in mid-flight has the potential to cause the plane to crash and thus to kill all on board. Barricade incidents on the ground, on the other hand, require fake or actual wiring of the location with bombs in order to be persuasive. This is precisely what the Chechens did in Moscow. Considering that in all similar incidents in the past the Russian troops had attempted to storm the location, this was a logical and rational action on part of the terrorists. And since the Chechen rebels had certainly proved their willingness to conduct suicide operations in the past, the deterrent value of their threats was high.[25] For this reason, it is difficult to blame the Russian authorities for believing the threats to be genuine and thus perceiving negotiations not to be an option.

At the same time, all past Chechen suicide operations have involved only the minimal amount of personnel necessary to carry out the attack. Since the Chechens rely heavily on small bands of 12–20 fighters to fight large Russian units in Chechnya, it is unlikely that they would be anxious to sacrifice some 60 fighters in a single operation against civilians, who are easy targets that can be attacked by alternative and less costly means. There is no question that members of Barayev's unit were *prepared* to die during the Moscow operation, it is however questionable whether their death was truly designed as the operation's *preferred outcome*. For this reason, the declared preparedness to die on behalf of the terrorists might have made negotiations extremely challenging, but certainly did not exclude the possibility of a nonviolent resolution altogether.

Indicators of De-escalation

Besides the above-stated indicators of high volatility, signs of de-escalation were also present as the incident progressed. The first such sign was the absence of cold-blooded executions (Strentz 1995). History shows that the vast majority of hostage casualties in barricade incidents occur in the opening moments of the siege, when the hostage-takers are aroused and highly nervous as they are trying to establish control over the panicking hostages. In very few instances do terrorists initiate executions later in the incident. On the one hand, it is true that the rebels in Moscow did in fact kill four hostages during the 58-hour ordeal, which might have led many on the outside to the conclusion that negotiations were simply not possible. On the other hand, however, not one of those killings was conducted in cold blood as a pressure tool; in actuality, the killings were not premeditated but rather came about out of "necessity". The first slain hostage was a woman who, according to witnesses, entered the concert room under heavy influence of alcohol and was very aggressive toward the rebels.[26] The second person killed was an intoxicated police officer who attempted to enter the theater despite all the warnings conveyed to him by the hostage-takers. The final two killings occurred by accident: the terrorists fired at a hostage who out of frustration attacked one of the female terrorists, but the shots missed their target and ended up killing the two other hostages. In sum, all of these situations absolutely required action by the terrorists, who would certainly not have been able to maintain control over the situation had they not acted. This, of course, does not acquit the Chechens of the responsibility for the deaths of the slain hostages, but understanding the circumstances under which these people were killed is critical for the negotiators, as it helps in assessing the stage and negotiability of an incident. While a cold-blooded execution of hostages as a negotiation tool significantly lowers the likelihood of a negotiated solution, circumstantial killing out of "necessity" does not necessarily have the same effect.

The fact that the Chechens let deadlines for fulfillment of their demands pass without incident was another positive sign. The hostage-takers did on at least two occasions threaten to kill a hostage per hour if their demands were not promptly met, but failed to follow suit. Experience shows that once a deadline is breached, it is easier to break through future deadlines and prolong the incident (McMains and

Mullins 2001). While the prolongation of the incident alone does not automatically guarantee a peaceful resolution, it does strengthen the chances for such an outcome. Further, it also provides the tactical unit with more time to study the behavioral patterns of the perpetrators and to prepare for an assault.

The final encouraging element in the ordeal was the periodic safe release of dozens of hostages, even without any demands attached. Such actions clearly indicated the willingness of the terrorists to deal with the authorities, as well as a desire to demonstrate their good will to the international audience. This specific factor is critical, and seems to support the assessment that killing as many people as possible was indeed not the principal goal of the operation.

The Negotiations: Successes and Missed Opportunities

As far as it is possible to analyze the negotiation approach to the Dubrovka crisis from open sources, there appears to have been a number of substantial mistakes and several key missed opportunities on the part of the Russians.

The first and possibly most significant blunder in the ordeal was the inability or unwillingness of the Russian authorities to establish an effective means of communication – without communication, there can be no negotiation. Further, the more reliable the communication links are, the greater the opportunities for the negotiator to establish a level of familiarity and rapport with the hostage-takers. The negotiator can then use active listening skills to express empathy with the hostage-takers in order to provide them with the feeling that they have someone who understands them, whom they can trust, and who has the ability to help them.

The negotiations in the Dubrovka incident (or "contacts", as one of the negotiators called them) were conducted mainly through face-to-face interactions and via a cellular phone that the hostage-takers had taken from one of the hostages. In addition, the hostage-takers made several of their demands indirectly, using journalists, media interviews, released hostages, pre-filmed video statements, and their website (www.kavkaz.org). The authorities also appear to have relied on indirect communication at times, making public announcements that carried a message for the hostage-takers with the knowledge that the people inside were watching the television broadcasts. One of the main problems of the selected communication strategy was that it relied too heavily on proxies. In fact, there seems to have been a complete absence of a trained principal negotiator conducting the majority of discussions with the terrorists! Among the people who spoke directly to the Chechens were Russian journalist Anna Politkovskaya, famous artist Iosif Kobzon, politicians Boris Nemtsov, Irina Khakamada, Aslanbek Aslakhanov and Ruslan Khasbulatov, doctor Leonid Roshal, several Red Cross representatives, and presidential plenipotentiary representative Viktor Kazantsev. Virtually all of these people were prominent cultural figures whose involvement was demanded directly by the rebels. And while all of these individuals should be commended for their courage and desire to help, there were several problems with their engagement. First, they lacked training and even basic instructions from the authorities on how to behave, what to say, what to do in certain situations, and what to avoid. In fact, the negotiators were given almost no overall guidance, and there appears to have been little interest in the negotiation progress achieved by their efforts – the authorities were much more interested in the tactical intelligence gained by their presence inside the theater (Politkovskaya interview 2003). The commanders of the operation also demonstrated alarmingly little hesitation to send the proxy figures directly to the rebels, despite the fact that face-to-face negotiations with hostage-takers are generally not advisable (Fuselier, 1986). This is especially true in cases where the presence of the persons doing the negotiating has been requested by the hostage-takers directly, as this request may be an indication of ulterior motives. And while the safety of those who went inside was largely self-evident since their selection by the rebels had likely been motivated by their favorable public stance on the Chechen issue, there was little reason for not attempting to conduct telephone negotiations first. Even if the hostage-takers had refused this offer, the situation would have opened up a vast array of opportunities for exchange. Negotiators should never give anything to hostage-takers without getting something back. Face-to-face negotiation with people of the terrorists' liking should therefore have been exchanged for the release of some hostages (after all, the release of a few people from among some 900 hostages may not have made a huge difference in the terrorists' eyes), or at least for a public guarantee of the negotiators' safety. While this may seem like a small concession, getting the hostage-takers in the habit of making promises not to hurt their hostages is a useful starting point for establishing mutual trust. Alternatively, a condition could have been attached allowing the terrorists to select only one person to act as the mediator throughout the entire crisis. This would have enabled the development of rapport between this individual and the hostage-takers, and would have made keeping track of events, demands and conditions much easier (Fuselier 1986).

Another critical flaw was the Russians' understandable yet unfortunate lack of patience. On one hand, it is comprehensible that prolonging the incident would have been difficult from a political standpoint, especially for president Putin, who had won his mandate precisely by taking a tough stance on the issue of Chechnya. Also, it is possible to understand the desire to end the suffering of hostages, who were subjected to very challenging mental and physical conditions. On the other hand, prolonging the incident would have improved the chances of a peaceful resolution of the incident and increased the hostages' chances for survival. And while the hostages would have suffered from the lack of food, water, medicines, and fresh air, so would the hostage-takers. This would have created an atmosphere of "shared misery" for everyone inside, which has a bonding effect. Such misery, combined with a common negative attitude toward the authorities because they seem to be doing nothing to resolve the crisis, creates a favorable environment for the formation of the Stockholm Syndrome, a mutually positive relationship between the hostage-takers and the hostages (Poland and McCrystle 2000). This relationship serves to humanize the victims to their captors, making it psychologically more difficult for the terrorists to proceed with executions. Since most hostages reported that they were not mistreated by the terrorists, the conditions necessary for the formation of the Stockholm Syndrome were most likely present. Thus, efforts of the Russian authorities should have focused primarily on enhancing this syndrome rather than on the political impossibility of meeting the instrumental demands made by the terrorists.

It also seems that the terrorists were interested in prolonging the incident as much as possible, as demonstrated by the fact that they requested to speak to people whose transportation to Moscow would take a significant amount of time.[27] One of the terrorists confirmed this point in a telephone interview with the Russian media, when he responded to the remark that pulling troops out of Chechnya would take time by stating that the commando unit was "in no particular hurry". In most barricade hostage incidents, it is the authorities who attempt to prolong the incident in order to apply the standardized negotiation approach. In Moscow, not only was the situation reversed, but the Russian leadership appears to have further enforced a self-imposed deadline on the negotiations. This was a colossal mistake – the ordeal was intense to begin with, and self-imposed deadlines only add to the pressure on everyone involved, particularly the negotiators. Even more importantly, once such a decision is made, any progress in the negotiation process is viewed by the command center with high skepticism, resulting in the de facto elimination of the chances for a peaceful settlement.

Another serious mistake, albeit a hypothetical one, was the offer made by Moscow Mayor Luzhkov to exchange himself as a substitute hostage. The introduction of a new hostage would have disrupted formation of the Stockholm Syndrome on the inside, and would have also unnecessarily raised tensions and fears among the responders on the outside (Fuselier, 1986). It is questionable, for instance, whether the authorities would still have been able to proceed so decisively with the assault had one of the most influential men in the country been a potential victim. Another reason why the exchange was a misguided suggestion is the fact that substitute hostages in general tend to have an increased sense of urgency and often feel compelled to try to change the situation from the inside. This usually brings them to the terrorists' attention, which in combination with the complete absence of the Stockholm Syndrome causes them to be the first ones selected for execution. This would have been a likely outcome with Luzhkov, who as a top politician would have also undoubtedly been perceived as a party to the Chechen conflict. Fortunately, the terrorists did not agree to the substitution of hostages.

The next significant flaw of the operation was the manner in which the authorities handled the question of the terrorists' demands. There seems to have been an unfortunate and excessive focus on the substantive nature of the demands, for example the unacceptability of withdrawing troops form Chechnya. However, this general demand had many expressive components to which the negotiations could have been diverted: the desire for peace, putting a stop to Russian mop-up operations, acknowledgement of the human rights violations in Chechnya, and so on. While some of the negotiators, including Boris Nemtsov, Anna Politkovkaya, and Iosif Kobzon, did intuitively incorporate the expression of understanding and empathy to calm the terrorists down and build rapport, there seems to have been no effort on behalf of the authorities to do the same. Also, the excessive focus on the nature of the general demand to end war in Chechnya prevented the authorities from focusing on specific opportunities that were provided to them. For example, Abu Bakar had stated on several occasions that 50 additional hostages would be released if the head of the Chechen administration, Akhmat Kadyrov, arrived in Moscow (FBIS ID# CEP20021024000326). Reprehensibly, this clear opportunity to save lives was missed. At another point, the rebels stated that "[they] shall be prepared to let go all hostages whose countries are not at war with Chechnya" (FBIS ID# CEP20021028000250). This provided a clear logic that should have consistently been used against the terrorists themselves until all foreign hostages were released. This is not to suggest that the lives of foreign nationals were more important but rather that sound logic for their release was provided by the terrorists themselves, creating the opportunity to reiterate that logic.[28] Emphasis should have also been placed on the large number of hostages, with the point being that the release of several people would not make much difference to the hostage takers. A similar rationale was apparently used with respect to other groups of hostages such as women, children, and the injured, but the terrorists refused this reasoning based on the principle of reciprocity: they argued that since Russian soldiers did not recognize the innocence of Chechen women and children, they did not feel compelled to do so either (Politkovskaya, 2002). While this explanation sounds rather cold-blooded, it reiterated that the terrorists did follow a certain pattern in logic, and that their actions were from this perspective quite rational.

Other problems with the way the negotiations were handled related to careless counteroffers. The terrorists had clearly stated in their discussions with Politkovskaya that the Russians were free to try to bargain for the hostages, but that the issue of the terrorists' safety should not even be brought up, as they were *sahedeen* (martyrs) who had come to Moscow to die. To support this claim, they stated that even if all the demands were met and the hostages were then released, they would still fight to the death with the Russian forces outside (Politkovskaya interview 2003). Nevertheless, on the second day of the standoff, the authorities offered them free passage in exchange for the lives of the hostages, which ultimately angered the terrorists and served as a pretext for rescinding an agreement to release all foreign nationals. Despite the failure of this tactic, the authorities made exactly the same mistake on day three of the standoff: a new deal to release the non-Russian hostages was stalled by a public promise to spare the lives of the terrorists if all hostages were released unharmed. This apparently led the hostage-takers to renew their threats to start killing hostages in the morning. Either by carelessness or by intent, the authorities' actions were responsible for the escalation of the situation. At the same time, certain indications exist that this criticism may be completely unfounded. According to anonymous sources within the FSB, the authorities were in fact eventually successful in striking a deal with the hostage-takers that featured precisely the exchange of hostages for a free passage out of Moscow (Soldatov interview 2003). The same source also claims that the terrorists were celebrating this deal in the bar area when the assault began, which would explain why many of them were killed in the corridors and why the trace odor of alcohol was reportedly detected on the breath of several of the terrorists.

Whether this claim is true or not is uncertain, but one thing seems clear: the Russian authorities, either due to inability or unwillingness, failed to fully exploit the opportunities to negotiate a peaceful settlement to the crisis. For instance, the authorities refused to grant some very concrete and feasible concessions, such as bringing in the Chechen official in exchange for 50 hostages, while at the same time making allowances without gaining anything in return, as in the issue of proxy negotiators. It seems that in Moscow, the political realities and the desire to teach the Chechens a lesson outweighed the concern for the lives of individual hostages.

Despite this notion, however, reaching a negotiated solution would not have been easy. The rebels had prepared themselves extremely well and had made arrangements that directly obstructed many elements that hostage negotiators commonly rely upon. For instance, the rebels were prepared to starve throughout the crisis, and even turned off the ventilation system in order to preempt the authorities from imposing agonizing conditions inside the auditorium. For the hostage negotiators, who normally seek to create such conditions in order to draw the hostage-takers' attention toward elementary needs such as hunger or thirst as opposed to their original demands, this presented a real obstruction. Under normal circumstances, items such as food, water, and air conditioning become commodities that can be exchanged for the release of several hostages or some other concessions on the part of the terrorists. In Moscow, however, the hostage-takers' tough stance on these issues created a reversed situation in which it was the authorities who had to make concessions in order to be allowed to bring in food. This effectively robbed the negotiators of much bargaining power by undermining their ability to create new items for trade. If in fact the Chechens took these preemptive measures intentionally, it only reiterates the meticulous preparation and planning efforts that went into the operation.

The Assault

Before any meaningful analysis of the assault can take place it must first be emphasized that once the decision to raid the theater was made, the primary objective of the operation became to negate the rebels' capacity to detonate their explosives, in order to avoid a "total loss" situation in which all hostages would have been killed. Limiting the overall number of casualties among the hostages was only a secondary objective, a point that is critical to the understanding of the assault. Illustrating this is the fact that Russian security agency analysts apparently preset a maximum number of casualties for the raid: 150 hostages (FBIS ID# CEP20021028000333). Given these objectives then, what can be said about the planning done and approach ultimately taken by the Spetsnaz?

Regardless of when the decision was made to raid the theater,[29] preparations by Spetsnaz units appear to have been ongoing from the outset of the crisis. While some reports suggest that these units had practiced the raid the previous day at the Meridian House of Culture (Myers 2002), a similar theater seven miles across the city, unit leaders deny any such rehearsal. Instead, they claim to have relied solely on a detailed floorplan of the Dubrovka theater, information gleaned from the thorough debriefing of released hostages, and intelligence on terrorist and hostage locales that was continually being acquired from auditory devices and covert surveillance cameras (Soldatov interview 2002). The presence of these cameras, not previously reported, may explain how the terrorists' leadership was so quickly located and eliminated as the assault began. The cameras may also have prevented the incidental targeting of the aforementioned "Nord-Ost" actors who, because their costumes consisted of camouflaged military uniforms, were strategically placed throughout the auditorium by the rebels with the apparent hope that an infiltrating assault team would shoot them. Certainly, training was of benefit in this instance as well: forces did not open fire without verifying their targets.

The diversionary approach ultimately taken during the assault, whether intentional or coincidental, was highly effective in drawing a significant number of hostage-takers out of the auditorium and away from the main explosive devices. The swift action by which Spetsnaz units eliminated the rebels' chain-of-command appears to have been a vital step toward achieving this objective as well. According to Politkovskaya, Chechen units are organized in a strict hierarchical order in which everyone has his or her specific role. It is quite possible that the explosives were never detonated because of the absence of a final order, which could only have come from the group's commander. On the other hand, according to inside sources, the explosive devices were not functional to begin with. Of course, there was another factor at play here: the gas delivered into the theater.

While the use of a chemical substance was largely viewed as a wholly novel approach to conflict resolution at the time of the raid, a number of precedents do in fact exist for such a tactic. Tear gas has historically been the agent of choice in this regard. The first such recorded use dates back to 1968, when a Pan Am DC6B was hijacked by a US marine in South Vietnam. Canisters of tear gas were thrown into the plane's passenger compartment as it was taxiing down the runway, providing the opportunity for a Pan Am flight engineer to overpower the marine (Mickolus 1980: 82). Throughout the 1980s and 90s, and as recently as the year 2000, similar cases have been reported.

Alternative approaches to using chemical substances have been documented as well. One of the earliest examples occurred during the infamous hostage-taking of Israeli athletes at the 1972 Olympic Games in Munich. Police involved in the subsequent hostage negotiations reportedly considered sending the terrorists food that had been poisoned (Mickolus 1980: 338–9).[30] In another incident three years later, negotiators considered ending an 18-hour standoff with hostage-takers holed up in a bathroom at France's Orly Airport by using a laser to create a hole in the bathroom door and then flooding the room with a nerve agent. This idea was eventually rejected because officials could not identify an appropriately fast-acting chemical (Mickolus 1980: 502–3). And in 1976, police successfully freed the seven hostages of a hijacked Indian Airlines B737 by using an unnamed sedative to taint the water that was given to the hijackers (Mickolus 1980: 643).[31]

The main problem with using a given chemical agent to resolve a hostage incident is limiting the level of hostage exposure to the agent in question.[32] For example, it has been reported that the US Army once rejected a plan to drug the food that was to be delivered to terrorists in an unidentified hostage situation, precisely because officials could not determine what dosage the hostages themselves might ingest (Barnard and Filipov 2002). This was of course the key question in the Moscow hostage crisis as well. In this instance, however, it was concluded that the potential benefits of terrorist exposure to the agent outweighed the costs in terms of hostage casualties, and in accordance with the primary objective of the assault, namely to avoid a total loss situation over all else, this reasoning holds.

What is far more difficult to rationalize, however, is why officials withheld a number of vital facts from medical responders both on the scene and at the hospitals where intoxicated hostages were eventually taken. First, it was not revealed that gas would be used until the assault was at hand, and as a result responders were inadequately prepared to treat the incoming patient load. Second, even when responders learned that gas had been used, they were not told what gas it was specifically, and thus treatment was either delayed, inappropriate, or in many cases not provided at all. Third, while multiple reports indicate that some responders were at some point informed that naloxone (Narcan) should be used to treat the hostages, this information was not provided early on. As a result, the drug was in vastly limited supply at the scene, and by the time hostages arrived at area hospitals it was often too late for such treatment to be effective. And finally, although the theater was reportedly littered with empty syringes after the raid, indicating that some Spetsnaz commandos had been armed with antidotes for the gas, it seems likely that this supply was rapidly depleted and ultimately of limited utility due to the overwhelming number of hostages in need of treatment. Therefore, what could conceivably have been a very manageable event from a medical standpoint had adequate consequence management measures been in place turned out to be a nightmare scenario in which 128 hostages ultimately died (Myers 2002).

Days after the assault took place, Russian Health Minister Yuri L. Shevchenko, apparently pressured by speculations that a substance prohibited by the Chemical Weapons Convention (CWC) had been used, announced that the gas delivered into the theater had been a derivative of the highly potent opioid fentanyl (Wines 2002).[33] This was not the first time that fentanyl had been used in a counterterrorist operation. In 1997, this chemical was reportedly utilized in the failed Mossad assassination attempt against Khalid Mishal, head of Hamas' political bureau in Jordan (Zanders 1999: 19). Commonly used in combination with other anesthetics in Western operating rooms, fentanyl is characterized by the rapid onset and short duration (15 to 30 minutes) of analgesia, and its analogs have similar effects. As is the case with all opioids, the most common and serious side effect of fentanyl is respiratory depression, the effect realized so tragically on 26 October 2002. This chemical has a notoriously narrow therapeutic index (therapeutic dose versus lethal dose), meaning that its administration in doses only marginally higher than those required to create the desired analgesic effect presents a significant risk to the recipient.

Given these properties, two arguments persist regarding the effects of the gas witnessed in the Moscow hostage crisis. The most prominent argument is that in calculating the amount of gas to be delivered into the theater, officials failed to consider that the debilitated physical and psychological status of the hostages would increase their susceptibility to the effects of the gas (Fisher 2002).[34] When fentanyl is used in a hospital setting, patients are similarly stressed, often resulting in a greater than expected effect of the gas. Respiratory depression in this setting can – and often does – occur. In a hospital setting, however, naloxone is readily available to reverse the effects of the drug, and ventilators are standing by if needed. These measures were not adequately available during the Moscow crisis, however, and thus the effects of the gas went largely unchecked. The alternative argument is that because rapid induction of anesthesia was seen as necessary in order to achieve the primary objective of the operation, and because such induction invariably causes respiratory depression, this effect was not only expected but in fact desired by officials at the scene (MacKenzie and Carrington 2002). The point to be taken from this discussion is that regardless of the amount of agent delivered into the theater and the motivation behind such delivery, losses would likely have been minimized had a rapid response capability been in place.

Conclusions

The negotiation attempt by the Russian authorities during the Moscow crisis suffered from many major flaws. At the same time, the Chechens' preparation and management of the operation were exceptionally professional, making *any* resolution extremely difficult. Whether the crisis could have been ended through negotiation is questionable, even though the authors of this article are convinced that many of the positive indicators suggesting this possibility were present. However, it seems that the Russian authorities had no intention of yielding to the terrorists in order to get the hostages out alive. The whole negotiations period seems to have been designed to provide a public relations alibi for exhausting all peaceful options and justifying the assault, as opposed to actually trying to accomplish a peaceful resolution. While the logic for not yielding to terrorists is sound from a political standpoint, it is unfortunate that the negotiation approach was never given a real chance, and that the time between the terrorists' takeover of the theater and the assault was not used more constructively.

The assault itself was carried out very well despite the dubious use of gas. A much greater flaw than the use of the gas itself, however, was the failure of the commanders to notify the medical responders of its use beforehand and to make all of the necessary arrangements for consequence management. It was precisely this part of the rescue mission that was responsible for the deaths of all but two of the 128 fatalities. The most unfortunate aspect of this is that while the decision to sacrifice the hostages was driven by political considerations, the consequence management blunders negated many of the political benefits that might have resulted from a forceful resolution in that they ultimately helped the terrorists achieve their objectives: the rebels succeeded not only in putting the issue of Chechnya back on the forefront of international debate but also in forcing the Russian government to kill its own citizens. And while the international community largely condemned the Chechen actions in Moscow, the Chechen leadership can effectively defuse these reactions by denying its role in the attack. Therefore, although unsuccessful in forcing the withdrawal of Russian troops from Chechnya, the Moscow operation served the Chechens' purpose very well.

There are several important implications of the solution used in the Dubrovka hostage crisis for the future. First, hostages in the future, having seen the casualties resulting from the Russian response, may decide that their chance of survival is so minimal that attacking the hostage-takers or attempting to flee is worth the risk. This effect is similar to the apparent mindset of airline passengers as a result of the September 11th attacks, but while fighting back on an airplane may be a good idea simply because the attackers are unlikely to be very well-armed, doing the same in barricade incidents will likely result in the deaths of many hostages. This in turn will complicate subsequent negotiation efforts by tarnishing the hostage-takers' "clean record" in terms of killing hostages, which is one of the strong persuasive elements negotiators use to facilitate surrender in the final stages of an incident. Further, the commanders of hostage response teams become less amenable to pursuing the negotiation option once hostages have been killed.

Another implication of the Moscow incident is that the possibility of gas being used in a rescue mission will undoubtedly translate into preparations for this measure on behalf of future hostage-takers. As a result, we are likely to see gas masks among the terrorists' equipment in future hostage incidents. Since incidents similar to the Dubrovka crisis are likely to occur in the future, this brings out the question of response: how does one respond to terrorist hostage incidents in which there seems to be little willingness to compromise and in which the terrorists are not just willing to die but actually desire such an outcome? One possibility may be to attempt to persuade them that their operation has already succeeded by drawing worldwide attention to their cause. The terrorist could then be reminded that this publicity could however very quickly turn against this cause if hostages are killed. While these attempts are likely to be refuted, the negotiator may then be successful in challenging the terrorists to die "honorably" in a fight against the "infidel" as opposed to murdering unarmed women and children in cold blood. The option of releasing hostages and then dying in an encounter with the security forces outside may be enough to satisfy those who have staged their operation with the ultimate goal of their own dramatic demise. While this option is by no means attractive, it may very well be one of the few negotiation approaches that could succeed in preventing significant loss of life among hostages as the outcome of suicide missions.

Acknowledgements

The authors would like to gratefully acknowledge the kind help of Ms. Anna Politkovskaya, Mr. Andrey Soldatov, and Mr. Boris Nemtsov, whose firsthand insights into the tragic events of the Dubrovka crisis were invaluable to this analysis. The authors would also like to thank Ms. Ekaterina Shutova for her excellent interpretation services and Mr. Bryan Traverso for his able research assistance.

Notes

1. Some sources say several jeeps, some several microbuses, some three minivans, and others two white buses.
2. According to some sources close to Basayev, the initial plan of the Budyonnovsk siege was to attack an unspecified target in Moscow. These sources claim that Budyonnovsk became a substitute target only after Basayev ran out of bribe money for Russian military checkpoints. (Aukai, Collins (2002) *My Jihad*, New York: Pocket Star Books).
3. Rudayev died on 15/12/02 of internal bleeding while serving a life sentence in Solikamsk prison in the Urals.
4. For instance, one of the Russian units did actually succeed in reaching the location where the hostages were held but was forced to retreat due to friendly fire from a Russian helicopter.
5. According to Russian authorities however, the operation was carried out with Maskhadov's blessing. This seems to be confirmed by the fact that one of the rebels encouraged the negotiators to speak directly to Maskhadov.
6. An unusual event that does not appear to have been directly involved in the triggering of the raid but which deserves mention nonetheless occurred around the time that the Spetsnaz forces were arriving outside. A man with bloodied hands and face suddenly appeared in the theater's lobby, claiming to be the father of one of the hostages. He said that he had forcefully penetrated police lines to reach the building's interior, hence his traumatized body. The Chechens immediately suspected that he was a Russian agent, a suspicion that is supported in most analyses of the incident. When the man's son could not be located, he was beaten, dragged off, and presumably shot. (BBC October 29, 2002); (*Moscow Times*, October 28, 2002); (CNN, October 28, 2002).
7. Some accounts suggest that this was the same bullet, which had continued on after passing through the man's head.
8. Both victims of the shooting were reportedly carried from the theater some time later but before the assault. (FBIS ID# CEP20021028000333); (*Washington Post* October 27, 2002).
9. Again, reports conflict: some hostages claim to have smelled the gas, some to have seen it, others to have felt its effects (namely disorientation, dizziness, and euphoria), and still others to have lost consciousness without any recognition whatsoever. Borisova, Yevgenia "The Gas Saved Them, the Gas Killed Them". (*Moscow Times* October 28, 2002); McGeary, Johanna and Paul Quinn "Theatre of War". (*TIME Europe* 160:19, 4 November 2002); Dunn, Newton Tom "Moscow Siege". (*Mirror*, pg. 11 October 28, 2002). Fisher, Matthew "Poison gas killed 115 hostages: Government slow to reveal details of raid". (*National Post* pg. A1); "Hostages speak of storming terror". (BBC October 26, 2002).
10. The Chechens had disabled the air conditioning system early on in the raid. Dunn, Newton Tom "Moscow Siege". (*Mirror* pg. 11. October 28, 2002); "How special forces ended siege". (BBC October 29, 2002).
11. These respirators likely offered only minimal protection against the gas, but some protection nonetheless. "A Man, A Bottle, A Shot, Then Gas". (*Moscow Times* October 28, 2002); Dunn, Newton Tom "Moscow Siege". (*Mirror*, pg. 11 October 28, 2002); "How special forces ended siege". (BBC October 29, 2002).

12. Areas removed from the influx of the gas are thought to include the corridor and balcony.
13. Some sources have stated that the mail explosive charge was found to be non-functional (Soldatov interview, 2003). Nevertheless, the authorities understandably had to operate under the assumption that the charge could be detonated at any moment.
14. These so-called "temporal associations" reflect the relative timing, based on witness descriptions, of gunfire, explosions, and actions both outside and within the theater.
15. FBIS ID# CEP20021114000199 Moscow Rossiyskaya Gazeta in Russian 12 Nov 02, Natalya Kozlova, interview in Rossiyskaya Gazeta's editorial office with five officers of the Alfa and Vympel special subunits, introduced only by their forenames and patronymics, not surnames; date of interview not given: "Soldiers of Last Resort. Fighters From the Alfa and Vympel Special Subunits Answer Our Newspaper's Questions", taken from HTML version of source provided by ISP (FBIS); *Hostages speak of storming terror* (October 26, 2002) BBC; *A Man, A Bottle, A Shot, Then Gas* (October 28, 2002). The Moscow Times.
16. One witness claimed that when the shots were first heard, those rebels still conscious told the hostages to take cover in their seats, a confusing action if the intention was to detonate the bombs and kill those same hostages upon identification of a hostile force within the theater. *How special forces ended siege* (October 29, 2002) BBC. Another hostage claimed that the reaction of the rebels did not in any way suggest a desire to inflict harm on the hostages. *Hostages speak of storming terror* (October 26, 2002) BBC.
17. For a list of names of all of the missing individuals see <http://zalozhniki.ru>.
18. He also reportedly ordered the beheading of three Britons and one New Zealander in 1998 who were building a cell phone network in Chechnya.
19. Abu Bakar is a allegedly pseudonym for a Barayev's close associate Yusupov, who however was supposedly killed two years ago, according to the Russian military.
20. This is sometimes reported as Prisoners of Islam, or the 29th Suicide Division.
21. Interestingly, Barayev was the head of the Special Purpose Islamic Regiment. Whether there is a difference between these – or any – Chechen groups is uncertain.
22. It seems that the group was keen on attacking a theater in Moscow from the very beginning, supported by the fact that a videotape indicating the Moskovky Dvorets Molodyozhi (MDM) Theater as another possible target was recovered from one of the dead hostage-takers. Abdullaev, Nabi: (6 November 2002) *Picture Emerges of How They Did It*, Moscow Times.
23. Tickets for the show were not cheap, selling for 450 to 1000 Rubles (approximately 14 to 42 US dollars). At the same time, the musical had played long enough for celebrities and the rich to have already attended the show.
24. In fact, the Chechen groups especially have a history of using suicide truck bombings with the principal goal of solidifying the fighters' morale.
25. Even before the Moscow hostage incidents, groups in Chechnya had conducted at least seven suicide truck bombings and a number of suicidal assassinations of Russian military officials, with the most significant operation being a coordinated attack of five suicide truck bombers who blew up military checkpoints and a police dormitory in 2000, killing 33 people and injuring 84. According to Anna Politkovskaya, the hostage-takers performed traditional Chechen preparations for death. Also, many of the terrorists spoke to Politkovskaya in a confessional mode and sometimes asked her to pass messages on to their families (Politkovskaya interview 2003).
26. The Chechens later claimed that this woman was a Russian intelligence officer, who was trying to infiltrate the scene. A similar tactic was reportedly used by the Spetsnaz in the Budyonnovsk siege as well.
27. Politkovskaya, for instance, had to fly in from the US, where she was receiving a prestigious jour-

nalist award. Among the other individuals with whom the terrorists demanded to speak was Yegor Yavlinsky, who was also out of the country.

28. In most hostage incidents, the negotiators task is to invent a logic for the release of a certain hostage (or a group of hostages) and than to persuade the hostage-taker(s) about the validity of this logic. Rarely do the hostage-taker(s) offer such logic voluntarily, and when they do, it is regarded by hostage negotiators as an excellent opportunity to achieve the release of a number of hostages. The failure of the Russian authorities to exploit such a great opportunity in Moscow was a colossal mistake.

29. Some sources say that the decision was made to raid the theater during the first hours of the crisis, on the very night of the theater's seizure, while others state that a final decision was made only hours before the actual assault took place. FBIS ID# CEP20021028000333 Moscow Moskovskiy Komsomolets in Russian 28 Oct 02 P 2, Natalya Galimova, Denis Belikov, Marat Khayrullin, and Yuriy Gavrilov: "Was Assault Scheduled As Far Back As Wednesday? Hostages' Bodies Piled Up" (FBIS); FBIS ID# CEP20021026000162 Moscow RTR Planeta TV in Russian 1010 GMT 26 Oct 02.

30. Interestingly, it has been reported that as a result of this event, the two 21-story towers of Montreal's Olympic Village – which housed athletes during the follow-up 1976 Olympic Games – were equipped with a security device capable of releasing incapacitating gas into any or all of the towers' individual suites. Brennan, Pat: (July 28, 2001) *Olympic Village still a champion site*, Toronto Star.

31. It has also been suggested that tunnels dug beneath the Japanese ambassador's residence in Lima, Peru during the 126-day hostage stand-off with Tupac Amaru guerillas were intended as conduits for the introduction of gas during a possible assault. Stead, Geoff: (April 23, 1997) *Freedom amid rebel firefight*, Daily Telegraph.

32. In the wake of 9/11, it was suggested that airlines might someday equip their planes with dispersal devices capable of flooding the cabin with a calmative agent in the event of a hijacking, particularly because current gas masks cannot be concealed at airport security checkpoints and thus hijackers would be largely unprotected against such an action. It is the authors' hope that passenger safety, as reflected by the level of hostage exposure to the agent in question, is of primary consideration if such a measure is undertaken. Shalom, Francois: (September 15, 2001) *Airline focuses on El Al's security tactics*, The Gazette (Montreal).

33. It should be noted, however, that the fentanyl derivative may have been delivered into Dubrovka theater in combination with another chemical, and further that a fentanyl derivative may in fact have not been used at all. Toxic analyses and insider accounts have named multiple other agents in the assault; some have denied the use of fentanyl altogether. The authors have accepted the official Russian declaration in this case but have formulated conclusions independent of the type of gas used.

34. In addition, subscribers to this theory note that a given hostage's proximity to the gas' point of release may have played a role in determining his or her outcome as well, with those individuals closest to the gas' infusion suffering the most significant effects. While conceptually this notion holds, no evidence, witness testimony or otherwise, has been brought to bear supporting or contradicting the theory in the Moscow theater hostage crisis.

References

Books, Articles, Interviews

Abdullaev, Nabi. "Picture Emerges of How They Did It". *Moscow Times* November 6, 2002.

Antokol, Nudell (1990) *No One a Neutral: Political Hostage Taking in the Modern World*. Alpha Publications.

Arquila, John and Karasik, Theodore (1999). "Chechnya: A Glimpse of Future Conflict?" *Studies in Conflict and Terrorism* 22: 207–229.

Baylon, Anne D. (1996) "Events of January 1996". Internet, available at <http://www.csdr.org/96Timelines/january96.htm> (accessed on 11/4/02).

Barnard, Anne and Filipov, David (2002) "Ways to subdue attackers probed". *Boston Globe* October 29.

Beaumont, Peter (2002) "The new romantics of death". *Observer* October 27.

Bolz, Frank, Jr., Dudonis, Kenneth and Schultz, David (2002) *The Counterterrorism Handbook: Tactics, Procedures and Techniques*. London: CRC Press 2nd edition.

Borisova, Yevgenia (2002) "The Gas Saved Them, the Gas Killed Them". *Moscow Times* October 28.

Boyle, Peter. Interview with Deynyseynko, Elley (2002) "*Rasskaz Cbiditeylnitsi zahvata zalozhnikov v Moskye*". ("Recollections of a Hostage in Moscow"). October 24. Radio Svoboda, available at <http://www.svoboda.org/ll/terror/1002/11.102402–6.asp> (accessed on 11/26/02).

Brennan, Pat (2001) "Olympic Village still a champion site". *Toronto Star* July 28.

Byrne, Cia (2002) "Journalist to negotiate in Moscow siege". *Guardian* October 25.

Dalziel, Stephen (2002) "Soviet methods for a Russian crisis". BBC News: World Edition October 28.

De Waal, Tom (1999) "Shamil Basayev: Chechen warlord". BBC News September 30.

Dolnik, Adam (2003) "Die and Let Die: Exploring Links between Suicide Terrorism and Terrorist Use of Chemical, Biological, Radiological, and Nuclear Weapons". *Studies in Conflict and Terrorism* 26,1: 17–35.

Dunn, Newton Tom (2002) "Moscow Siege". *Mirror*, pg. 11 October 28.

Dutton, Don (1986) "Hostage-taker shot with tear-gas powder". *Toronto Star* June 5.

E-mail correspondence with Andrey Soldatov. March 26, 2003.

Feifer, Gregory (2003) "Russia: Murky Information Complicates Hostage-Crisis Conclusions". Radio Free Europe. Internet, available at <http://www.rferl.org/nca/features/2002/11/12112002163511.asp> (accessed 7/3/2003).

Fisher, Matthew (2002) "Poison gas killed 115 hostages: Government slow to reveal details of raid". *National Post* pg. A1 October 28.

Fuselier, Dwayne (1986) "What Every Negotiator Would Like his Chief to Know". *FBI Law Enforcement Bulletin*.

Fuselier, Noesner (1990) "Confronting the Terrorist Hostage Taker". Internet, available at <http://www.emergency.com/host-tkr.htm> (accessed 1/29/02).

Glasser, Susan B. (2002) "Rescue Ended Days of Horror And Uncertainty". *Washington Post* pg. A1 October 27.

Glasser, Susan B. and Baker, Peter (2002) "Russia Seizes Theater From Rebels". *Washington Post* pg. A1 October 27.

Golovnina, Maria and Bullough, Oliver (2002) "Armed Chechens seize hundreds in Moscow theatre". *Muslim News* October 23.

Gousseva, Maria (2002) "Terrorists Had Laid Over 30 Explosives in the Theatre". *Pravda* October 26, 2002.

Hayes, Richard (2002) "Negotiations with Terrorists". In Victor Kremenyuk (ed.), *International Negotiation*. San Francisco: Jossey-Bass.

Hudson, Rex A. (1999) *Who becomes a terrorist and why*. Guilford: The Lyons Press.

Interview with Anna Politkovskaya. March 19, 2003.

Kline, Chris and Franchietti, Mark (2002) "The woman behind the Mask". *Timesonline* November 3. Intertnet, available at <http://www.timesonline.co.uk/printFriendly/0,,1–3505–469538,00.htlm> (accessed 3/24/03).

Leinwand, Donna and Bowles, Scott (2000) "Gunman fires shots in Maryland". *USA Today* March 21.

MacKenzie, Debora and Carrington, Damian (2002) "Russia finally names mystery gas". *NewScientist.com* October 30.

Main, Frank (2000) "Bringing them out alive". *Chicago Sun-Times* August 25.

McGeary, Johanna and Quinn, Paul (2002) "Theatre of War". *TIME Europe*, 160: 19. November 4.

McMahon, Colin (2002) "Why didn't the Russians negotiate?" *Chicago Tribune* November 3.

McMains, M.J., and Mullins, W.C. (2001) *Crisis negotiations: Managing critical incidents and hostage situations in law enforcement and corrections* (2nd ed.). Cincinnati, OH: Anderson.

Mickolus, Edward F. (1980) *Transnational Terrorism: A Chronology of Events, 1968–1979*. Westport: Greenwood Press.

Myers, Steven Lee (2002) "From Anxiety, Fear and Hope, the Deadly Rescue in Moscow". *New York Times* November 1.

Poland J.M. and McCrystle, M.J. (1999) *Practical, Tactical, and Legal Perspectives of Terrorism and Hostage-taking*. Lewiston, NY: E. Mellon Press.

Politkovskaya, Anna (2002) "Inside a Moscow Theatre with the Chechen Rebels". International Women's Media Foundation. Internet, available at <http://www.iwmf.org/features/anna> (accessed on 11/21/02).

Quinn-Judge, Paul (2002) "The Man Who would be Martyred". *Time Europe* November 4.

Robertson, Ian and Lamberti, Rob (1995) "Siege ends with volley of tear gas". *Toronto Sun* July 8.

Royson, James (1988) "OPP probes police killing of hostage taker". *Toronto Star* August 27.

Shalom, Francois (2001) "Airline focuses on El Al's security tactics". *Gazette* (Montreal) September 15.

Shleynov, Roman (2002) "*Posleoperatsionniy period. Spasti mozhem. Vykhodit-net*". ("Post-operation period: Rescue is possible, escape is not"). *Novaya gazeta* October 31.

Singh, Charu (2002) "Terror in Moscow". *Frontline* 19: 3 November.

Stead, Geoff (1997) "Freedom amid rebel firefight". *Daily Telegraph* April 23.

Strentz, Thomas (1995) "The Cyclic Crisis Negotiations Time Line". *Law and Order*.

Strentz, Thomas (1991) "13 Indicators of Volatile Negotiations". *Law and Order*.

Traynor, Ian and Paton-Walsh, Nick (2002) "Tension binds captors and captives". *Guardian,* October 26.

Tsvetkova, Maria (2002) "Chechen women to drive killer trucks". *Gazeta.ru*. October 29. Internet, available at <http://www.gazeta.ru/2002/10/29/Chechenwomen.shtml> (accessed 7/3/03)

Tyler, Tracy (1990) "Police use tear gas to nab hostage-taker". *Toronto Star* pg. A20. March 18.

Venzke, Ben and Ibrahim, Aimee (2003) *The al-Qaeda Threat: An Analytical Guide to al-Qaeda's Tactics and Targets*. Alexandria: Tempest Publishing.

Warner, Margaret (2002) "Terrorism in Moscow". Newshour with Jim Lehrer October 24.

Williams, Brian (2000) "Shamil Baseyev, Chechen Field Commander: Russia's Most Wanted Man". *Central Asia Caucus Analyst.*

Wines, Michael (2002) "Hostage Toll in Russia Over 100; Nearly All Deaths Linked to Gas". *New York Times* October 28.

Wines, Michael (2002) "Russia Names Drug in Raid, Defending Use". *New York Times* October 30.

Zanders, Jean Pascal (1999) "Assessing the risk of chemical and biological weapons proliferation to terrorists". *Nonproliferation Review* 6: 19.

Zartman, I. William (1990) "Negotiating Effectively With Terrorists". In Barry Rubin (ed.), *The Politics of Counterterrorism.* Washington, DC: The Johns Hopkins Foreign Policy Institute.

Authorless Press Reports

"A Man, A Bottle, A Shot, Then Gas". *Moscow Times* October 28, 2002.

"A package of Caribbean news briefs". Associated Press February 10, 1999.

"Barayev v prinsipe ni isklychayet vozmozhnoct osvobozhdeyniya zalozhnikov". ("Barayev does not rule out the possibility of releasing the hostages"). 25 October 2002. Internet, available at <http://www.gazeta.ru/cgi-bin/lastnews.cgi>.

"Hostages speak of storming terror". BBC October 26, 2002.

"How special forces ended siege". BBC October 29, 2002).

"Captives freed". *Independent* February 1, 1996.

"Chechen rebels' hostage history". BBC October 24, 2002.

"Tantrum' Sparked Theatre Raid". CNN October 28, 2002.

"Two hostages flee Moscow theatre". BBC News: World Edition 24 October 2002.

"Russia: Authorities Negotiating With Hostage Takers". October 24, 2002. Internet, available at <http://www.rferl.org/nca/features/2002/10/24102002095817.asp> (accessed on 11/26/02).

"Russia: Press Faces New Restrictions Following Hostage Crisis". October 24, 2002. Internet, available at <http://www.rferl.org/nca/features/2002/11/01112002183716.asp> (accessed on 11/26/02).

"Moscow Hostage-takers Threaten to Blow up Theater". October 24, 2002. Internet, available at <http://www.ict.org.il/spotlight/det.cfm?id=839> (accessed 3/12/03).

"Newspaper publishes interview with Barayev". *Russian Journal* October 28, 2002.

"Non-stop nightmare for Moscow hostages". BBC News: World Edition October 25, 2002.

"Nord-oct: ofitsialniye dahhye". ("Northeast official news"). November 5, 2002. Internet, available at <http://www.ng.ru/events/2002–11–05/10_official.htm>.

"Leading Chechens Negotiate with Moscow Hostage Takers". *People's Daily* October 24, 2002.

"Gunmen release chilling video". CNN.com: World October 25, 2002.

"Hostages speak of storming terror". BBC News: World Edition October 26, 2002.

"In quotes: Moscow hostage crisis". BBC News: World Edition October 25, 2002.

"Death toll among Moscow theatre victims rises to 120". November 4, 2002. Internet, available at <http://archives.tcm.ie/breakingnews/2002/11/04/story75389.asp> (accessed on 3/11/03).

"Film of siege from inside theatre shown on Russian TV". November 4, 2002. Internet, available at <http://archives.tcm.ie/breakingnews/2002/11/04/story75339.asp> (accessed on 3/11/03).

"Gas was only solution, says Moscow siege doctor". November 4, 2002. Internet, available at <http://archives.tcm.ie/breakingnews/2002/11/04/story75416.asp> (accessed on 3/11/03).

"Capture of Hostages in Moscow Museum of Peacekeeping Operations". October 25, 2002.

"Chechen warlord Basayev's statement on Moscow siege". *Johnson's Russian List* November 2, 2002.

"Rusko odškodní rodiny obětí z divadla". ("Russia will compensate the families of victims from

the theater"). iDnes. October 31, 2002. Internet, available at: <http://zpravy.idnes.cz/zahran-icni.asp?r=zahranicniandc=A021031_154003_zahranicni_kotandt=A021031_154003_zahran-icni_kotandr2=zahranicni>.

"*Rusko zvyšilo pocet obětí z divadla*". ("Russia increased the number of casualties inside the theater".) iDnes November 7, 2002. Internet, available at: <http://zpravy.idnes.cz/zahranicni.asp?r=zahranic-niandc=A021105_155047_zahranicni_andt=A021105_155047_zahranicni_andr2=zahranicni>.

"*Mrtvy šéf teroristů: Poslal nás Basajev*". ("Dead chief of terrorists: we were sent by Basayev"). iDnes October 26, 2002. Internet, available at: <http://zpravy.idnes.cz/zahranicni.asp?r=zahran-icniandc=A021026_150040_zahranicni_kotandt=A021026_150040_zahranicni_kotandr2=zahran icni>.

"*Rukojmí jedli cokoládu, komando hladoví*". ("Hostages ate chocolate, commandos are starving"). iDnes October 25, 2002. Internet, available at: <http://zpravy.idnes.cz/zahranicni.asp?r= zahranicniandc=A021025_122235_zahranicni_kotandl=1andt=A021025_122235_zahranicni_ kotandr2=zahranicni>.

"*Komando separatistůvede Movsar Barajev*". ("The separatist commando is lead by Barayev"). iDnes October 25, 2002. Internet, available at: <http://zpravy.idnes.cz/zahranicni.asp?r=zahranic-niandc=A021025_124233_zahranicni_kotandl=1andt=A021025_124233_zahranicni_kotandr2=z ahranicni>.

"*Čecenci vyhrozují zabíjením rukojmí*". ("The Chechens are threatening executions of hostages"). iDnes October 24, 2002. Internet, available at: <http://zpravy.idnes.cz/zahranicni.asp?r=zahran-icniandc=A021023_203718_zahranicni_kotandl=1andt=A021023_203718_zahranicni_kotandr2= zahranicni>.

"*Basajev se hlásí k prepadení divadla*". (Basayev claims credit for theater operation"). iDnes November 1, 2002. Internet, available at: <http://zpravy.idnes.cz/zahranicni.asp?r=zahranicniandc= A021101_153316_zahranicni_kotandt=A021101_153316_zahranicni_kotandr2=zahranicni>.

"Spetsnaz: Russia's elite force". BBC News: World Edition October 28, 2002.

"Transcript of hostages phone call". *Russia Journal* October 26, 2002.

"*Kto takoy Movsar Barayev*". ("Who is Movsar Barayev?"). (2002). Internet, available at <http://grani.ru/Events/Terror/m.13000.html> (accessed on 3/17/03).

FBIS ID# CEP20021026000162 Moscow RTR Planeta TV in Russian 1010 GMT 26 Oct 02 (FBIS).

FBIS ID# CEP20021028000333 Moscow Moskovskiy Komsomolets in Russian 28 Oct 02 P 2, Natalya Galimova, Denis Belikov, Marat Khayrullin, and Yuriy Gavrilov: "Was Assault Scheduled As Far Back As Wednesday? Hostages' Bodies Piled Up". (FBIS).

FBIS ID# CEP20021030000064 Moscow Rossiyskaya Gazeta in Russian 29 Oct 02 PP 1, 2 [Interview with unnamed chief of staff responsible for liberating the Moscow theater hostages by Natalya Kozlova; date, place not given: "Special Liberation Detachment. One of Chiefs of Staff for Liberation of Hostages Gives Exclusive Interview to Rossiyskaya Gazeta Correspondent"] (FBIS).

FBIS ID# CEP20021030000407 Moscow TVS in Russian 1800 GMT 29 Oct 02 (FBIS).

FBIS ID# CEP20021114000199 Moscow Rossiyskaya Gazeta in Russian 12 Nov 02, Natalya Kozlova, interview in Rossiyskaya Gazeta's editorial office with five officers of the Alfa and Vympel special subunits, introduced only by their forenames and patronymics, not surnames; date of interview not given: "Soldiers of Last Resort. Fighters From the Alfa and Vympel Special Subunits Answer Our Newspaper's Questions". Taken from HTML version of source provided by ISP (FBIS).

FBIS ID# CEP20021028000250 "Chechen Hostage Negotiator Nemtsov Interviewed on Talks". 10/28/2002 (FBIS).

FBIS ID# CEP20021024000569 "Russian source talks of 'pause' in developments surrounding hostage crisis". 24 Oct 02 (FBIS).

FBIS ID# CEP20021024000326 "Chechen hostage-takers set conditions for release of 50 more captives". 10/24/2002.

.

Negotiating with Villains Revisited: Research Note

BERTRAM I. SPECTOR

In 1998, I wrote an article that examined the decision process and conditions under which sovereign states sometimes agree to engage rogue states through peaceful negotiation rather than practice a no-negotiation policy or engage in hostilities (Spector 1998). The article reviewed the reasons for cutting off the negotiation option, the psychology of villainizing the enemy and its influence on closing the options for peaceful resolution of conflict between states. While the article focused on villains as states, its analysis is still current, given the US government's recent pronouncements about rogue states comprising the "Axis of Evil". But the article ignored another type of villain that has become a central focus of contemporary international relations – non-state villains, in particular, terrorists. This research note seeks to extend the ideas of the former article to examine if there are circumstances under which negotiation with *terrorist* villains is feasible.

Who constitutes a villain in international relations? A villain is an international actor that is perceived as believing or acting in a threatening or hostile fashion in contravention of or in a manner that is totally indifferent to accepted norms of particular societies and the international community. Participation in or support for terrorism, trafficking in illegal drugs, disregard for human rights, the routine use of torture, exporting revolution, explicit deception in international affairs, and illicit trade in banned weapons are often sufficient to label a state or group as a villain. For some of these issues, international agreements define the criteria for asserting villainy; some countries, like the United States, have developed their own criteria in national law.

The perceptual nature of this definition is critical in understanding villainization. Villainy is a relative concept. It is determined through the lens of the beholder. A terrorist to some might be considered a freedom fighter to others. It is often the case that villainy is a mutually held belief; a state that views another as a villain is likely to be viewed as a villain in return. So, just as the United States government labeled Iraq under Saddam Hussein as a villain because of state support for terrorism, human rights breaches, the use of torture, and the alleged development of weapons of mass destruction, Saddam's regime labeled the US as a villain for its alleged imperialist actions and support for Israel.

International Negotiation Series 1:
I.W. Zartman (ed.) Negotiating with Terrorists, 165–173
© 2006 *Koninklijke Brill NV. Printed in the Netherlands.*

Deciding to Negotiate with Villains

Dealing with villains poses a dilemma. Once labeled as a villain by the international community, it has become customary for a state or group to be ostracized from normal interaction. Because it does not abide by the rules and norms of international society, it gives up its rights to deal and be dealt with in a traditional way, and the "no-negotiation" doctrine takes effect. Negotiation is usually eliminated as an option to resolve conflicts with villains because the process is viewed as according legitimacy to the villain or worse yet, appeasing the villain. Accordingly, villains are usually given an ultimatum and if they do not comply, negative sanctions are made stricter, threats are hardened and violent conflict may be unleashed.

While these are the norms by which villains are managed, there are some who disagree with the policy. Eban (1994) argued that national leaders are obliged by their constituents to negotiate directly and early with villains, no matter how detestable, to achieve pragmatic compromises that will save lives if security is in danger. The ethical imperative of democratic leaders is to ensure the safety and security of their population, no matter what. Jimmy Carter (Rose 1995) also believes in this ethical imperative of leaders to practice negotiation, even with unsavory characters, to open communication and gain the respect and trust of the villain, in the hopes of resolving conflict peacefully. From a practical perspective, Fisher, Ury and Patton (1991) also encourage negotiation with villains, not for the ethical reasons of saving lives, but because that is the only way to exert meaningful influence over them and to search for a viable formula.

Empirically, several researchers have found that negotiation is indeed a viable mechanism to resolve conflicts with villains – especially in intrastate conflicts. Gurr (1992) concluded that negotiation was used successfully to find short-term peaceful solutions in ethnopolitical struggles where both sides are typically villainized. Richardson (1992) found that the negotiation process was helpful to leaders in managing deeply rooted disputes. Stedman, Rothchild and Cousens (2002) present many cases in which negotiation and mediation were used to successfully implement peace agreements that ended civil wars among parties that mutually viewed each other as villains.[1]

The suspension of the no-negotiation doctrine for villains, while still taboo in the international community, has been exercised in a discrete fashion and to good effect in some intrastate and international contexts. The 1998 article examined four such cases that occurred between 1993–94: Israel-Palestine Liberation Organization, US-Haiti, US-North Korea, and Great Britain-Sinn Fein. In these cases, several approaches were used to overcome the no-negotiation impediment:

- One party temporarily suspended the stigma of being a villain from the other side. It submerged ideology and emotion and took a very pragmatic approach to the problem.
- The leaders reframed the villain and communicated their new vision to their constituents. They indicated that the villain was still an enemy, but one that can be trusted sufficiently to implement a peace initiative.
- An historic moment was sensed whose opportunity should not be missed.
- The leaders presented themselves as tough and self-interested with strong credibility among their constituents. They were viewed as looking out for their country first.
- The leaders saw themselves as figures who have to take risks for peace.
- The negotiation mechanisms used were cautious and secretive – unofficial mediators were sent as envoys to send up trial balloons with the villain and with the domestic population. If the attempts did not work, the mediator could be scapegoated.
- The negotiation offer presented overwhelming incentives to the villain – extreme costs (imminent military invasion) or extreme reward (massive foreign aid) – and it was presented as the villain's last chance.

These mechanisms enabled leaders to transform the prevailing no-negotiation-with-villains policy. It is interesting to note that in all of these cases, save Haiti, the agreements reached through the ensuing negotiations were shortlived. The so-called villainous state, and in some cases, the other party as well, failed to live up to the agreed provisions after only a few years. However, the negotiated settlements did defuse the immediate situations that threatened violence and potential loss of life; from this perspective, the ethical "duty" of leadership to ensure the safety and protection of citizens was exercised effectively.

Deciding to Negotiate with Terrorist Villains

There are some clear differences between villains that are sovereign states and those that are terrorist organizations, which will have direct implications for the decision to negotiate. Terrorist groups are not legitimate representatives of a physical territory or population. They lack formal accountability to any constituency and thereby may not abide by international law, norms or principles, and may not act as reliable negotiation partners who faithfully implement agreements. They typically hold extreme positions, values and beliefs that are not shared by many in their country or internationally. Terrorist groups also do not participate in the same traditional channels of communication and interaction as nation states.

Negotiation is not often thought to be a relevant mechanism for terrorist organizations. Prerequisites for successful negotiation often include the cessation of
hostilities, open communication channels, a belief in reciprocity, and trustworthiness. Most of these factors are antithetical to terrorist activity. Violence is the terrorist's principal mode of operation. Terrorist communication is often one-sided,
heralding threats and demands, but not necessarily responding to the outside world.
Reciprocity in the negotiation sense is also not a typical terrorist attribute; interactions are generally conflictual, sporadic, and unpredictable. Terrorists do not
preach reciprocation, but resignation of the other side. And there is little confidence
that terrorists will comply with negotiated agreements if they are not perceived as
producing victory for their ideological objectives.

Much as terrorist violence promotes an atmosphere in which negotiation is
inoperable, so a government doctrine of "no-negotiation with terrorists" plays to
the strength of the terrorists. If not negotiation, then what? Interaction can become
a deadly tit-for-tat, escalating the conflict with no apparent way out other than capitulation or retreat by one side. Nonetheless, "no-negotiation" is the doctrine because
it is believed that open government engagement in negotiation is simply an unrea-
sonable option in the face of violence and threat.

From the position of the state, there are several decision options available when
confronting a threatening terrorist organization. They can declare a war on terrorism and attack with greater force, hoping to disable and obliterate the threat. They
can threaten the terrorist group with future attack and establish obstacles for their
operations. They can initiate a preventive campaign to build an internal fortress
capable of fending off future terrorist attacks. And they can decide to negotiate with
the terrorists.

For all the reasons described above, negotiating with terrorists is not an easy
decision to make. But it is not an impossible decision. There have been examples
of negotiations with rebels and spoilers of peace agreements considered to be terrorist groups at an intrastate level – in Sri Lanka, South Africa, Mozambique, Mali,
Mexico, and elsewhere (Rothchild 1997; Zartman 2001; Stedman 2000). This
negotiation option need not occur through traditional or formal mechanisms. It can
proceed in indirect talks through a trusted third party in secret (Zahar 2003),
impersonally via the mass media or through nonverbal demonstrations that seek
reciprocation. Small initiatives to generate mutual confidence or larger formulas for
agreement can be attempted as trial balloons. Threats, warnings, promises and
rewards can be transmitted to persuade and influence. Particular initiatives that will
have known meaning to the other side can be implemented to induce a tit-for-tat
reciprocation that reduces tensions (Osgood 1966). If none of these work, the ini-
tiators can disassociate themselves from the attempts without loss of face. History
has shown that tough negotiating with terrorists has a chance of being productive
if appropriate opportunities are found where the state has ample capacity to back

out gracefully or secretively and escape capitulation and charges of appeasement if the attempt fails.

Accounting for Terrorist Interests

Terrorists are often viewed as criminals. However, they differ from ordinary criminals in that their intentions are usually political. And unlike traditional political interest groups, terrorists pursue their objectives through violent means; their interests often seek a revolution to the current political order. Under normal negotiation circumstances, parties would seek to address their competing interests through a give-and-take process. However, the sovereign states that are targets of terrorists often react solely to the terrorists' violent actions and tactics, not to their motivating ideas and interests; they either do not attend to their interests or refuse to acknowledge them. A stark example of this is the US State Department's latest *Patterns of Global Terrorism* report (2002) where the goals and interests of most terrorist groups are not discussed. Another example is a database project on intrastate terrorism in Europe where the researchers (Engene and Skjølberg 2001) have collected time series information on terrorist events using 61 variables, 59 of which deal with incidents and fatalities, and only 2 that deal with group ideology and attitudes toward the state. One might conclude from these efforts that terrorist groups pursue violence for no reason other than to wreak havoc; while some terrorist acts in fact are random and senseless, others most assuredly are purposeful. The point is that without acknowledging terrorist interests, no matter how heinous they might be, negotiation certainly is not possible.

Terrorists usually are motivated by intense, often extreme, interests – interests to overthrow their national or neighboring regimes, transform economic relationships, and expel foreign troops or foreign culture, for instance. Parties that have interests, at least in theory, can be engaged in negotiation to achieve their objectives if they see it as legitimate channel where they might succeed. Terrorists resort to violence, in part, because they see it as the only way to achieve their objectives or gain attention to their interests. If there are other paths to their goals, perhaps they can be nudged in those directions.

For terrorists, the negotiation mechanism might be acceptable if they believe that they will not be sullied by interacting with their erstwhile target. They need to be convinced that they can, in fact, achieve their goals through negotiation *and* that they will never achieve them through continued violence, because of impenetrable barriers or overwhelming force.

At the same time, if state leaders have the political will to promote negotiation as a response to terrorism, they will need to attend to terrorist interests and intentions, not only their actions, strategies and tactics. In doing so, states will have to look "between the lines" at terrorist interests to evaluate where progress can be made legitimately. Only then will there be the possibility to engage them in negotiation.[2]

It is very likely that in certain cases, addressing terrorist interests effectively will be impossible for the threatened state. Terrorist intentions may be entirely irrational or totally absolute and irreconcilable. In the case of suicide terrorists, negotiation is a non-starter, but for hostage or hijack terrorists, for example, negotiation is an alternate way out to achieve their goals. The challenge will be to dissect and dissemble terrorist interests to identify and separate those that can be negotiated from those that cannot. If this can be done, peaceful transformation of the terrorist may be feasible.

Feasible Negotiation Strategies

Some strategies described in the 1998 article that proved useful for leaders deciding to negotiate with state villains are not likely to be appropriate in negotiating with terrorists:

- It will be difficult to deny the villainous stigma of the terrorists and assert their trustworthiness without some concrete evidence that the terrorists have reformed themselves.
- Taking risks for peace with terrorists is likely to be viewed as foolhardy.
- Positive incentives are likely to be viewed as bargaining from weakness.

Terrorists may be seen as more dangerous than state villains, in part because they are not accountable to a constituency. Their actions are more random and anarchic, generating greater fear than more traditional enemies. The ethical path for state leaders confronted with such terrorist threats is a conundrum. How best to secure the safety for their citizens: by eliminating the terrorist threat through counterattack, by threatening extreme retaliation in the future, by engaging in preventive security measures, or by negotiating? The first two options risk the safety of more lives. The third option may save some lives, but 100 percent prevention is impossible. The fourth option – negotiation – offers the opportunity to transform the engagement from one of antagonism to one of strong but peaceful competition. Negotiation with terrorists, if possible in a particular case, can be framed as coopting the villain – to mollify and soften their tactics from violence to talk and persuasion. Negotiation would preempt the terrorists' approach and channel it into socially acceptable paths.

What negotiation paths with terrorists are available and feasible? To overcome the no-negotiation impediment, state leaders will need to respond in a special way to:

- Seek an understanding of terrorist interests and intentions, translate those interests into politically acceptable terms, and respond to them appropriately.
- Negotiate with complete deniability, using the media, dispensable third parties and go-betweens in unofficial processes.
- Implement symbolic initiatives to signal an interest in negotiation.
- Employ coercive diplomacy (sanctions, ultimatums, threats and warnings) to practice tough bargaining (George 1991), making high demands and threatening great costs for non-compliance.
- Establish limited short-term goals and seek to get the terrorists to abide by some rules.
- Practice tough bargaining, while not giving up principles or excusing crimes.

While terrorist tactics cause tangible destruction and loss, it is, in essence, psychological warfare that terrorists are waging. Reciprocal violence will not stop terrorism over the long term; there are always more to fill the ranks and there only needs to be a few terrorists to wreak havoc. State objectives should focus on reciprocal psychological transformation: finding the opportunities for change and communication.

New Research Directions

Many questions need to be examined. Not all terrorists are alike. Which kinds are more prone to be interested in the negotiation track? Are there particular terrorist attributes that might predict their readiness for negotiation or when overtures to negotiation would be a non-starter? For example, are terrorists that are motivated by clear nationalist objectives more likely to have political goals that can be satisfied by negotiation? In general, how can terrorist intentions be deconstructed to reveal those that may be negotiable?

In comparison with nation-states, terrorist groups serve very different functions, abide by different rules, have very different relationships with their constituencies, and maintain a different basis for legitimacy. Can such differences be broached in negotiation? As well, interests, stakes and the consequences of action are very different to terrorist groups than to nation-states due to the absence of accountability for terrorists. How do such fundamental differences impact the course of possible negotiation?

Options to negotiate with terrorists can also be advanced by research on how states negotiate with non-state actors. While non-governmental groups are getting more involved in negotiation in general, they still do not participate at an equal level as states; they influence, pressure, create public opinion, but do not negotiate per se. Our current negotiation frameworks do not clearly represent how negotiation processes work among non-equivalent entities. Individual-to-individual or state-to-state negotiation has been analyzed extensively, but state-to-nonstate negotiation is not well understood. How does the power imbalance and structural difference impact negotiation and what can be accomplished reasonably?

While the reasonableness of state negotiation with terrorists may be highly questionable in many circumstances, research on these types of issues may shed light on the opportunities where negotiation is feasible. And if negotiation is deemed feasible, it is the appropriate path for national decision makers.

Acknowledgements

Thanks are extended to I. William Zartman and an anonymous reviewer who provided useful insights and suggestions. The author also gratefully acknowledges the United States Institute for Peace that supported the initial research under Grant No. SG-37–95. The conclusions reported do not necessarily represent the views or opinions of the Institute.

Notes

1. However, in another piece, Stedman (2000) presents cases where groups become *spoilers* in post-conflict situations, sometimes using terrorist tactics to undermine the emerging peace if they see their power or interests threatened by the new order. Recent examples of success by spoilers include Angola (1992) and Rwanda (1994).
2. Stedman (2000) concludes that effective spoiler management requires a correct diagnosis of the spoiler problem to assess their intentions and motives objectively. If this assessment is accomplished, appropriate strategies can be implemented that either threaten, promise, or induce the spoiler to transform terrorist tactics into cooperative approaches. Zahar (2003) extends these ideas: importance is given to understanding how spoilers assess their own costs and benefits and why they spoil the peace process in the first place.

References

Eban, Abba (1994) "The Duty to Negotiate", *Washington Post*, September 9 (op-ed page).
Engene, Jan Oskar and Skjølberg, Katja (2002) "Data on Intrastate Terrorism: The TWEED Project", paper presented at the 2002 International Studies Association Annual Convention, New Orleans, LA (March 24–27).
Fisher, Roger, Ury, William and Patton, Bruce (1991) *Getting to Yes*, 2nd edition. New York: Penguin Books.

George, Alexander I. (1991) *Forceful Persuasion: Coercive Diplomacy as an Alternative to War*. Washington, DC: US Institute of Peace Press.

Osgood, Charles E. (1966) *Perspective in Foreign Policy*, 2nd edition. Palo Alto, CA: Pacific Books.

Rose, Charlie (1995) "Always a Reckoning", *The Charlie Rose Show*, Transcript no. 1293, broadcast by PBS, 17 January 1995.

Rothchild, Donald (1997) "Ethnic Bargaining: Conflict Management in Pluralistic Societies: Special Issue", *International Negotiation* 2 (1): 1–174.

Spector, Bertram I. (1998) "Deciding to Negotiate with Villains", *Negotiation Journal* 14 (1): 43–59 (January).

Stedman, Stephen (2000) "Spoiler Problems in Peace Processes", in Paul Stern and Daniel Druckman (eds.), *International Conflict Resolution After the Cold War*. Washington, DC: National Academy Press.

Stedman, Stephen, Rothchild, Donald and Cousens, Elizabeth (eds.) (2002) *Ending Civil Wars: The Implementation of Peace Agreements*. Boulder, CO: Lynne Reinner Publishers.

United States Department of State (2002) *Patterns of Global Terrorism 2001*. Washington, DC: Office of the Coordinator for Counterterrorism, US Department of State. May.

Zahar, Marie-Joëlle (2003) "Reframing the Spoiler Debate in Peace Processes", in John Darby and Roger MacGinty (eds.), *Contemporary Peacemaking*. New York: Palgrave Macmillan.

Zartman, I. William (2001) "Negotiation of Internal Conflicts: Special Issue", *International Negotiation* 6 (3): 297–469.

INDEX

DATE DUE

FEB 1 0 2016	